BASE BUILDING *for*
CYCLISTS

BASE BUILDING *for* CYCLISTS

A NEW FOUNDATION FOR ENDURANCE AND PERFORMANCE

THOMAS CHAPPLE

Boulder, Colorado

The Ultrafit Cycling Training Series
BASE BUILDING FOR CYCLISTS
Copyright © 2006 by Thomas Chapple

 1830 N. 55th Street • Boulder, Colorado • 80301–2700 • USA
303/440-0601 • Fax 303/444-6788 • E-mail velopress@insideinc.com

Library of Congress Cataloging-in-Publication Data
Chapple, Thomas.
  Base building for cyclists : a new foundation for endurance and performance
  / Thomas Chapple. — 1st ed.
    p. cm.
  Includes index.
  ISBN-13: 978-1-931382-93-9 (pbk. : alk. paper)
  ISBN-10: 1-931382-93-X (pbk. : alk. paper)
  1. Cycling—Training. 2. Cardiovascular fitness.   I. Title.
  GV1048.C43 2007
  796.6—dc22
                              2006029049

Cover design by Anita Koury
Cover photo by Getty Images
Interior design by Samira Selod
Interior layout/production by Jessica Xavier
Illustrations by Tom Ward, power graphs courtesy CyclingPeaks, kilojoules graphs courtesy TrainingPeaks

Printed in the United States of America
10 9 8 7 6 5 4 3

To purchase additional copies of this book or other VeloPress titles, call 800/234-8356 or visit us at www.velopress.com.

To my Mom for her constant support, whatever my adventure,
and for teaching me about generosity.

To my Dad for developing my sense of humor and
understanding of things mechanical.

Thanks to

Joe Friel for his support and willingness to share
all that he knows with anyone who asks;

Renee, Jade, Iris, Liza, and David
at VeloPress for their hard work and sense of humor;

the athletes I've coached, learned from,
and who encouraged me to write this book.

CONTENTS

FOREWORD

In 1995 I wrote *The Cyclist's Training Bible* strictly for my own purposes. I wanted to make certain that I could logically explain and defend my coaching methods, which I had developed over 15 years of working with athletes of all abilities. That book truly became an overnight success. Athletes all over the world read it. I know because they've sent me e-mails with questions for the last 10 years, many of which have to do with the base period of training.

The base period is undoubtedly the least understood and the most perplexing of all of the periods in a season. Athletes are simply puzzled by what appears on the surface to be a rather straightforward time of the season.

For decades the base period meant only one thing to serious cyclists—ride a lot of miles. That's hardly the case anymore. There is far more to early season training than simply logging distance. Athletes who only look at their odometers during the base period will spend the race season trying to get back onto the peloton. I tried to explain that in *The Cyclist's Training Bible* but somehow many cyclists failed to learn the lesson. In *Base Building for Cyclists*, Thomas Chapple devotes an entire book to the concept I tried to explain in one chapter. After reading this book you will come away with a much greater depth of understanding of this all-important time of the year. And you'll race better because of it.

I met Thomas in 2002 and shortly thereafter invited him to join Ultrafit Associates, an association of like-minded endurance coaches that I founded in 1992. As of this writing we have 34 members in our coaching association. I have personally selected only the best and brightest and trained each in my unique coaching methodology. What you will find in this book is a summary of the training concepts the Ultrafit coaches follow with the athletes they train. Thomas clearly describes here how to train during the most crucial period of the year. Follow his teachings and you will start the season with a platform for excellent fitness.

Joe Friel
Scottsdale, Arizona
November 2006

INTRODUCTION

All cyclists have a *fitness ceiling,* or highest level of fitness, that they will realize each year. The height of that ceiling and the duration that it can be maintained depend on the size of the athlete's base. It is this aerobic, or base fitness that serves as the foundation for all levels of cycling activity. The elements of fitness that make up your base are endurance, strength, and efficiency. It takes months, and ultimately years, to develop and build your base fitness.

The fitness elements that you will focus on during base training must be in place before higher-intensity training and racing can be supported. Strength, endurance, and efficiency must be developed before you can begin specific-event preparation or race simulation, and race simulation must be completed before you attempt your first high-priority event. This means that the base building phase alone can take 8 to 24 weeks *or more* depending on the athlete's experience, strengths and limiters, and goals.

What base building entails for individual cyclists varies depending on where they live, their experience, personal strengths and limiters, and cycling goals. Some climates allow for year-round training outdoors, while others require more indoor training. Cyclists living in flatter regions often incorporate strength training, as will masters cyclists, female cyclists, or those with limited muscle mass or muscular imbalances. Some athletes find that their goals necessitate positive changes in their body composition, while certain athletes benefit from crosstraining, while others need to focus their energy on cycling-specific drills.

You may get fitter by just going out and riding without any specific plan or structure. You will, however, reach your ceiling early, and improvements will stop before your fitness reaches the highest possible level. Most cities have weekly training rides that are really weekly races. Cyclists ride so hard that they can barely breathe and do so during times of the year when they should be riding easily enough to carry on a conversation. Easier rides develop your aerobic system. You can't do that if you are continually trying to crush the competition in the weekly rides because these efforts train your anaerobic fitness too much. If you ride hard all year round, you effectively detrain your aerobic system. The goal of base training is to take an activity that is currently dependent on a high level of anaerobic energy contribution and ultimately make it a predominantly aerobic effort.

If you train hard all the time, you will never realize your potential. Sometimes athletes come off the race season feeling fast and try to maintain that fitness throughout the winter. They may be able to keep their speed a while longer, but by the time the next cycling season begins, they are often sick, injured, or burned out. The concept that you must slow down and even lose some high-end fitness for a time in order to achieve greater levels of fitness down the road is difficult for many highly motivated athletes to accept. But it is necessary!

Should you be riding more or fewer miles? You may be surprised by the answer. Some athletes need to increase their mileage or training hours in order to see gains, while others see improvements by training less. Sometimes less is more! Some athletes benefit from strength training. Every athlete can benefit from following general training principles, but each athlete benefits more from individualizing the training program to fit his or her unique needs. There is no one training plan that is appropriate for every athlete.

I am often approached by serious athletes who want to compete at the highest level in their sport after just one year. Such an accomplishment is very rare and unlikely to happen. It takes years of training to fully develop your potential. Success requires planning, and your plan should look at the entire year and beyond. Athletes preparing for the Olympics have a training plan outline for four or more years. They set short- and long-term goals and measure their progress along the way. It may be necessary to make adjustments to their training or goals based on their progress, but the plan provides direction and motivation. If you have already been training for several years and feel that your improvements don't measure up to the time you are investing, or if you seem to be losing fitness, then you may be training in a manner that is holding you back rather than moving you toward your potential. The ideas outlined in this book have proven to be successful. If you apply them to your training you will see results.

Base Building for Cyclists will show you how to train your body to be more economical, using less energy or fuel to perform a given task. This will leave you with more energy for longer or harder efforts such as a climb or a sprint to the finish. Smart base training will allow you to ride faster or with more power while maintaining a lower heart rate or rate of perceived exertion. By better understanding the concepts and how to apply them to address your needs, you'll be able to get the most out of the time you have available for training.

Part I, The Cyclist's Engine, explains how your body uses energy. Fat and carbohydrates are the primary energy sources for your body, but it is more efficient to use fat because it is abundant in even the leanest of cyclists. Chapter 1 explains the need to condition the body to prefer fat over carbohydrates as you build your base fitness. This will not happen if you don't take the time to ride at low to moderate intensities. Chapter 2 explains the energy systems that deliver power to the pedals. In order to ride farther and faster you have to increase your aerobic capacity. How well your body can deliver and utilize oxygen will have the greatest impact on your fitness ceiling. Chapter 3 will help you determine what you need to eat to meet your body's daily energy needs. By assessing your body composition and following basic nutrition guidelines, you can drop some extra pounds, build muscle mass for increased power, or maintain your current weight more easily throughout the training season. Once you understand how your body uses energy, the benefits of base building will come into focus.

Part II, Diagnosing the Engine, will help you determine how to shape your training. Chapter 4 will measure your existing fitness and give you proven methods for testing performance over the course of your training, taking into account your unique physiology.

Chapter 5 applies your fitness testing to identify the different training zones and the heart rate or power level you should be training at, and when. Chapter 6 will help you identify your personal limiters and ways to improve them. For most cyclists, these limiters are rooted in underdeveloped base fitness elements: endurance, strength, and efficiency.

Part III, Planning Your Training Year, will help you develop a training plan that will better prepare you for specific events throughout your cycling season.

Chapter 7 explains the factors that impact training load and how you can measure your training load from week to week. This is important, because knowing how your body adapts, or responds, to a given training load is critical in determining an appropriate training load for you. Chapter 8 explains the shape your base training should take based on your experience level and goals. Chapter 9 tackles training volume and progression, and outlines how to best structure your training days and weeks. Gains in fitness are a delicate balance between applying a training stimulus and providing adequate recovery so that your body can continue to make ongoing adaptations. Chapter 10 covers the key to tracking your training. Throughout the season, adjustments will need to be made, and by regularly recording your "vital signs" and training details, you can make better decisions that will bring more productive workouts.

Part IV, Building a Stronger Engine, breaks down each component of base fitness to make you a better cyclist, raising your fitness ceiling and sustaining it longer into your season. Chapter 11 will develop your aerobic fitness with a base training progression that takes you from moderate-intensity, high-cadence rides in early base training to rides that use low-rpm strength and strength-endurance intervals, and comfortably hard "tempo" and upper-threshold intensities, by the end of late base training. Chapter 12 describes the phases of strength training off the bike. Even if you are not looking to build muscle mass, you need to maintain a strong core and avoid the imbalances that result in injury. Chapter 13 gives you pedaling, skills, sprinting, and riding drills that you can do every time you get on the bike. Ultimately, these drills will help you achieve the results you are working toward with less effort or more efficiency. Chapter 14 covers the basics of mental training because the base period is a great time to improve your mindset for competition. Finally, Chapter 15 will help you transition to specific event preparation or advanced fitness concepts.

Base Building for Cyclists is about losing unnecessary body weight and gaining strength. It's about recovering from nagging injuries and training in a way that prevents injuries from happening in the first place. You will learn how to test your fitness, identify your personal strengths and limiters, create a training plan that addresses your needs and goals, and measure your progress along the way. It is your base fitness that will allow you to ride and race faster. Whether you've been training and racing for years or if this will be the first year you follow a training plan, *Base Building for Cyclists* will show you how to achieve a greater level of aerobic fitness in the coming season and how to continually push your fitness ceiling higher in the seasons ahead.

PART ONE

THE CYCLIST'S ENGINE

1
ENERGY SOURCES

When you turn the ignition key in your car, some source of fuel (gas, diesel, or fermented organic manure) must be delivered to the engine for it to fire. Even though the spark to ignite it may be there, if the fuel tank is empty, the engine will not fire. Muscles burn a substance called *adenosine triphosphate* (ATP) and, like a car engine, must have an ongoing supply available to continue doing work. Whenever you place a demand on the muscles to perform a task, such as turning the pedals, the energy systems must work continuously to convert energy sources into ATP to keep up with that demand.

The fuel necessary for activated muscles to contract is delivered through one of the body's two energy systems—*aerobic* and *anaerobic*. Energy stored in the body is converted to fuel and delivered to the working muscles through one or both of these energy systems. The energy sources that supply these energy systems are carbohydrates, fats, and, to some extent, proteins.

When you are riding, the preferred source of fuel changes as your intensity increases. At slow, easy paces, the body can burn mostly fat to produce enough energy to support muscle contractions. As you ride faster and harder, your muscles will start craving carbohydrates to keep up with the demands of a higher effort level. Carbohydrates ignite and burn much like the matches and kindling that you use to start a fire. Fats are more like the logs on the fire that burn slowly and can produce a long-lasting fuel source. Your body has a limited supply of matches to burn, so you need to learn to use them sparingly and replenish them frequently.

CARBOHYDRATES AS FUEL

Carbohydrates are a powerful but limited energy source that can be quickly converted to fuel for muscle contractions. Carbohydrates are either stored in the body within the muscles and liver or are moving around within the blood. Those stored in the liver and muscles take on a slightly different configuration called *glycogen*. Glycogen stored in the muscles is available for rapid conversion to fuel but can be depleted quickly once you step on the gas. Muscles can develop the ability to store larger quantities of glycogen and to spare, or conserve, those carbohydrates.

The way you train plays a major role in how your muscles work and use carbohydrates. One of the main objectives of *Base Building for Cyclists* is to teach you how to train your muscles to store more carbohydrates but use less of that stored energy to perform a given task. This will make you a more fuel-efficient athlete. Efficiency is a major factor in athletic performance. One clear advantage of using fewer carbohydrates to accomplish a given effort is that you have more of this high-power energy available for when you need it most. Conserving fuel means that you can ride longer or harder when you need to. Your muscles will demand carbohydrate energy when you're chasing a breakaway, battling a headwind, climbing a tough hill, or outsprinting an angry pit bull. These are all good reasons to ration your limited supply of carbohydrates!

The small amount of carbohydrates found circulating in the blood take a form called *glucose*. The amount of glucose in your blood is also referred to as your blood sugar level. If your blood sugar levels run low, the body will release glycogen stored in the liver to maintain appropriate glucose levels. The liver can store only a few hundred calories of carbohydrate, which will quickly become depleted, so it is best to maintain healthy blood glucose levels through ingestion and digestion of a carbohydrate source such as a sports drink or gel and water while cycling for extended or intense periods of time. The liver will also release stored glycogen into the bloodstream throughout the night while you're sleeping to maintain blood sugar levels. This means that your liver will be low or depleted of glycogen in the morning and will need to be refilled if you want to have your carbohydrate stores fully loaded to support that day's activities. The process of ingesting, digesting, and storing carbohydrates within the liver can take three to four hours; so if you have an important event that will demand a lot of carbohydrate energy, you'll want to eat a meal several hours before the start of your event. Liquid fuel sources tend to digest faster and may be a better choice for prerace meals.

Your body will have a limited total amount of carbohydrates (glycogen in the muscles and liver and glucose in the bloodstream) at any given time. The total amount depends on your state of fatigue (or recent level of physical activity), how well your body has developed its ability to store carbohydrates, and when and how much you last ate. Depending on your size, you could have from 1,500 to 2,000 calories stored when your body is at full capacity. Most of that is within your muscles. This is enough carbohydrate energy to support a high-intensity effort lasting about 60 to 90 minutes.

Carbohydrate stores must be replaced before, during, and after high-intensity or long-duration cycling activities. The depletion of carbohydrate stores is the main cause of fatigue related to longer, harder efforts, and it can also lead to the breakdown of proteins in the body. It is important to maintain carbohydrate stores in the body because they must be present in order for the body to be able to access and burn fat. When carbohydrates are broken down, they produce by-products that facilitate the use of fat for fuel. "Fat burns in a carbohydrate flame"—in other words, the body uses carbohydrates to burn fat.

The terms *hitting the wall* and *bonking* refer to the point when there is not enough carbohydrate energy left in the body to support the effort levels being demanded of the working muscles. When you run out of carbohydrates, you will need to slow down or stop because your body will be forced to begin breaking down proteins (such as muscle fibers). In effect, this cannibalizes the body for fuel. Some research indicates that your body will bonk before you totally deplete your carbohydrates. This may be a built-in protective mechanism to prevent you from running the tank completely dry.

The total amount of fuel needed from carbohydrates to support a given effort depends on several factors. In addition to how hard and long you ride, it also depends on how well you've trained your body to conserve carbohydrates. The harder you ride, the more likely you are to be using a higher percentage of carbohydrates to support the effort. Cyclists who ride hard every workout are more likely to be teaching their body to prefer carbohydrate over fat utilization.

In addition to being a limited energy source, carbohydrates also have another limitation. When carbohydrates are broken down and used as an energy source, other by-products, including lactate, are released into the bloodstream. Most cyclists are familiar with lactate. It is most commonly associated with the burning sensation that you feel in your muscles during hard efforts. More recently, however, scientific research indicates that lactate may not be to blame for this problem. What is important here is that you realize that when you are burning carbohydrates, you are also releasing by-products into the blood that could potentially interfere with muscle contractions and force you to slow down. One of these by-products released is hydrogen ions. Research now points to these ions as being responsible for the burning sensation you feel when you are climbing a steep hill fast, riding all out in a time trial, or trying to hang on to the wheel in front of you at 30 mph. If you start burning carbohydrates too quickly and your body has not developed the ability to process the by-products fast enough, lactate levels, and consequently hydrogen ions, begin to accumulate in the blood. If you continue to push the pace, your breathing will increase rapidly and muscle contractions will become inhibited—forcing you to slow down. If you've attempted to go all out on a long climb, you've no doubt reached this point.

CARBOHYDRATES AS NUTRIENT

Carbohydrates are necessary to supply the body with energy but can also be a source of high-quality nutrition. Many athletes eat a diet that includes large quantities of carbohydrates from sources that are high in starches and refined sugars—pasta, bread, and cereal, for example. These foods can sometimes provide the extra carbohydrates necessary for recovery from challenging workouts, but making them your daily staple limits the quality of your calories. Fruits and vegetables are foods that contain carbohydrates along with large quantities of vitamins, minerals, and fiber. Your body needs these nutrients on a daily basis to maintain optimum health. It's not enough to be a fit athlete; you also have to make healthy choices for that fitness to last.

Inadequate intake of quality carbohydrates can also result in a suppressed immune system and make you more susceptible to fatigue, illness, and injury. Moreover, the brain burns blood glucose almost exclusively. This is one reason why you might feel light-headed or disoriented when your blood sugar levels get low and you bonk.

Carbohydrates should make up 45 to 60 percent of your diet, depending on which training phase you are in. During the base building phases, training emphasizes fat burning and carbohydrate intake can be at the lower end (50 percent). Your intake will need to increase in proportion to training intensity and duration.

FAT AS FUEL

Fat is a long-lasting fuel source stored throughout the body and it's available in abundant supply even in the leanest of athletes. Fat stores can support muscle contractions for long periods of easy to moderately hard efforts without any risk of being depleted. You are not likely to run out of fat! On average, an athlete may have 60,000 to 100,000 calories of fat available. Compared with the possible 2,000 calories of available carbohydrate, it is easy to see why it is preferable to train the body to burn fat. However, fat is converted to energy more slowly and cannot support faster and harder efforts in the same way that carbohydrates can. The process of converting fat to fuel requires more oxygen than carbohydrate burning does, which is one reason that you have to slow down when you run out of carbohydrates. Also, as mentioned before, for fat to be converted to fuel an ongoing supply of carbohydrate must be present. A high percentage of the body's muscles can be trained to run on, or favor, fat even at moderately high intensities. These muscles can also be trained to burn carbohydrates as the preferred fuel choice. Since there is a limited supply of carbohydrates in the body at a given time and the body can burn it faster than you can replenish it, teaching your muscles to utilize fat is the more fuel-efficient option.

If you are trying to burn fat, you should avoid spending too much time training at high intensities that demand carbohydrates. This can teach the muscles to prefer carbohydrates over fat. There is clearly a place and time in training for high-intensity efforts; but by developing your base fitness first through easy to moderate efforts, you will establish a better capacity for burning fat; which means you'll be sparing carbohydrates. By developing your utilization of fat, you begin to lay the foundation necessary to support those harder efforts that will allow you to raise your fitness ceiling. Even though there is a natural tendency toward carbohydrate burning as cycling intensity increases, you can still train in a way that will sustain fat-burning longer.

At effort levels that are easy to moderate, fat may supply as much as 70 to 90 percent of the energy being consumed. As the intensity goes up, more and more of the energy comes from carbohydrates. As effort levels near maximum, 100 percent of your energy will be coming from carbohydrate sources (see Figures 1.1a and 1.1b). When I review the fitness data for athletes, I often find that their bodies burn too much carbohydrate at even easy to moderate effort levels. In some cases they burn more than 60 percent carbohydrates at the easiest effort levels.

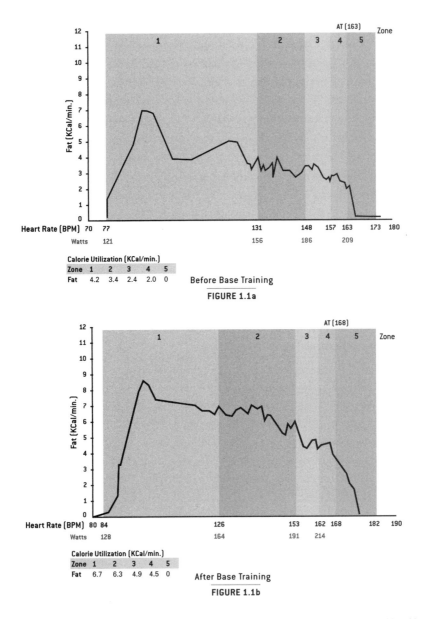

Before Base Training

FIGURE 1.1a

After Base Training

FIGURE 1.1b

Graphs showing how, after following the base training program outlined in this book, this athlete improved fat burning, raised the upper training threshold (or fitness ceiling), and increased power output relative to heart rate. The athlete did so by training at lower intensities than in previous base training. Although the athlete slowed down, he became faster.

These athletes typically have a history of training at high intensities frequently, and they commonly "floor it" as soon as they get on the bike, rather than warming up gradually. Once they begin a training program that emphasizes base building, their fat-burning capacity usually improves within six weeks. In turn, this causes their fitness ceiling to reach all-time highs.

Since carbohydrates are in limited supply and fat is in abundance, training to use fat and spare carbohydrate makes sense. This is one of those aspects of training that seems counterintuitive. To support your body's ability to ride harder longer, you need to teach it to spare carbohydrates. To develop your body's fat-burning ability, you need to ride at slower to moderate intensities. In other words, you have to slow down, to get faster.

If you are attempting to reduce your body fat percentage, you will also find that riding at slower to moderate intensities will lead to more success than riding hard all the time. Riding longer durations (longer than four hours) at easy to moderate intensities has also been shown to improve fat utilization as long as adequate carbohydrates are available to keep the fat fire burning.

FAT AS A NUTRIENT

Not all fat is bad for you. There are certain types of fat that should be avoided, but your body needs an adequate daily supply of the "good" fats that play a role in repairing cells and maintaining healthy tissue for strong immune and nervous systems. This topic is described more fully in Chapter 3.

Recent research has shown that a diet higher in fat can increase fat metabolism and utilization during training. For this reason, it may be worth increasing fat intake and reducing carbohydrate intake during the base-building phase. Fats can make up as much as 30 percent of your calories. The key is to consume healthy fats. A pint of ice cream a day will increase your fat intake, but it will also increase your risk of heart attack.

PROTEIN AS A NUTRIENT AND FUEL

Protein is essential for daily rebuilding of body tissues (including muscles) and blood cells and it also supports the immune system. It is clearly important for recovery, and nutritionists recommend that you include protein in your postrace or workout meals to enhance carbohydrate uptake into the muscles. Recovery drinks are an easy way to get this protein at a ratio of about 4 to 1, carbohydrate to protein. Look for whey or egg protein powders that contain 6 grams of the branch chain amino acids (luecine, isoluecin, and valine) and glutamine.

Protein is not stored in the body and is not a preferred fuel source. As we discussed previously, if carbohydrates run low the body will eventually break down muscle tissue during extended exertion. If you are participating in ultraendurance events lasting four hours or longer, you may benefit from consuming some protein along with your carbohydrates. Over very long durations some protein will inevitably be broken down, but by periodically replacing it you may be able to delay or repair the damage. Protein should make up 25 percent of your total daily calories.

———•———

The choices you make about the foods you eat will affect your cycling as well as your overall health. Be mindful of how your body's engine uses fuel and how it uses that fuel differently when burning carbohydrates versus fat. Start paying more attention to the total amount of calories you take in and what sources they come from. After training, consume recovery foods to rebuild tissue on a daily basis, support the immune system, and replenish carbohydrate stores. The foods you eat should be high in micronutrients (vitamins and minerals). Whenever possible, it's better to choose natural foods like fruits and vegetables rather than foods that are "enriched" with micronutrients. Lean meats provide the best source for the high-quality proteins that the body needs.

Balance your macronutrients (carbohydrates, fats, and proteins) so they fall within an appropriate range. Protein should be consistently 25 percent of your total calories. Carbohydrates can make up 45 to 50 percent during base training, with healthy fats making up as much as 30 percent. After the base phase, you'll move into event-specific training and it will be time to increase the carbohydrates to 60 percent of your caloric intake to meet the higher demands of your training.

2
ENERGY DELIVERY

To make the bike move, you must push on the pedals. The harder and longer you can do that, the happier you are. The ability to get the pedals moving and keep them moving is dependent on a combination of physiological and neurological processes working in conjunction with one another. They're tied together through the cardiovascular (heart, lungs, and circulatory system) and muscular systems and are responsible for delivering and using oxygen and converting energy sources into muscle activity. Through base training, we're developing the physiological abilities that translate to being able to ride longer and faster.

Our body's ability to deliver and utilize oxygen is a limiting factor in endurance sports like cycling, but how and when we use our muscles and our limited energy supplies will also influence how far—and how fast—we can go. Base training focuses on developing the following areas:

- Increased flow of oxygen-rich blood to the working muscles by raising cardiac output, or the total amount of blood that the heart is able to pump per minute. This is affected by how much blood the heart can pump with each stroke. A reduced resting heart rate indicates that the heart is able to pump more blood per stroke.
- Greater blood flow within the working muscles due to an increase in the number of capillaries. These microscopic blood vessels help diffuse oxygen-enriched blood into the muscle fibers and remove the by-products of energy metabolism from the working muscles. The more capillaries we have surrounding the working muscles, the greater their ability to work aerobically.

- Higher levels of aerobic enzymes to allow for energy sources to be converted to fuel aerobically.
- Improved ability to process metabolic by-products such as lactate. Lactate can be processed back into an energy source or utilized as fuel directly by organs such as the heart. The ability to convert metabolic by-products more effectively means they accumulate in the blood more slowly and lactate turnover is faster.
- Increases in the size and number of mitochondria. Mitochondria are small factories within the muscles that convert energy sources into fuel aerobically. This is one case when more and bigger is actually better.
- Greater glycogen (carbohydrate) storage capability within the muscles and an increased ability to spare those carbohydrates through the ability to better utilize fat for energy production.
- An increase in actual blood volume.
- More activated muscle fibers capable of producing a higher level of force.
- Better muscle firing patterns. By improving the coordination of how we use our muscles, we can reduce the energy required to keep the bike moving forward.

ENERGY SYSTEMS

As mentioned in Chapter 1, exercise intensity and duration are limited by the amount and type of fuel sources available. They are also limited by the rate and efficiency that our body's energy systems can convert that available fuel supply into the ATP that muscles need. Training can improve how well our bodies perform this task, but the way we train also affects how and which of the energy systems are developed.

We have two energy systems, the aerobic and anaerobic systems. The most distinguishing feature between the two is that the aerobic system must have an ongoing supply of oxygen available at all times to do its job, whereas the anaerobic system works without using, or needing, oxygen. Another difference is that the aerobic system can convert fat, carbohydrate, and, to some extent, protein into fuel for muscle contractions. The aerobic system is like the hybrid engine, and the anaerobic system is like the muscle car engine. The anaerobic system is limited to using only carbohydrates or a substance called creatine phosphate, which is stored within the muscles in very small quantities. Creatine phosphate can be converted to energy immediately, but its supply can last for only about 8 to 10 seconds before it is depleted and needs several minutes to replenish. This substance is available for sudden bursts such as sprints and the start of rapid accelerations. Given that we have such a limited supply of carbohydrate available and an ample supply of fat, our goal should be to produce as much of the needed energy as possible through the aerobic system.

Another way the systems differ is in how much energy they produce and how fast they accomplish it. The aerobic system will deliver more fuel for a given amount of energy source (carbohydrate, for example) being converted, but it takes longer to accomplish this than the anaerobic system. The anaerobic system will produce energy faster, but the end result is less total fuel from the carbohydrates being processed. The lesson here is that the aerobic system is more fuel efficient and the anaerobic system is a gas hog. You need to be able to produce as much of your needed energy as possible through the aerobic system and wait to tap into your anaerobic system until you need that extra boost of power.

The common perception that there is a point when the aerobic system shuts down and the anaerobic system fires up and takes over is misleading. This point is most commonly referred to as the lactate or anaerobic threshold (see the sidebar "Threshold" in Chapter 4). This threshold is a marked point in energy usage, but the body does not switch from one energy system to another. Both energy systems are active and contributing to keep up with the demands for energy production at the same time, but the amount that one system is contributing at a given effort level is what can make the difference. The more the aerobic system is able to contribute before the anaerobic system is needed, the longer and faster you can ride.

That said, many cycling events do demand some short, high-intensity efforts that require an ability to produce energy through the anaerobic system. If you are riding and racing in events that involve drafting and will need the ability to "put the pedal to the metal" to hold onto the draft when the pack attacks or accelerates, then you'll need to develop anaerobic endurance and power. So, if your events dictate it, you'll need to develop the anaerobic system to an appropriate level. In contrast, ultraendurance events are not dependent on the anaerobic system's contribution. You should be cautious, therefore, in overdeveloping anaerobic pathways if your focus is on individually paced ultraendurance events.

One common mistake athletes make is spending too much time training the anaerobic system and not enough time developing the aerobic system. The idea that to get faster you have to ride faster or harder all the time is misleading. The anaerobic system is supported by the aerobic system and therefore depends on the strength and quality of your aerobic base fitness. Each year we have an opportunity to raise our fitness ceiling to a new high. The depth and quality of our aerobic base fitness will determine how high our fitness ceiling is raised, and how long it will stay up. This is where the idea that you have to slow down to get faster finds meaning.

The rate at which energy systems can produce the energy (or ATP) necessary for ongoing muscle contractions is dependent on which energy source is being used and which energy system is doing the converting. The objective of base training is to move toward a higher percentage of aerobic system contribution at all intensity levels.

Aerobic Energy System: Our Hybrid Engine

The aerobic energy system is responsible for supporting efforts lasting longer than a couple of minutes and is the foundation that supports cycling activities. It is dependent on an adequate supply of oxygen being delivered to and used by the body to convert fat, carbohydrates, and (to some extent) protein into ATP so that muscles can continue to push on the pedals. The aerobic system, which takes years to fully develop its capabilities, plays a major role in supporting the anaerobic system, which can be brought to its peak in about 6 to 9 weeks. Knowing this, which system would you spend the most time developing each year? The correct choice is the aerobic system, yet I see athletes actually detraining their aerobic system by frequently riding very hard five months before their first race or event. You need a larger aerobic engine to get faster, and riding at slow to moderate paces will develop your aerobic system. This doesn't mean that every workout will be so slow that you'll fall asleep, but effort levels should progress from easy to moderate to comfortably hard intensities during your base training to emphasize aerobic system development.

Our goal through base training is to advance our aerobic fitness to a point where an activity that may currently be dependent on a high percentage of anaerobic system contribution can be supported by a higher percentage of aerobic system contribution. So, for example, if you can currently ride at 20 mph or 270 watts for 30 minutes before you have to slow down or stop, the goal might be to ride at 21 mph or 290 watts for 30 minutes. This progress is largely dependent on the development of your aerobic system. An improvement like this would be an indication that the aerobic system is better able to keep up with the energy production demands. You will also be developing your strength and efficiency throughout base training, which will help your ability to maintain a faster pace longer; but by improving your aerobic fitness, you will be able to remain predominantly aerobic up to a higher pace or power output than before.

You can also see aerobic system improvements through heart rate response. If, for example, you can currently ride steadily at 200 watts at a given heart rate, then when you can consistently ride at the same wattage at a lower heart rate and perceived exertion, you'll know that your aerobic system is better developed.

A lower heart rate for a given effort or power level does not always mean increased fitness, however. You may also experience a lower heart rate or even an inability to get your heart rate to increase regardless of how hard you try. This is usually the result of accumulated fatigue and an indication that you need more rest. Your body may actually be inhibiting your heart rate from increasing to protect you from potential harm, sort of a built-in speed limiter.

To see an improvement in your aerobic system through a lower heart rate, you should be seeing lower heart rates gradually over time, when your legs are feeling fresh. Your rate of perceived exertion is another way to determine whether the effort level feels easier than it did a month or two before. Your morning resting heart rate can also provide some insight into aerobic system improvements. As the heart becomes stronger and is able to pump more blood with each stroke, it will be able to supply the body with the blood it needs with fewer beats per minute. You can plot this by consistently checking your morning resting heart rate (see Chapter 10).

The aerobic system, unlike the anaerobic system, can burn or convert fat into ATP. By training correctly, you can improve the aerobic system's ability to supply energy for your cycling efforts through the abundant supply of stored fat that even the leanest of athletes has. When athletes are tested in a lab, we can see how much fat they are burning compared with carbohydrate at various effort levels. It's clear when an athlete has not developed his aerobic system adequately, because we'll see that he is burning too many carbohydrates at lower effort levels. In some cases, his fat burning will shut down well before it should. This is also accompanied by an increase in heart rate, breathing rate, and blood lactate accumulation. All of these physiological responses lead to an earlier onset of fatigue or having to back off and slow down. As you better develop your aerobic system, you'll be able to ride at faster paces or higher power outputs for longer durations before running out of gas. The aerobic system also supports the anaerobic system by helping shuttle metabolic by-products like lactate.

Anaerobic Energy System: Our Muscle Car Engine

Anaerobic Lactate

The anaerobic system actually has two subsystems: lactate and A-lactate. The anaerobic lactate system can convert carbohydrates into fuel without oxygen being present and also provide energy faster than the aerobic system. That's the good news. The bad news is that the total amount of energy produced per unit of carbohydrate through the anaerobic system is not as great as what would result from that same amount of carbohydrate being processed through the aerobic system. This means that whenever you engage the anaerobic system, you are dipping into your limited supply of carbohydrate stores, or "burning your matches"—much like when you slam your car's gas pedal to the floor and see the fuel gauge needle heading to "E." Engaging your anaerobic system also means that you're producing lactate (exhaust emissions) at a greater rate, since lactate is one of the by-products of carbohydrate metabolism. The anaerobic lactate system will not burn fat and requires carbohydrates to function. Once you use up your carbohydrates you'll be forced to slow down, so it's best to train your body to conserve carbohydrates by increasing the aerobic system's ability to support your efforts.

Anaerobic A-Lactate

The anaerobic A-lactate system uses creatine phosphate, which is stored within the muscles, to produce immediate energy for muscle contractions lasting about 8 to 10 seconds. This system also functions without oxygen; but since it's not burning carbohydrates, it will not result in lactate production. This is why it is referred to as being anaerobic A-lactate. The anaerobic A-lactate system is in place to support sudden accelerations and sprints while the other energy systems are getting fired up.

MUSCLES

Neuromuscular Stimulus

Muscles contract and relax in response to stimuli from the brain. These stimuli can be voluntary or involuntary. Involuntary stimuli keep us alive by contracting muscles such as the heart and diaphragm without our having to think about it. If we want to perform a specific task, we must instruct the muscles to contract by delivering a stimulus to them. This instruction can be a reflexive or intentional action. The level or strength of this stimulus can be affected by our current motivation, will, and state of fatigue. Training specific muscle groups to perform certain tasks, such as moving the pedals correctly and forcefully, can lead to more efficient movements that require less energy to perform. We can also train the body to recruit a higher percentage of available muscle fibers when we need them—during high levels of fatigue or for explosive movements, for example. Muscles need to use one of the energy system processes to accomplish this. The way we train influences how our muscles work and can change how much or which type of fuel they use.

Muscle Fiber Type

We'll be training two types of muscle fibers: type I (slow-twitch) and type II (fast-twitch). Type I fibers are more able to handle the demands of longer-duration efforts. Type II fibers are capable of producing more explosive movements and higher power output for shorter efforts. The most successful endurance athletes have a high percentage of type I fibers. The best sprinters tend to have a greater percentage of type II fibers.

The ratio of type I to type II fibers varies from one cyclist to another. What will influence this the most is your parents, since the ratio is genetically determined. It won't help if Lance Armstrong adopts you, since you must be bred into your specific genetics. Training, however, can influence how well the different fibers produce force and use energy. Base training is designed to improve the recruitment patterns of muscle fibers and develop the aerobic pathways to and within the muscles. Your muscle fiber type is seldom what holds you back. You may find that your dominant muscle fiber type may influence which types of races you do well in; but your skills, tactics, nutrition, and training will have a greater effect on how well you utilize the muscles you do have.

Type I

Type I fibers are known as aerobic or oxidative fibers, which indicates that they use oxygen. More specifically, oxygen must be present for the fuel to be converted to energy (ATP) for muscle contractions within these muscle fibers. Since type I fibers are aerobic, they can burn either fat or carbohydrates for fuel. They have a high mitochondria concentration, are more resistant to fatigue, and have a slower shortening or contracting speed. This is why they are also referred to as slow oxidative, or SO, fibers.

Type II

The type II fibers are either type IIa or type IIb. Type IIa fibers are known as fast oxidative gylcolytic, or FOG, fibers. Glycolytic means that they can burn carbohydrates without using oxygen, and oxidative means that they can also burn carbohydrates aerobically. They have a faster shortening or contracting speed than do the type I fibers. One of the goals of mid and late base training is to influence how these fibers prefer to function. Training them to contribute aerobically as much as possible is an advantage for endurance events.

Type IIb fibers are anaerobic fibers that burn carbohydrate anaerobically, or without the use of oxygen. They can contract very quickly and are used for producing rapid, forceful movements. They are also referred to as fast glycolytic, or FG, fibers. When we activate these fibers, we start going through our supply of carbohydrates like a race car consumes high-octane premium fuel.

Air Supply

One important point here is that for type I and type IIa fibers to function, they must have a continuous supply of oxygen available. Having an adequate supply of oxygen is critical if you want to utilize your aerobic energy system and not have to rely on the anaerobic system as much. You will also use up your limited supply of carbohydrates more quickly if you are engaging your anaerobic system frequently, either through choice or necessity. This is why it's important to develop the physiological aspects responsible for delivering oxygen to the working muscles through base training. The limiting factor here is not how much air we can breathe in but rather how much oxygen we can extract from what we inhale, how much of that oxygen we can deliver to the working muscles, and how much of it we can utilize within those muscles.

Muscle Size

Training, or not training, can change the size but not the quantity of your muscle fibers. Trained muscle fibers can increase in size. This is called muscle hypertrophy. The opposite is true of muscle fibers that are not trained. When fibers decrease in size it's called muscle atrophy. As we get older, muscle fibers have a natural tendency to atrophy. This is accompanied by a natural increase in fat storage. Yes, nature can be cruel, but you can fight it by training your muscles regularly. This will be covered more in the chapters on strength and endurance training.

Absolute versus Relative Strength

So why does size matter? We measure strength in two ways as cyclists: absolute strength and relative strength. Absolute strength is how much force your body can produce; relative strength is that force divided by your body weight in kilograms. Chapter 6 explains how to measure your absolute and relative power output. This is significant because climbing is affected by gravity. It takes more strength or power output to move weight up a hill. This is why a cyclist will shell out $1,000 to shave a pound of weight off his bike. I suggest spending the money on lighter wheels, since rotating weight is even more of an issue than total weight when climbing.

As muscle fibers grow in size, they will usually also be able to produce more force. There is a trade-off between your ability to produce more force and the amount you're increasing your body weight with the added muscle fiber size. This is why climbers tend to be smaller and sprinters have larger muscles. The sprinter is not as concerned with the climbs and needs the ability to produce as much power as possible. The climber has to be more concerned with relative power. The sprinter will have a higher relative power for shorter durations (5 to 20 seconds), and the climber will have a higher relative power output for longer durations (20 to 60 minutes). This doesn't mean that you're better off letting your muscles atrophy down to weigh as little as possible in order to become a climber. On the contrary, there is often an increase in the power-to-weight ratio, or relative power output, with the addition of a pound or two of muscle fibers if the increase in the power output outweighs the increase in body weight. Chapter 12 discusses ways to develop strength.

Muscle Attachment Points

Muscles are attached to bones through tendons. It's important to know this because cyclists often face an overuse injury that results in a condition called *tendinitis*. This is when the tendon is worked harder or longer than it's been prepared for, and becomes inflamed or even torn. Patella tendinitis is very common because it is the tendon that connects the powerful quadriceps muscles to the front of the knee and to the lower leg. This happens in part because muscles will develop the ability to create force production and resistance to fatigue more quickly than tendons will. You must be careful when increasing your training so you allow enough time for the tendons to catch up and develop before demanding more from them.

Another factor that can contribute to the development of patella tendinitis as well as tendinitis in the back of the leg is an improperly adjusted saddle height. Although it is not always the case, an improper saddle height can cause pain in both the front and back of the knee. If the saddle is too low or too far forward, you can injure the front of your knee. A saddle that is too high or too far back can cause pain in the back of the knee. Pain in and around the knee can be caused by a variety of factors related to bike fit (see the section "Bike Fit" at the end of Chapter 6), rapid increases of training or strength demands, cleat alignment, or other physical issues not related to training. If you experience any lingering aches or pains, you should check with a sports medicine doctor or physical therapist who is familiar with cycling. The beginning of your base training is the best time to address these and any other issues you might be having relating to bike fit or injuries. You'll need to resolve them before you can ramp up your training. You don't want such issues to interfere with your training progression or force you to stop training altogether and have to start over.

MUSCULAR FATIGUE

Muscles are responsible for moving the pedals and the energy systems are responsible for supplying the muscles with the fuel they need to keep working. As energy sources are depleted or when the demands placed on the muscles are greater than what your energy systems are capable of keeping up with, your muscles will begin to lose their ability to contract with enough force or duration to continue. This is one form of fatigue.

Fatigue can be physiological and neurological. As the burning sensation associated with the accumulation of metabolic by-products becomes too much for you to tolerate, or as your carbohydrate stores become depleted, you may find yourself starting to shut down or struggling to maintain muscular contractions at the same effort level you'd like to (see the sidebar "Lactate"). The exact physiological and neurological causes for this shutting down are still being researched, but they may be associated with built-in protective mechanisms designed to keep us from becoming completely depleted or causing harm to ourselves. I've seen athletes shut down when they still had something left in the tank and others who have pushed themselves past or through fatigue and kept going. It's not easy to keep going when we feel the sensations of fatigue, but through training we can develop an ability to tolerate and even resist fatigue, both physically and mentally. Even when your fitness is greater, however, you'll still find someone out there who will challenge you and make you go harder than is comfortable and force you to make greater demands on your body. It never gets easier; you just get faster. Racing, for example, is always hard. If it's easy, you're in the wrong category!

I'm not suggesting that you often push yourself to or beyond your personal limits. That is not the best way to see continual improvements. Bringing yourself

---

LACTATE

Lactate is released as a by-product of carbohydrate metabolism. Years ago, lactate was believed to be a waste product that interfered with our performance and made us shut down. It has since been given a pardon, and its status has been upgraded from waste product to by-product. Researchers have shown that lactate is not the culprit it was once believed to be and is actually a fuel, or energy, source. The heart can burn it directly for fuel, and it can be converted back into an energy source for working muscles. It appears that there is another source of that burning sensation we get in our legs during hard efforts at higher intensities (called acidosis). Hydrogen ions are currently getting blamed for that and are taking the same rap that lactate took for years.

Because hydrogen ions are released along with lactate, measuring the levels of blood lactate is still one method for determining threshold points and energy system contributions. One threshold point is where lactate levels (and presumably hydrogen ions) begin to rise faster than the body can process it. As the intensity increases and the body shifts to more carbohydrate burning to keep up with the demand for energy, more

(continues)

LACTATE *continued*

tate will get released into the blood. Evidence indicates that the accumulation of lactate is not related solely to the increase of carbohydrate burning but also to the body's lack of ability to shuttle it around efficiently. The aerobic system is involved in shuttling the lactate out of the working muscles and moving it to where it can be re-synthesized (or recycled) back into a carbohydrate source that can then be reintroduced into the muscles as usable fuel. Some of this process actually takes place within the muscles. Lactate is actually a form of carbohydrate. Increases in blood lactate levels may even indicate that the body is not able to process a metabolic by-product called pyruvate, rather than producing more lactate. Some research points to lactate playing a role in reducing acidosis, or burning in the legs. So, even though we may still continue to use blood lactate levels to help define training zones, it doesn't mean that lactate is the enemy. Increases in blood lactate levels are associated with metabolic activity and related to muscle fiber type recruitment, so it still provides insight into energy system activity.

to the point of complete failure should be limited to races. The time necessary to recover from such efforts will interrupt your training progression and place you at greater risk for injury and overtraining. (See the sidebar "Symptoms of Overtraining" in Chapter 9.) You can challenge yourself without having to take yourself to complete failure. During base training, these challenges will focus on being able to sustain easy, moderate, and some comfortably hard effort levels for longer durations, as opposed to the challenge of going as hard as you possibly can for a given duration. That level of effort will be reserved for fitness testing throughout the base training. You should be aware that we all have limits, and build up our physical and mental fitness gradually over time. Placing gradual, progressively more challenging demands on your body will result in continued fitness improvements without the setbacks associated with training too hard, too often. This is where the concept of "less is more" comes into play.

⎯⎯•⎯⎯

The body is burning fuel even when you're resting. At rest, the body will use only a small amount of carbohydrates and should be able to rely on mostly fat. As you step on the gas and your effort level increases, your fuel consumption goes up. The rate at which your body becomes dependent on carbohydrates to support the demands of that activity is affected by how well your aerobic system pathways are developed. You must be able to deliver an adequate supply of oxygen to the working muscles to be able to continue to burn fat and produce energy aerobically.

When you demand more energy production than your oxygen delivery systems can keep pace with, you'll have to move to more anaerobic energy system involvement. The more you rely on your anaerobic system, the faster you'll go through carbohydrate stores, the faster metabolic by-products (lactate and hydrogen ions) will accumulate in the blood, and you'll have to slow down.

Muscle contractions require that both neurological and physiological processes take place and that enough energy sources (carbohydrates and fat) are available and turned into ATP fast enough to support the muscle contractions at the level you demand of them. To sustain longer, harder efforts, you need to train your body to favor fat as its fuel source over carbohydrates and to shuttle lactate. This is achieved through training that allows the body to develop the aerobic system. If you're riding at an intensity that requires the anaerobic system to support much of your effort too often, then you're likely teaching the body to favor that system. Back off during your base training because you have to slow down to get faster.

You want to start your base training by addressing any injuries or bike fit issues you might have. Ease into your training and build fitness gradually and consistently. Other considerations as you begin your training are your weight and general health, which are the topics of the next chapter.

3

WEIGHT AND HEALTH MANAGEMENT

The base training phase is the time to turn your attention to making positive changes or maintaining appropriate body composition through good nutritional habits. Your goal may be to drop some unneeded body fat, gain some useful muscle, or just maintain your current weight. I've seen too many cyclists store away extra body fat during their off season only to struggle to lose it later on. I have also seen cyclists gain a benefit from an increase in muscle even though that development added some weight.

Cycling is affected by gravity and therefore weight, especially when you ride uphill. An athlete who is carrying around excessive or unnecessary weight or is lacking the necessary muscle development will be at a disadvantage. During the advanced race preparation training and cycling season, energy needs are usually higher, and cutting back on caloric intake can lead to reduced carbohydrate stores in your racing legs, general fatigue, a higher risk of injury, and even full-blown overtraining. During early base training, your body can more easily tolerate a reduction in energy supply and is less likely to suffer the setbacks that can occur during training at a higher volume and intensity.

ASSESSING YOUR NEEDS

If your goal is to lose some unnecessary body fat, be realistic. Take into account your current energy needs, focus on foods high in nutrients, and reduce caloric intake no more than 300 to 500 calories a day less than your actual total daily energy expenditure (TDEE). If you are already at an appropriate body weight and your goal is to maintain that composition, then tracking your daily caloric intake can help you keep a balance between intake and expenditure. This could also be a good time to reexamine your food choices and make a step toward improving your overall nutrition. If you could benefit from developing increased force production by adding a pound or two of muscle mass (usually in the legs), use the early base training for specific strength training and slightly increase your intake of healthy calories, especially lean protein. Strength training is covered in Chapter 12.

Body Composition Test

To start, have your body composition tested. You'll want to establish a baseline of what your lean body mass is compared to your metabolically inactive tissue (aka body fat). Choose an accurate method that can be repeated. Skinfold caliper testing is often the easiest and can be accurate if the tester is experienced. Try to use the same tester each time to assure consistency. Bathroom scales that include body fat percentage measurements are usually not accurate enough for athletes, and readings can vary with hydration. They may be useful for noting general trends in body composition changes, but investing in a professionally measured test will give you a better indication of your progress. The person who tests you should be able to calculate how much body fat you can lose without having adverse side effects.

There are limits to how lean a machine you can be and still maintain good health. The body needs some fat for such things as insulation, protection of vital organs, and nervous system function. Many cyclists also report that they perform better with slightly more body fat than would be considered the absolute minimum they could survive on. Body fat percentages vary for elite competitive cyclists and can range from 4 to 12 percent for men and 12 to 20 percent for females.

Cycling, like many sports, can place unrealistic expectations on athletes regarding body weight, and your overall health should always be your main concern. I've witnessed many lean cyclists get beat up a hill by a larger cyclist. Emphasizing how you train will take you farther than focusing on just being lean. If you need some guidance with finding the body composition that is healthy for you, consider working with a licensed nutritionist.

As you move closer to your body weight goals, you can take another test to see how your body composition is changing. One of the reasons that it is important to monitor body composition and not just weight is that your weight can stay the same, even as composition improves. This means that muscle mass is increasing and body fat is reduced (muscle weighs more than fat). So you can be leaner even if you weigh the same or gain weight. Gaining more muscle mass in your legs can be useful if your power output increases along with it.

If you find that you're losing weight but your body fat percentage is the same or higher, then you may be losing muscle mass. If you are not trying to lose muscle mass, then this is not a good thing and usually means that you are not eating enough and your body is cannibalizing (breaking down) muscle tissue to provide energy to meet your daily needs. There are times when it is appropriate to drop some unneeded muscle mass. I've worked with very muscular athletes who wanted to improve their climbing ability but were already at their minimum fat percentage composition. They did, however, have a very muscular upper body. This upper-body muscle mass looked great but was slowing them down on climbs. Every extra pound of chest or bicep muscle they had required a few extra watts to move up a hill at the same speed. I had them use lighter weights during upper-body strength training and in some cases stopped all upper-body lifting and focused on core exercises until they were able to reduce their upper-body muscle mass.

Food Log

If you don't already, this is a good time to start tracking your daily caloric intake. Buy a small notebook that you can carry with you and write in it everything you eat each day. Web sites like TrainingPeaks.com also feature food logs to help you track what you eat. Include the morning latte and even the energy drinks while training. At the end of the day or throughout the day as you learn the caloric content of foods you consume regularly, calculate your total intake. You might be surprised to see the sum of what you eat every day.

Daily Energy Needs

You'll need to compare what you consume to your total daily energy expenditure (TDEE). Your TDEE is the sum of your resting metabolism rate (RMR) and your energy expended during the day through physical activity (training and any other normal daily physical work).

Each of us has a minimum daily intake needed to sustain vital body functions and activities besides training. We then have to add energy used during training to get TDEE. Three to four hours of hard training can more than double our daily caloric needs. It may also be necessary to add energy expenditure from job-related activity. If you load and unload boxes from trucks all day, for example, then you'll need to add calories to your daily intake to offset that extra energy expenditure. You can find several formulas online to help you estimate your RMR. Each of them may yield a slightly different total, but you can use them to get close. You can also have your resting metabolism measured in a lab.

Estimating your energy expenditure during exercise can be done using the kilojoules (kj) feature included on most power meters used for cycling or by having it measured while riding your bike during a lab test with a gas exchange analyzer. The kilojoules will give you a guide for total calories burned during that workout, but this measurement does not specify how much of that energy came from carbohydrates and how much came from fat. The ratio will vary depending on your fat-burning efficiency and the intensity and duration of the workout. Some software available for analyzing power meter data files estimates how much of the calories burned during a ride are from carbohydrates and fat, but measuring your metabolic energy usage while cycling during a lab test will give you a better idea of what the energy source is. You'll need to know how much time you spend at a given intensity and then calculate your energy expenditure based on what the lab test data indicate you burn. Calories burned during other types of exercise, like running, can also be measured while performing that activity in a lab.

If you use a power meter while cycling, use kilojoules as an equivalent of calories burned. On some power meters, like the Power Tap, kilojoules are marked as the E (for energy) on the computer. So if your ride records total kilojoules as 1,000, then you can estimate that you burned 1,000 calories (±10 percent) during that ride. As ride duration or intensity increases, so will your kilojoules or energy expenditure. Add the workout energy to your RMR and daily activities so you can estimate your TDEE. That's how many calories you need to consume that day to maintain an energy balance.

If losing weight is your goal, then subtract up to, but no more than, 500 calories in order to lose 1 pound of body fat per week. One pound of body fat is 3,500 calories (7 × 500 = 3,500). Attempting to lose more than that per week can affect training, recovery, overall energy levels, and overall health. A reduction greater than 500 calories a day can also lead to loss of muscle rather than

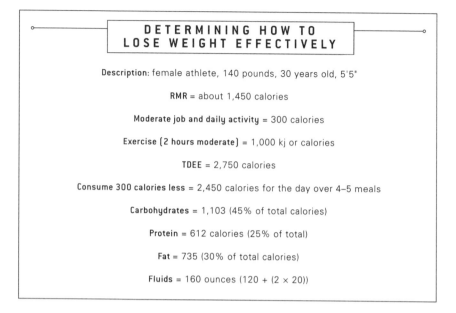

DETERMINING HOW TO LOSE WEIGHT EFFECTIVELY

Description: female athlete, 140 pounds, 30 years old, 5'5"

RMR = about 1,450 calories

Moderate job and daily activity = 300 calories

Exercise (2 hours moderate) = 1,000 kj or calories

TDEE = 2,750 calories

Consume 300 calories less = 2,450 calories for the day over 4–5 meals

Carbohydrates = 1,103 (45% of total calories)

Protein = 612 calories (25% of total)

Fat = 735 (30% of total calories)

Fluids = 160 ounces (120 + (2 × 20))

fat. Remember, if you run your energy systems out of carbohydrates, your body may have to break down muscle fiber (protein) to produce energy. I recommend a goal of 300 calories per day less than your estimated daily expenditure to ensure that you err on the side of caution and manage a gradual weight loss while maintaining consistent, healthy training. This approach will give you a starting point. Monitor your body weight over several weeks to see if you are on track, and adjust your daily reduction up or down 100 calories accordingly. If you record your calories and activities, you'll be better able to dial in your daily needs and look for trends in body weight changes that will indicate whether you're on the right track.

I find that athletes will often just eat the same amount day after day. This routine often leads to eating too much on their rest or easy days and not enough on their longer, harder training days. One problem with this is that their body will store excessive calories as fat on their easy days, and muscle protein may be used on their big training days. They may also not be able to replenish their carbohydrate stores on their harder training days. You must adjust your intake on a daily basis to balance your needs on that day.

If you are going to weigh yourself each day, try to do it consistently in the morning after you wake and use the bathroom. Doing so can serve as a guideline for adequate hydration. If you are down a few pounds from the previous day, you are missing some body fluids. A pound on the scale equals a pint of water. What you are looking for is a trend in your body weight up or down over a couple of weeks. If your weight is dropping faster than a pound a week and the loss is not related to hydration, then you are not eating enough.

As mentioned before, it's important to consider the quality of the calories you are consuming. Eating foods high in micronutrients (vitamins and minerals) as well as fiber, iron, and healthy fats is necessary to maintain overall health and energy from day to day. Your body needs adequate nutrients each day to repair tissue and support the immune system. You also have to replace energy stores within the muscles that are used up during moderate exercise lasting more than 1.5 hours or shorter high-intensity efforts. As the total quantity of calories consumed is reduced, the quality needs to increase, too, to ensure that you're getting adequate nutrients.

GENERAL NUTRITION GUIDELINES

Load Up on Colorful Carbohydrates

Carbohydrates should make up 45 to 60 percent of your daily calories. Eat three to five servings of a variety of both fruits and vegetables every day. Include as many different types as you can. Think colorful: green, red, yellow, and orange fruits and vegetables for a variety of vitamins and minerals, fiber, and carbohydrates.

One way to consume a variety of produce is to steam fresh vegetables. Place them in a bowl with a small amount of water, and put them in the microwave for three to four minutes. Bags of frozen fruit can be blended into smoothies. You can also chop up fresh fruits and for a change, add nonfat vanilla yogurt and a small amount of honey.

Add different fruits and vegetables, as well as mixed nuts and raisins, to salads. Add steamed vegetables, sliced avocado, olives, nuts and raisins, fresh berries, or apple or pear slices, along with some grilled salmon or beef filet, to a bed of spinach.

Although you will not be able to always meet your daily carbohydrate needs from fruits and vegetables, every time you eat carbohydrates less rich in nutrients, you're missing an opportunity to take in necessary vitamins and minerals. So choose your carbohydrate sources wisely.

Eat Healthy Fats

Eat healthy, good fats every day. Your body needs these fats for building new cells and to support the immune system daily. Include avocado, flaxseed oil, salmon, and canola oil in your daily diet. Avoid foods high in saturated fats that are also low in nutrients. Having a treat now and then is fine, but keep it in moderation. Foods containing polyunsaturated and monounsaturated fats are better choices. These include lean meats and fatty fish like salmon. Include free-range or wild meats and fish whenever possible.

Some research suggests that eating a diet containing slightly more fat can increase fat burning. This means that your caloric intake could include up to 30 percent of the calories from fat during the base training phases. Keep these calories in the healthy fat category by choosing foods high in omega-3 fatty acids. As you move to longer and higher-intensity efforts, you should move toward more carbohydrates and less fat to ensure that your carbohydrate needs are being met.

Choose Lean Protein

Protein is essential for the daily repair of body tissue and supporting the immune system. It should make up about 25 percent of your daily calories.

Eggs are the only food that can be called a complete protein because they provide the best possible mixture of amino acids. Use egg whites in your diet regularly as a protein source. Other sources of quality protein are lean meats and fish.

Go for the Iron

Iron is important because it plays a key role in the body's oxygen-transporting capacity. Eating lean red meat at least three times a week can supply the iron you need.

Lean red meats contain the most easily absorbed form of iron available. Other sources of less easily absorbed iron include beef liver, pork, tuna, and clams. Sources of less easily absorbed iron include spinach, dried figs, oatmeal, beans, and lentils.

Since the body can absorb only a small percentage of the actual iron consumed, it is essential that you include adequate quantities of it in your diet. You can boost your body's ability to absorb it by combining foods high in vitamin C with iron-rich foods. For example, try grilling kebobs made with lean chicken, tomatoes, and peppers. Also note that coffee, tea, and some antacids can decrease iron absorption, as can consuming calcium at the same time as your iron sources.

Consume Enough Calcium

Daily calcium intake is essential for maintaining strong bones as well as muscle contractions and nerve impulses. Cyclists can develop low bone density even if they are otherwise healthy and young, because cycling alone does not provide enough load-bearing stimulus on our bones to cause positive changes in their density. This is one of the reasons to consider running as a form of crosstraining (see Chapter 11).

Consume 1,000 to 1,500 milligrams of calcium each day. Vitamin D facilitates the uptake of calcium. Remember to consume your calcium at different times than your iron-containing meals to enhance the absorption of both minerals. If you are not getting enough calcium from your daily diet, you can take chewable calcium supplements.

Stay Hydrated

Develop a habit of drinking plenty of water for appropriate hydration. Aim for about half your body weight in ounces of water per day as a baseline, and add 20 to 40 ounces per hour of exercise depending on your body size, ambient temperature, and your personal sweat rate. You can estimate your sweat rate by weighing yourself, naked and dry, before and after workouts. Every pound you lose represents a pint of fluid more that you lost (through your sweat and breath) than you consumed. You must replace twice that amount after exercise, since your body will be flushing waste by-products from your blood through urine as part of the recovery process.

Skin dryness, power output, joint fluids, digestion, and waste removal are all affected by fluid consumption. Your goal should be to finish a long workout with close to the same amount of fluid in your body that you started with. A loss of 2 to 3 percent of water can lead to a significant reduction in power output.

Eat around Training

Developing a habit of eating before, during, and after training will lead to being more successful at meeting nutritional needs during hard training and racing weeks down the road. For rides longer than 1.5 hours, you should consume calories during the ride. Consuming 200 to 300 calories an hour is a good starting point. Lighter riders can start at 200. Riders over 150 pounds should start at 250; over 175 pounds, at 300 an hour. The longer the rides, the more you should be consuming an hour.

Athletes I've coached have improved their success in ultraendurance events like solo 24-hour mountain bike races by increasing their caloric intake during those events. They practice this during training and dial in what their body can tolerate before racing. I have coached 165-pound athletes who can consume 400 to 600 calories an hour during long events. The fuel they take in allows them to keep going and delay fatigue. As pace or intensity increases, the amount of fuel your body can tolerate will decrease significantly.

Boost Your Metabolism

You may be able to increase your metabolism by eating more frequently. In other words, if your daily caloric intake needs to be 3,000 calories, then eating five 600-calorie meals may be more effective at keeping your metabolism active than eating three 1,000-calorie meals that day. This method tends to also keep blood sugar levels more stable throughout the day.

Another way to keep your metabolism active is to split your training up so you workout twice a day. Your metabolism remains active for some time after you finish exercising. Some athletes find that training once in the morning and then again in the early afternoon or evening helps reduce body fat stores.

SPECIAL CONSIDERATIONS

It is a good idea to get baseline bloodwork done each year to determine cholesterol and iron levels. Knowing that your iron levels are normal or low can be valuable down the road if you are feeling fatigued. You can retest to see if your iron levels have fallen during a period of lingering fatigue that you are at a loss to explain. Some research indicates that even having iron levels in the lower portion of the normal range can affect performance in endurance athletes. Since excessive iron intake can have serious health risks, iron supplementation should be done only under the supervision of a medical professional.

Some research indicates that taking large doses of vitamin C (about 600 to 1,000 milligrams a day) may reduce the frequency of upper respiratory tract infections (URTIs) in endurance athletes. However, supplementing with mega-doses of vitamins (especially B_6) may be harmful.

Check with your physician before starting an exercise program or changing your diet.

•———•

Remember that the body needs enough calories every day to support basic functions as well as daily activities. Carbohydrates supply fuel for energy to keep the muscles moving and the brain thinking, and they should make up 45 to 60 percent of your total daily intake. Poor concentration, mood swings, or low energy can all result from inadequate carbohydrates. Protein is used to rebuild tissue and support the immune system and should make up 25 percent of your daily calories. Fat is used to support the immune system and can be 15 to 30 percent of your daily intake.

Injuries and frequent illness can result from inadequate amounts of protein, carbohydrates, or fats. Don't try to lose or gain a lot of weight too quickly. Aim for steady, gradual changes. Cutting too many calories out of your daily intake can lead to fatigue and a suppressed immune system. The risk of getting sick or injured is not worth the possibility of losing more weight faster, since getting sick or injured will interrupt your overall training progress.

With weight and health issues addressed, you'll be ready to start seriously assessing your fitness level, the topic of the next chapter.

PART TWO

DIAGNOSING THE ENGINE

4

FITNESS ASSESSMENT

Fitness assessment determines an athlete's current fitness level, outlines personal strengths and limiters, establishes training zones, and measures for improvements to determine the effectiveness of training. *Strengths* are areas of fitness that we're already strong in, and *limiters* are the areas of our fitness that are holding us back from achieving our goals. It's important to find your cycling fitness strengths and determine your fitness limiters so you can design the training program that is most appropriate for you and your goals. It's also important to see your improvements through testing to help build confidence as you train.

Fitness testing can be done in a lab or on your bike (preferably with a power meter). Testing at a lab can determine physiological markers that can be used to establish appropriate training zones. Fitness testing done on the bike with a power meter during individual time trials, fast group rides, and races can determine performance markers and establish training levels based on power, or watts. *Physiological markers* are useful for determining potential and establishing training zone guidelines, but *performance markers* are what ultimately determine how fast you are able to go on the bike.

Fitness can also be assessed subjectively through questionnaires regarding your personal cycling experiences. When cyclists talk about their personal experiences, usually they describe their individual strengths and limitations: "I get dropped on the short steep climbs," or "I get dropped on the long steady climbs," or "I can outsprint my friends but can't hang on very long when it's windy." These are a few examples of how your cycling experience can tell you what fitness elements you need to improve.

Fitness tests can be done to determine training intensities based on heart rate, rate of perceived exertion (RPE), blood lactate concentrations relative to power and heart rate, or average power output for specific sustained durations. Each has advantages and disadvantages.

Without a fitness assessment, you won't know whether you are training at the appropriate intensity to achieve the goals of the workouts outlined in Chapter 11. I frequently see athletes training at an excessively high intensity during those times of the year when their focus should be on building base fitness. By defining specific zones, or levels, you'll know whether you are accomplishing the objectives outlined in the workouts.

HEART RATE, POWER, AND PERCEIVED EXERTION

Testing and training with a heart rate monitor can be relatively effective at lower to moderate steady intensities but not as effective during harder, shorter efforts. This is in part because heart rate is a response to the effort level rather than a direct measure of it. The heart's response also lags behind the effort. I'm sure you've done a short all-out sprint and seen that your heart rate was still climbing well after you stopped. Power output, on the other hand, is a direct measure of your effort at the moment you push on the pedals and power is measured throughout the sprint (see Figures 4.1a and 4.1b). Once you stop the sprint, your power drops instantly, even though your heart rate continues to climb. This is one example where power, not heart rate, would be useful to measure the effort. With a power meter you can see your peak power (displayed as watts) as well as the point that power begins to drop.

Power is variable, which can make monitoring an ongoing moderate effort difficult, whereas heart rate has a sort of built-in smoothing component. When you're riding steadily on a moderately rolling course, your heart rate will usually remain steadier than power and show gradual changes up and down. Even slight variances in pressure on the pedals can make significant changes in the power readout. Although heart rate may make it easier to monitor a steady, easy-to-moderate effort, it will not necessarily provide an accurate outline of time spent in a given zone. Since heart rate rises and falls gradually and power readings will change instantly along with changes in effort, the heart rate may still be reading that you're working at a high effort level well after you've actually stopped pushing on the pedals, or that you're not working hard yet when you actually are.

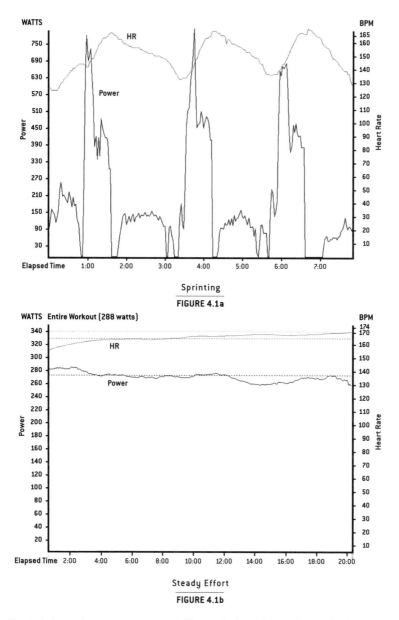

Sprinting

FIGURE 4.1a

Steady Effort

FIGURE 4.1b

Heart rate is not always an accurate method for monitoring and measuring training intensity. In these examples, you can see how heart rate response lags behind the actual effort level (displayed by power). Figure 4.1a shows a cyclist doing sprints. Notice how heart rate continues to climb after power has dropped off. Figure 4.1b shows heart rate increasing over time, even when power is dropping off.

If your heart rate monitor provides you with data regarding time spent in zones, it will be only an estimate of time at a given effort level. In other words, heart rate provides a guide for effort level, but power *is* the effort level.

Heart rate is also affected by variables like your state of hydration, rest, anxiety, illness, medications, and ambient temperature. If you are dehydrated, your heart will have to work harder, which will lead to a higher-than-normal reading. Since blood is mostly water and you have less blood volume when you're dehydrated, your heart has to work harder to keep up with demand by the working muscles for blood flow. In hot temperatures, your heart may have to beat faster even if you are fully hydrated because in addition to supplying the muscles with adequate blood flow, it also may need to direct blood to the surface area of the skin to aid in cooling. I see this condition frequently during indoor workouts where a cyclist's heart rate is sometimes higher for the same power or effort level than it would typically be outdoors, where the body can often stay cooler. A large cooling fan is essential when training indoors. I like one with a remote control, so I can adjust it without getting off the bike.

Adrenaline and caffeine can also elevate heart rate. I can recall standing in line at the start of a downhill mountain bike race and watching my heart rate climb 40 beats for no reason other than the excitement and anticipation of my turn approaching. Your heart rate may also be elevated in the morning if you are still recovering from the previous day's workouts. The heart will be working overtime along with the rest of your body as it tries to take care of whatever is going on. An unexpected increase in resting heart rate can also indicate that you're coming down with an illness. Your morning resting heart rate is one of the vital signs that should be monitored to assess your ongoing state of recovery (see Chapter 10 for more details). If your heart rate is higher than normal while exercising, it's a good idea to find out why. If you suspect that you are dehydrated, consume a sports drink and slow down or stop until your heart rate is normal again.

Heart rates can also be suppressed, or lower than normal, when you are in a state of ongoing fatigue known as ***overreaching***. The body's nervous system seems to have a built-in governor of sorts designed to protect the heart under these conditions. One sure sign that you are carrying a lot of fatigue is that your heart rate will not rise like it normally would regardless of how hard you ride. Such a sign means it's time to back off, cut the ride short, and take a few days of rest. This is one example when heart rate provides us with valuable feedback.

Power Variables

Power, unlike your heart, could care less how sick or dehydrated you are. Power can tell you whether your legs are tired or fresh, however. If you can't reach or maintain a power level that you normally could, then your body is giving you feedback about your current state of fatigue, health, or fitness level. When your legs are fatigued or you're sick or dehydrated, you may not be able to maintain the same power levels you could even as recently as a few days ago.

It is also normal to see upper-level sustainable power levels decrease during early base training. This is the time that we are working on our low end, or base, and we will lose some of our top-end power until we start ramping back up later. To raise our fitness ceiling higher each year, we must bring the ceiling down while we are building our foundation. You will also see a reduction in power output when you travel to higher elevations. Speed, relative to power output, will increase at higher elevations.

If power levels seem easier to reach and maintain and you've checked to be sure that your power meter is calibrated, then you may be realizing a jump in fitness or freshness in your legs. It's a great feeling to be questioning the accuracy of the power meter when it seems to be reading higher than normal!

Rate of Perceived Exertion (RPE)

Your rate of perceived exertion, or RPE, also provides a great deal of insight into the effort level you are riding at as well as your current state of fitness, fatigue, or health. It can take years for an athlete to get dialed into his or her RPE, but some pick it up rather quickly and can use it as one more form of feedback.

There are two standard scales for RPE, 1–20 and 1–10. Although the 1–20 scale is the standard used in lab testing, I prefer using the 1–10 scale because there are fewer choices, which makes it easier to compare from day to day. The "Rate of Perceived Exertion" sidebar explains how to use the 1–10 RPE scale.

RPE, when used along with heart rate and power, can be an excellent aid in determining effort, fitness progression or digression, and deviations from normal body function, so try to learn how your body feels at a certain heart rate and power level under normal conditions. As you learn to recognize effort levels through perception, you'll be better able to race and train at an appropriate effort level and recognize deviations from your normal rested state. By comparing RPE and power to heart rate, you can determine if the heart rate

RATE OF PERCEIVED EXERTION (RPE)
1–10 SCALE

1: VERY EASY

Sitting on your bike waiting to start the ride.

2–4: EASY TO MODERATE

Comfortable; you could ride all day at this pace and carry on a conversation. Breathing rate begins to increase at about an RPE of 4. This range is where your lower training threshold will fall (also see the sidebar "Threshold").

4–6: COMFORTABLY HARD

Steady, comfortably hard effort, commonly referred to in cycling as tempo. There is a noticeable increase in your breathing rate, and if you talk, your speech will be slightly interrupted by the need to breathe. It takes focus and desire to maintain this effort level, but if you are rested, you could hold this effort for up to 90 minutes.

5–7: HARD

This range will be where your upper training threshold will fall. Breathing is rapid and steady, but not yet labored. You will not want to talk, and if you do say anything, it will usually be very short sentences. You are just below the point when you feel the burning sensation in

[continues]

you're seeing at a given time is an accurate depiction of your effort or is being affected by other circumstances, such as heat, dehydration, illness, fatigue, or stress. The idea is that if you establish what an effort level of 4 feels like relative to heart rate and power day after day, then if you reach an RPE of 4 and your heart rate and power are lower than normal, you may be overreaching and need rest. If RPE and power match but heart rate is higher than normal, you may be dehydrated, anxious, or getting sick. If you are feeling light-headed, you should stop riding and consume a sports drink. Usually, both heart rate and RPE will gradually climb during a long, challenging, steady-state effort, even when power level stays constant.

This increase in heart rate is referred to as *cardiac drift*. The exact cause of cardiac drift is still under investigation, but it is currently believed that either a reduction in the heart's output (called *stroke volume*) creates the need for an increased heart rate to keep up with demands, or an increase in core temperature requiring that additional blood flow be directed to the skin for cooling and loss of blood volume through sweating requires that the heart work harder to keep up (see Figures 4.2a and 4.2b).

If you combine heart rate, RPE, and power, you have three great measuring tools to help you dial in your effort levels. Fitness testing gives you guidelines and starting points for using these three measurements of effort level.

PHYSIOLOGICAL TEST MARKERS

Three main physiological measurements can give insight into your current fitness and help define your training zones. They are maximum aerobic capacity, or VO_2max, and your upper and lower training thresholds. Maximum aerobic capacity is a measurement of your maximum ability to process and utilize oxygen throughout your body. Training thresholds are defined in several ways but are points that can be marked as a percentage of your VO_2max.

Your lower training threshold is called the *lactate threshold*. Your upper training threshold may be called one of many names: *anaerobic threshold, maximum lactate steady state,* or even *lactate threshold,* depending on what method is used to determine it and who does the test. You'll want your thresholds to be at a high percentage of your VO_2max during the time of the season that you need your fitness to be the highest. But you can't keep them up at their highest potential all year; if you try to do that, you will be limiting the height of your fitness ceiling by neglecting your aerobic base. (See the sidebar "Threshold" later in this chapter.)

RPE *continued*

your legs. If you are rested, fresh, fit, and motivated, you could hold this effort level for 50 to 75 minutes.

6–8: VERY HARD

You feel that burning sensation in your legs, breathing is rapid and labored, and you have to be very motivated to maintain this effort. If you're rested and motivated, you could hold this effort level for about 20 to 40 minutes. Breathing rate will make it difficult to talk at this level, and if you do, it will be one or two words at a time.

7–9: VERY, VERY HARD

You could hold this effort level for about 5 to 8 minutes. The perception of this effort, along with heart rate, will lag behind actual effort. So, for example, if you start out at 25 miles per hour or 325 watts, it may feel like an RPE of 4–6 and seem manageable, but after a couple of minutes, that same speed or power will begin to feel much harder.

9–10: MAXIMUM

Maximum effort, such as a hard sprint after a long race; talking is not an option.

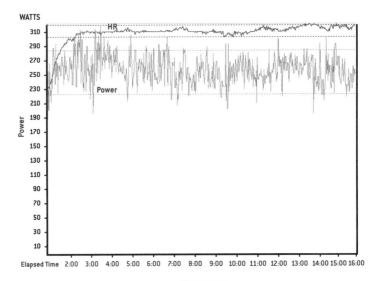

FIGURE 4.2a

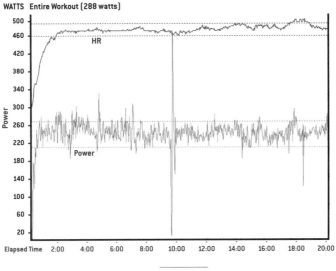

FIGURE 4.2b

Above are two examples of cardiac drift. Even at a steady power-level effort, heart rate can climb over time even when power, or effort level, remains constant. This "cardiac drift" can be greater if the athlete is dehydrated or if ambient temperature is high.

Maximum Aerobic Capacity

VO_2max can be estimated through mathematical formulas involving various data, but it can be measured only with sophisticated equipment and is usually expressed in terms of milliliters of oxygen processed per kilogram of body weight per minute (mL/kg/min). Therefore, two cyclists may be able to process the same volume of oxygen per minute, but a lighter athlete will have a higher VO_2max number when expressed relative to body weight.

There are genetic limits to what our VO_2max potential is, but it can increase through training and decrease when you are not training for extended periods. If you want to see your highest VO_2max numbers, you should be tested at a time when your fitness is high. You can also be tested when you are not at your peak fitness and then be retested in 8 to 12 weeks to help determine how effective your training has been.

Testing your VO_2max is very difficult, and it takes a great deal of freshness and motivation to reach your true maximum. It involves wearing a mask over your nose and mouth or having your nose pinched off and breathing though a tube secured in your mouth. You ride for several minutes at a progressively harder and harder effort level until you can't pedal anymore. Your exhaled air is compared with the inhaled air content to determine how much of the ingoing oxygen your body utilized. Ranges among elite cyclists are 70 to 80 mL/kg/min for males and 60 to 70 mL/kg/min for females. Don't expect to reach these levels, since they are the numbers achieved by the best cyclists in the world. Also remember that your VO_2max is sport specific and will be different for cycling than it would be for running, for example.

Determining Training Thresholds

Although VO_2max can be a measure of your athletic "potential," your threshold measurements are a better indicator of what your actual performance will be and are what we use to establish our training zones and measure progress. The threshold levels will also change throughout the training year but can go up or down independent of VO_2max.

During the base training phase, the upper threshold will usually drop and the lower threshold will rise. It's odd to think that we are getting temporally slower to get faster down the road, but it does happen. Think of it as bringing the fitness ceiling down so that you can build a larger foundation that will support a higher, stronger ceiling. It does not take as long to put the ceiling back up as it takes to build a larger foundation. Having your upper training threshold at 90 percent of your VO_2max means that you are capable of using more of your maximum ability than if it was at 80 percent. This is where planning is important, since the objective is to have your fitness ceiling at its highest point to coincide with your most important events (see Figure 4.3).

Training thresholds measured in a lab test are useful, but, as noted in the sidebar on thresholds, the method of measuring thresholds can change how the training levels, or zones, are determined. For base training you will use two "training thresholds" for determining your training intensities: the lower and upper training thresholds.

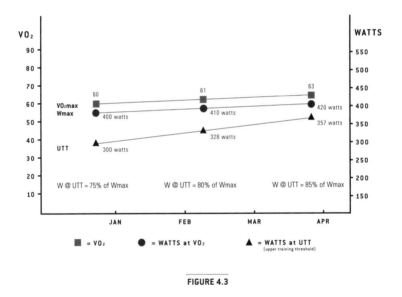

FIGURE 4.3

Your fitness ceiling can increase independently of your maximum aerobic capacity. The goal of training is not only to increase your aerobic capacity but also to raise your fitness ceiling so you are capable of using a higher percentage of your aerobic capacity. This athlete was able to increase power output at the upper training threshold as a higher percentage of the maximum power output at the athlete's aerobic capacity.

ESTIMATING YOUR LOWER TRAINING THRESHOLD (LTT)

Your LTT is 55–75% of your current CP30 power level.

CP30 = 250 watts

250 x 0.55 = 137.5

250 x 0.75 = 187.5

LTT = 138 – 188 watts

Lower Training Threshold

The lower training threshold, as mentioned earlier, is called the lactate threshold (although some coaches refer to it as the aerobic threshold, or AeT). You will come across various definitions of what the lactate threshold is; if you haven't already, this would be a good time to read the sidebar "Threshold" later in this chapter. This lower training threshold, or LTT, is when the level or concentration of lactate in your blood begins to rise above your baseline blood lactate levels.

Some labs do not use a lactate analyzer or specifically test for your lower threshold, but you can estimate it by using your upper threshold and subjective markers. If you have determined your upper threshold in a lab and set your heart rate zones, you can start out by estimating your lower threshold to be at the top of zone 1. (See zones listed in the heart rate zone chart, Table 5.1, in the next chapter.) If you're using power and you determine your critical power (CP) for 30 minutes, as outlined later in this chapter, then you can estimate that your LTT will fall between 55 percent and 75 percent of your current CP30 power level. (See the sidebar "Estimating Your Lower Training Threshold.") The location of your lower threshold will vary slightly depending on how well you've developed your aerobic fitness base up to this point. The greater your aerobic base, the higher your LTT will be—70 percent of CP30 rather than 60 percent, for example. For base training, you will be doing a lot of riding around this lower threshold, so it's important that you know where it is.

A subjective way to estimate your LTT includes riding at an intensity where your heart rate just begins to rise and breathing is up just a bit. You should feel that you are making an effort, just not pushing yourself. There should be no burning sensation in your legs or significant increase in your breathing rate. You should be able to carry on a conversation without having to stop midsentence to breathe. You should be able to ride for 30 minutes to 3 hours (depending on your level of base fitness and current regular ride durations) steadily at this effort level without feeling overly challenged on almost a daily basis. Your heart rate should not drift up at this workout intensity. If you find your heart rate increasing by more than a few beats over the duration even when effort is steady, then the effort level is a bit too high for you right now to be considered your lower threshold, and you should ride a bit slower or not as long. Since dehydration and heat can affect your heart rate, make sure you are staying well hydrated.

Upper Training Threshold

The upper training threshold, or UTT, is the highest level of intensity at which your body is able to process the by-products associated with carbohydrate metabolism at the same rate they are being produced. As your effort level or intensity increases, your body will demand more energy production from carbohydrates, which results in the release of more lactate and hydrogen ions into the blood. (See the sidebar "Lactate" in Chapter 2.) At lower intensities, the body is able to shuttle the by-products and keep up with production, but there is a point where production overwhelms your body's ability to process the by-products. Your UTT is where production and processing remain at the highest level currently possible. If you are tested using a lactate analyzer, then it would be your maximum lactate steady state (MLSS).

Some labs will test you using the same gas exchange analyzer used to measure your VO_2max and will determine your upper threshold based on various physiological markers, or parameters, without taking blood samples. This can be used to estimate your heart rate training zones by plugging that number into the heart rate zones chart. Many labs will refer to this upper threshold as your "lactate threshold." That's fine as long as you know that it's your *upper* threshold they are referring to rather than your lower threshold.

One advantage of having your upper threshold determined in a lab using a gas exchange analyzer is that the lab staff should also be able to measure your energy expenditure. This will provide you with an outline of how efficiently you burn fat and how many calories you burn while riding at a given intensity. This information is useful for calculating daily energy needs and measuring again for improvements in fat usage down the road.

ESTIMATING YOUR UPPER TRAINING THRESHOLD (UTT)

Your UTT is 85–95% of your current CP30 power level.

CP30 = 250 watts

250 x 0.85 = 212.5

250 x 0.95 = 237.5

UTT = 212 – 237 watts

PERFORMANCE TEST MARKERS

A power meter used during training and racing is becoming the standard for providing ongoing feedback on performance and appropriate training intensities. Power meters currently range in price from about $700 to $3,400 and are housed in the rear hub, the bottom bracket, or the cranks. One advantage of riding with a power meter on your bike is that each workout can provide valuable performance data, and each test is also a workout. That's not to say that each time you ride your bike your objective is to reach a higher power level than the last ride. It means that if you are riding, and especially racing, the data you get from that workout can be reviewed and used to determine how well you are doing on that day. Testing with a power meter on your bike means that when you are doing one of the specific critical power tests outlined later, you are also getting a great workout.

One interesting aspect of this feature is being able to view how hard an athlete is working during a given race. I've had two cyclists in the same race have vastly different finishes: one of them finished in the field sprint, and the other was dropped halfway through the race. After reviewing their power files, I could see that the athlete who finished the race did so with far less power output than the athlete who was dropped. The course was a flat criterium, and they both had similar power-to-weight ratios. The athlete who finished was doing a better job of staying protected in the pack and not wasting energy. The other rider spent too much time at the back and was having to work harder to stay with the field. She had to put out more power to stay at the back than the rider up in the pack. Remember, you have a limited supply of "matches" to burn, and you want to save them for when you need them the most. Power files can teach us to race smarter, not harder. Most athletes will set personal records (PRs) for power levels during races, since their motivation (and often fitness) is highest at that time.

I have also seen files from races where an athlete thought her fitness was low because she could not stay with the group, but the file clearly showed that she was not putting out the same level of power she was able to just a week earlier. After talking with the athlete, I discovered that she had a lot of work and life stress the week before this race, and she was fatigued. After a week of recovery, her power levels came back up to where they should be, and she was able to race with the pack again.

Critical Power Testing

Critical power (CP) as used here means the highest average power you can sustain for a given duration. With a power meter on your bike, you can determine the highest power level you can average for a specific duration and then outline training intensities based on power levels from these tests to meet certain training objectives. Durations of interest commonly measured are 20 or 30 minutes, 10 to 12 minutes, 5 or 6 minutes, 1 minute, and 5 to 12 seconds. Some test durations are more relevant during different training phases and to the type of races that you are preparing for, so not all athletes will need to test at all durations. If, for instance, you're a mountain bike racer who specializes in solo 24-hour events, then you don't need to know what your highest 5-second power output is because you won't be training that proficiency. You will need to know what your 60-minute power level is, since most of your training will be based on the longer durations. You can estimate the 60-minute power level as 5 percent less than the average power you can sustain for a 30-minute test. Your average, or CP, power levels for 6 and 12 minutes will also be used. If you race shorter mountain bike cross-country events, then you'll need to train at your 1-minute power level to prepare for fast starts, so testing at this duration is useful. A road racer will need to train at all power levels, since different points throughout the race will require output at every level. Knowing which of the power levels are your limitations helps you fine-tune your training so you can improve at that duration.

You'll want to repeat CP tests about every six to eight weeks to check for increases or decreases in performance (see Table 4.1). An increase means that fitness is improving, and you will need to adjust your training zones accordingly.

TABLE 4.1: CRITICAL POWER ZONE BENEFITS AND RACE APPLICATIONS

DURATION	CP ZONES	FITNESS BENEFIT	RACE APPLICATION
12 sec.	CP0.2	Explosive power	Finishing sprint Short hill Start
1 min.	CP1	Lactate clearance	Fast starts Short climbs
6 min.	CP6	Velocity at VO_2max	Moderate duration climbs Short, high-intensity segments
12 min.	CP12	Aerobic capacity (VO_2max)	Fast starts
30 min.	CP30	Lactate superthreshold	Long steady efforts
60 min.	CP60	Lactate threshold	Short duration race endurance
90 min.	CP90	Sublactate threshold	Moderate duration race endurance
180 min.	CP180	Basic aerobic function	Long duration race endurance

From *The Cyclist's Training Bible* by Joe Friel (VeloPress).

A decrease in your power output may mean that you are in a state of overreaching and are carrying fatigue in your legs. This tells you that you may need to be resting more so your body can continue to absorb the training load and make improvements. One mistake I see repeated frequently is when an athlete sees his performance decreasing and adds more training when he really needs to back off and allow his body to recover. Fitness improvements happen during recovery or rest. You have to apply the training stimulus, or load, but then you have to allow the body time to adapt to that training stress before you'll see gains in fitness. If you are coming off the cycling season with a lot of fitness, you will also see your upper threshold power (or power you can sustain for about 50 to 75 minutes) drop a bit during your base fitness training. This is normal—and necessary—to bring it up higher down the road.

PROTOCOL FOR 30-MINUTE CRITICAL POWER TEST

Terrain: Well-paved road with little traffic or long, steady climb (3–5% grade).

Goal: Complete 30:00 test, riding as hard as possible.

Warm-up: See the sidebar "Warm-up" for details.

Test: For first 5:00, hold back. Gauge your speed every 5:00 thereafter, adjusting your pace incrementally.

Cool-down: 10:00–20:00 easy spinning.

Note: Record your average power, cadence, and heart rate for the entire test. If you choose to ride a steady climb, find one that allows you to keep your rpms above 80 for the duration of the test.

Performance Field Testing

Critical Power Tests

The first test you should perform is a 30-minute CP time trial. This will provide the starting point for determining your baseline fitness and training intensity profile.

The testing can be done with a power meter outdoors or on an indoor trainer. The testing protocols that follow describe outdoor tests, but they can easily be adapted for the trainer. One consideration for indoor testing is that many athletes will produce less power indoors (3 to 10 percent lower) compared with what they can do outdoors. Hard workouts or tests done on a stationary trainer can create higher heart rates and perceived exertion. Motivation can also be lower indoors for many cyclists, since one of the passions of cycling is to be outdoors and moving around.

It's important that the testing follow a specific, repeatable protocol so that future test results are a reliable comparison. That means that you should be fully rested and healthy before the test and warm up the same way before each test (see the sidebar "Warm-up" for guidelines), eat the same meal, make sure that you are fully hydrated and carbohydrate loaded, and that you do the test at about the same time of day. Environmental conditions such as temperature and wind can also affect the consistency of the testing, which is one advantage of doing the testing indoors (see Figures 4.4a and 4.4b).

Treat the test as if it were a race. I recommend that cyclists test at the end of an easy or recovery week so the legs are rested. Make sure that your power meter is correctly calibrated and that the batteries are fresh before you begin.

A good warm-up is essential to the performance tests described in this chapter. An adequate warm-up is usually 45 minutes or longer. The shorter the test duration, the longer the warm-up should be. I find that some athletes do well with a 45-minute warm-up, while others need up to 90 minutes to reach a point where they are able to put out their best efforts. You'll need to experiment with different warm-ups to find out what works best for you. Once you get your warm-up routine perfected, write it down and use it each time before a test or race to ensure consistency. The warm-up sidebar describes a warm-up that's effective for both indoor and outdoor workouts.

WARM-UP

[for critical power tests]

Use a high cadence for most of the efforts during the warm-up. A good starting point for a warm-up includes the following (suggested in minutes):

20:00 easy pace
Zones 1–2

10:00–15:00 moderate effort
Zones 2–3

5:00 hard but not all out
Zones 3–4

5:00 easy,
1:00 at 95% max
just below CP1 watts

3:00 easy,
1:00 at 95% max
just below CP1 watts

3:00 easy,
5:00 hard but not all out
Zones 3–4

5:00–10:00 easy

At this point, you can start the test. Good luck!

Tests using a power meter will also help you develop a pacing strategy for time trials, because they can help you determine appropriate effort levels from perceived exertion as they correlate to power output and heart rate. For this type of test, use a road with good pavement that allows you to ride all out for about 20 minutes in one direction, make a U-turn, and ride back along the same route. It should also have little or no traffic and as few driveways, turns, and cross streets as possible, since you will have to watch for traffic while you're doing this test.

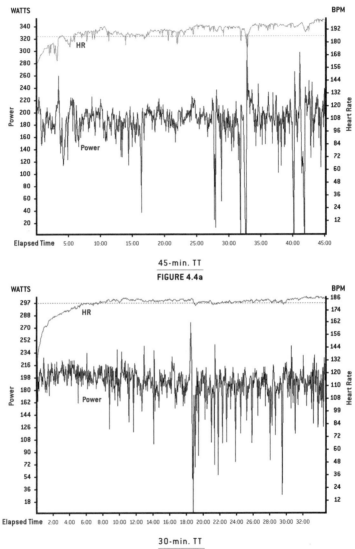

45-min. TT

FIGURE 4.4a

30-min. TT

FIGURE 4.4b

These examples are from the same athlete performing time trial efforts within a few weeks of each other. In the first time trial, she was able to average 180 watts for 45 minutes and spent a lot of the effort with her heart rate above 180 bpm. She also averaged 180 watts during another time trial a few weeks later that lasted about 30 minutes. Given that she was able to average 180 watts for a 45 minutes just a few weeks earlier, she should have been able to average more than 180 watts for an all-out 30-minute effort. The lower heart rate she obtained during the second time trial demonstrates that her motivation may have been lower or that she may have been carrying fatigue in her legs.

PROTOCOL FOR 12-SECOND CRITICAL POWER TEST

Warm-up:	See the sidebar "Warm-up" for details.
Test:	Stand and sprint all out for 0:12.
	Spin easy 3:00–5:00.
	Repeat the 0:12 effort and easy spin 2–3 times.
Cool-down:	10:00–20:00 easy spinning.

Note: Record your highest average power for each 12-second interval and the maximum wattage you hit.

You can also use a long, steady hill climb for your time trial. Choose a climb with a moderate grade (3 to 5 percent) that will take you at least 30 minutes to climb and will allow you to keep your rpms above 80. You will usually see slightly higher power output numbers for the same duration while climbing than you will on a flat course. Once you find a safe road, warm up well and do your time trial. Mark the test using the interval mode on your power meter.

I recommend that you ease into the test to be sure that you can maintain the intensity for the duration of the effort. Since heart rate and perceived exertion will lag behind, you might feel like you can put out more power during the first few minutes than you actually can over the entire test. The most common mistake is going out too hard. Keep reminding yourself during the first 5 minutes to hold back a bit. About 5 minutes into the test, check in with yourself and decide if you are going too hard, too slow, or just right. You then have three choices: slow down, speed up, or maintain the same effort level. Make any changes in your pace small and then wait another 5 minutes to see how it feels. Every 5 minutes of the 30-minute test, check in with yourself and note your power level, heart rate, and perceived exertion level. Adjust your effort level based on that information to ensure that you will be able to complete the test but are also going as hard as possible over the 30 minutes.

PROTOCOL FOR 6-MINUTE CRITICAL POWER TEST

Terrain: Moderate hill with steady grade (to keep speed down and power up).

Warm-up.   See the sidebar "Warm-up" for details.

Test: Manageable pace, 1:00–2:00

                Hard pace, 3:00–4:00

                Very hard pace, 5:00–6:00, with final minute being all you can do to finish

Cool-down: 10:00–20:00 easy spinning.

Note: Record your average cadence, power, and heart rate as well as maximum heart rate reached.

At some point during the test, you may begin to wonder whether you can maintain the effort level for the entire test. If you've done a hard time trial, you'll know this feeling well. If this happens during the first 10 minutes, then you went out too hard. You should reach this point somewhere after halfway through the test. This is a good time to use or practice a mantra (see Chapter 14). During hard efforts like time trials or races, your mental fitness plays as big a role as your physical fitness in getting you to the finish.

After completing the test, cool down for about 15 to 20 minutes by spinning easy. Record all the data in your daily log. You can also use the test data profile sheet in the Appendix B to track all your information.

Many regions will have time trials on the same course throughout the year and from year to year. You can also use these races for your power testing. Motivation is usually higher during races, so your output should be higher, too. You can also do the tests with riding buddies and teammates to increase motivation.

For base training, we will test at the durations of 12 seconds, 6 minutes, 12 minutes, and 30 minutes. Don't do all these tests on the same day. If you want to get started, you can do all the tests over the course of one week, but allow a couple of days between tests. You could combine the 12-second and 6-minute tests on the same day, but do the 12-second effort first. Also be sure

---

PROTOCOL FOR 12-MINUTE CRITICAL POWER TEST

Terrain:	Moderate hill with steady grade (to keep speed down and power up).
Warm-up.	See the sidebar "Warm-up" for details.
Test:	Manageable pace, 1:00–4:00.
	Hard pace, 5:00–8:00.
	Very hard pace, 9:00–12:00, with final minute being all you can do to finish.
Cool-down:	10:00–20:00 easy spinning.

Note: Record your average cadence, power, and heart rate as well as maximum heart rate reached.

---

to give yourself adequate recovery between the two tests by spinning easy for 10 minutes before starting the 6-minute test. For example, after a week of rest, you could do the 12-second and 6-minute testing on Saturday, rest or ride easy and short on Sunday and Monday, test for 12 minutes on Tuesday, rest for 2 or 3 days, and test for 30 minutes on Friday or Saturday. That's a very tough week! Make sure you're eating and resting well that week. And don't try this the same week you are experiencing unusual stressors, such as moving into a new house or taking finals.

For the 12-second efforts, stand and go all out like you are sprinting for the finish line. Spin easy before your next 12-second sprint. Do three or four of these 12-second efforts, and record the one with the highest average power. Also note the maximum wattage you reach. For the 6-minute test, use a moderate hill that is as steady a grade as possible. This will help keep your speed down and your power up. Use whatever cadence you feel most comfortable with, but note your average cadence. Ease into this effort, too. Split it into 2-minute segments. The first time you try this duration, start out conservatively and try to build more power, or go harder, every 2 minutes.

The 12-minute test should be done on a steady climb as well. Use a similar pacing approach for this test to the one for the 6- and 30-minute efforts.

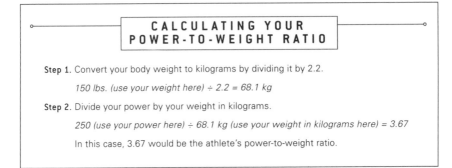

CALCULATING YOUR
POWER-TO-WEIGHT RATIO

Step 1. Convert your body weight to kilograms by dividing it by 2.2.

150 lbs. (use your weight here) ÷ 2.2 = 68.1 kg

Step 2. Divide your power by your weight in kilograms.

250 (use your power here) ÷ 68.1 kg (use your weight in kilograms here) = 3.67

In this case, 3.67 would be the athlete's power-to-weight ratio.

You still may find that you'll go out too hard or too easy the first time you try these tests. That's fine. You'll learn from them and have a better idea what power level to use the next time you test.

Record Your Data

Keep track of all your power test data. Even if you don't feel you were able to put out as much power as you can, it's good to have the reference points for future tests. If, for instance, you start your 30-minute test and blow up 15 minutes into it, forcing you to stop, you can look at the power level you averaged for those 15 minutes and start a bit lower the next time you test.

I recently started working with an athlete who had not raced in over 5 years. He did have all his power test data from 5 years ago, which provided some great information on where he needed to be in order to get back to where he left off. He had also kept track of his body weight, so that information gave us insight into his power-to-weight ratio.

Don't underestimate the importance of your training data. The first thing I ask for when I start coaching a new athlete is his or her daily training log. Accurate information about what a cyclist has been doing can tell me a lot about what that individual needs to be doing now.

Remember to take into consideration the weather any time you conduct performance test outdoors. Wind, rain, and heat can all affect your power output regardless of fitness. Weight can also affect your climbing speed, so be sure to note your body weight as well as bike and wheel set for comparison later.

Power Profiling

One guideline that you can use for estimating your strengths and limiters is the power profiling chart found in *Training and Racing with a Power Meter* by Hunter Allen and Andrew Coggan. Their profile chart is set up for test durations of 5 seconds, 1 minute, 5 minutes, and 60 minutes. Once you feel you have your personal best average power levels for those durations, you can plug them into the chart (based on the power-to-weight ratio of your body weight in kilograms) and see what your profile is and what aspects of your fitness need improvement to reach your goals.

Again, you don't need to be a good sprinter to be a great mountain bike racer, but you do need to be able to sprint if you want to race criteriums. Use Allen and Coggan's power profile chart as a guideline, and don't worry about what category the chart places you in. I've seen athletes with power profiles in the category 4 range who have done very well in category 3 races, for example. I have also seen athletes win sprints even though their power profiles indicated that they were not strong sprinters.

You can estimate your 60-minute critical power level from your CP30 average watts. CP60 is estimated to be 5 percent less than CP30. For example,

$$CP30 = 300w \times 0.95 = 285 \text{ watts for CP60}$$

(See the sidebar "Calculating Your Power-to-Weight Ratio.")

A cyclist with a high CP12 and CP30 power will do better in time trials and in longer events with rolling or steady hills. If you have a high CP1 and CP5 to 6-minute power average, you will usually do better in shorter events with short, steeper climbs or events with a lot of surges, like criteriums. The higher your power-to-weight ratio number is, the better you will climb. In the same way, the higher your absolute power output is (regardless of weight), the stronger you'll be on a flat course. If you have a high average power for 5 to 12 seconds, you should be a strong sprinter. It is less common to see a cyclist with a very high 5- to 12-second power average and a relatively high 30-minute power average. What is common are cyclists who are good at one end of the power durations or the other or are somewhat balanced across all durations.

The more you train at a given duration, the better you generally become at that range, but there will be limits to what you can achieve based on your muscle fiber type. Cyclists with a high percentage of fast-twitch type II fibers tend to be better at the shorter critical power durations; those with more slow-twitch type I fibers tend to do better at the longer durations. Developing your overall base fitness elements should allow you to improve across the board at all power durations.

Heart Rate Time Trial

If you don't have access to a power meter, then do a 30-minute effort the same way you would with power but note heart rate and perceived exertion. I have found that most athletes will average 8 to 15 heartbeats higher than their upper threshold heart rate for a 30-minute time trial. If you estimate your upper threshold heart rate this way, be aware that it is only an estimate and that you are always better off underestimating your upper threshold heart rate than over-estimating it.

You can also time yourself up a climb and estimate fitness changes based on whether you climb the same hill slower or faster. You'll need to mark a specific distance on the climb so you know exactly where to start and stop your watch or computer. Make sure these reference points are permanent so you can use them year after year.

Fitness assessment plays a critical role in helping you determine appropriate training levels and then monitor your improvements throughout your base training. This chapter has defined various thresholds—including the different terms that you may come across that are various ways to refer to the same point. The reference points we are most concerned with are referred to as your upper and lower training thresholds throughout this book.

Physiological testing can be done in a lab, where sophisticated equipment can assess lactate levels, VO_2max, and other reference points. Performance testing may be done during a time trial or even a race, during which you use a power meter on your bike. Power, heart rate, and perceived exertion can all provide insight into determining your training zones, as discussed in the next chapter.

Keep track of all your testing and training data. It is very valuable information that can tell you whether your training is effective or not.

THRESHOLD

If you've been cycling for very long, you've probably heard of lactate threshold (LT) or anaerobic threshold (AT). Other terms you may come across include maximum lactate steady state (MLSS), ventilatory threshold (VT), aerobic threshold (AeT), and the latest, functional threshold power (FTP). These terms are all used to describe significant reference points for setting up training zones and measuring fitness progression throughout the training year, but they are measured in different ways and have different meanings. The higher you can raise your thresholds, the greater your fitness. I call this "raising your fitness ceiling."

As a cyclist, you're limited by the power you can sustain at these thresholds. The more power or speed you can generate at these thresholds, the faster you can ride. Understanding what is being measured is important because each can have a different function regarding training.

LACTATE THRESHOLD (LT)

Technically, lactate threshold is the point where lactate levels in the blood first increase over your baseline levels. This is the point that I'll be referring to as your lower training threshold (LTT) throughout the book. Some coaches also refer to this point as the aerobic threshold (AeT), in part because lactate threshold is commonly used to describe or define a reference point at a higher intensity. The term aerobic threshold is not popular among exercise physiologists because it implies that there is a point when energy metabolism switches from aerobic to anaerobic. Since both systems are working at the same time, this term can be misleading. However, many coaches, cyclists, and even lab testing technicians use the term lactate threshold to define a point of exercise intensity that is much higher and results in a greater amount of lactate in the blood. You may also see this lower lactate threshold called LT1 and the upper reference point referred to as LT2.

Lactate is present in the blood even at rest, which is why you have a baseline level. The levels, expressed as millimoles per liter of blood (mmol/L), are low and stable until you start activating more muscle fibers and burning more carbohydrates. Baseline levels, or concentrations, range from about 0.07 mmol/L to about 2 mmol/L. If you start out at a very easy cycling pace or power level and gradually increase the effort level by a small percentage every 3 to 5 minutes, the lactate levels will begin to rise above your normal resting range. This is a point when your body begins to produce lactate faster than it is processing and utilizing it. When your lactate levels reach a point that is 1 mmol/L above your baseline, it is referred to as your lactate threshold, or LT. From this point on, lactate levels begin to rise along with the effort level.

(continues)

Measuring the blood lactate levels at the end of each of the 3- to 5-minute steps or increases in effort level will create a profile that will show at what effort level and rate (relative to power and heart rate) the lactate levels rise. The longer it takes before your lactate levels begin to climb, the better. I often see athletes with a poorly developed aerobic base have lactate levels rise very quickly and early relative to effort level. This means they are moving from burning fat to carbohydrate too soon, and their aerobic system is failing to keep up with lactate production, which results in an accumulation of lactate as well as hydrogen ions. The hydrogen ions are currently being blamed for the burning sensation that you feel in your muscles during prolonged hard efforts. (See the sidebar "Lactate" in Chaper 2.) This rapid increase of lactate levels results in a lower fitness ceiling because you have to shut down or slow down as the by-products in your blood (lactate and hydrogen ions) overwhelm your aerobic system's ability to manage them. These athletes usually have a history of training at higher intensities too often. After I've had them slow down or train at lower intensities for 6 to 8 weeks, I've seen significant improvements in their low-end lactate profiles (see Figure 4.5). This allows them to raise their fitness ceiling, which means they can ride faster and longer before fatiguing. This supports the concept that you have to slow down to get faster.

Lactate threshold is measured by taking the small samples of blood after each 3- to 5-minute step and analyzing them to determine the level of lactate present. A few smaller portable lactate analyzers are available, including the Lactate Pro and Lactate Scout, which allow you to do this with the help of an assistant. You can also have it done in an exercise physiology lab.

MAXIMUM LACTATE STEADY STATE (MLSS)

After that initial 1 mmol/L rise, if you continue your progressive step test, lactate levels will begin to increase quickly. There is a point within this increase that is frequently referred to as your lactate threshold. Some testers will use a specific blood lactate level like 4 mmol/L as the lactate threshold point for everyone. The 4 mmol/L point can be used to measure performance increases and decreases, but it is not necessarily the "upper training threshold" that we are looking for to determine our appropriate training zones. You can use 4 mmol/L as a reference point to compare your heart rate and power levels at 4 mmol/L down the road to see if you are putting out more power or have a lower heart rate at that lactate level, but it gets a bit complicated in determining what exactly is causing that shift. Overall, using 4 mmol/L to establish training zones is not practical or appropriate.

(continues)

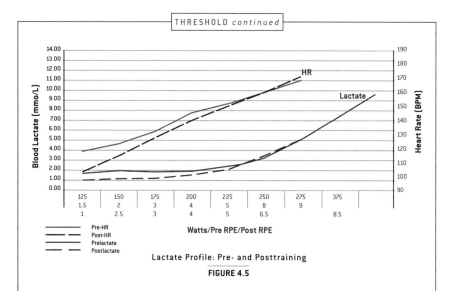

Lactate Profile: Pre- and Posttraining

FIGURE 4.5

A better way to figure out what is an appropriate upper training threshold using blood lactate levels requires more testing to pinpoint your highest possible effort level (measured relative to heart rate and power in watts), where you can maintain the highest possible steady level of lactate in the blood during a steady 60-minute effort. One method of doing this is to take measurements every 10 minutes during a steady effort to determine if your body is actually able to maintain a balance between lactate production and lactate clearing, or processing. The highest effort level at which you can maintain this balance is referred to as maximum lactate steady state (MLSS). This is an excellent reference point for establishing training intensities, since you can be certain that you are at or just below the point where you are overwhelming your body's ability to process lactate and the other by-products associated with exercise metabolism. The idea here is that staying at or just below this point allows you to train longer and, therefore, obtain greater benefit without the additional training load stress associated with higher accumulations of the metabolic by-products.

ANAEROBIC THRESHOLD (AT)

Another common way of determining training zones based on a progressive exercise step test will determine what is referred to as your anaerobic threshold, or AT. Anaerobic threshold is measured using a gas exchange analyzer that measures the rate that you consume and process (or utilize) oxygen. To do this, you will be breathing into a device through either a mask

(continues)

┌─────────────── THRESHOLD *continued* ───────────────┐

worn over your mouth and nose or through a tube in your mouth. You can find these testing devices at university labs and exercise testing facilities around the country. You can also find portable gas exchange analyzers that allow you to test while riding outdoors. These devices are very expensive, and the data from them can be inaccurate if the person doing the test is not experienced enough or the equipment is not calibrated correctly.

Several parameters are measured by the technician or coach doing the testing in order to determine your AT. They include lactate levels (although not directly measured through blood samples), heart rate, oxygen inhaled and exhaled, carbon dioxide exhaled, and breathing rate. From these data, we can determine a threshold called the anaerobic threshold. Some exercise physiologists prefer not to call this the anaerobic threshold because it is not a point when the body shifts from aerobic to anaerobic metabolism. Both systems are "on" at the same time (just like the aerobic threshold). So, some labs will refer to this point as the lactate threshold, or LT2. Whatever they call it, it's a reference point that can be used to establish training zones based on heart rate and, to some degree, power. Find out what they are referring to so you'll know which threshold it is that they are measuring.

This is also done as a step test, with effort level being increased at given durations throughout the test. Training zones, usually based on heart rate, can then be established as a percentage of your AT heart rate. The same equipment used for this test is also used to measure an athlete's maximum aerobic capacity, or VO_2max.

One drawback to using just AT to determine training intensity is that it does not pinpoint the MLSS but just estimates it. If you are at the point when you will be training near your upper threshold, then AT can overestimate the appropriate intensity at which you should be training. This does not mean that you need to have several tests done to establish perfect training levels. You can use other parameters like heart rate, power, and perceived exertion to help you determine your training intensities as well. If you have access to a lactate test, then you can pinpoint your MLSS by starting at your prescribed AT level and working up or down from there until you find it.

FUNCTIONAL THRESHOLD POWER (FTP)

When using a power meter to assist in setting appropriate training levels, you will be able to test your maximum sustainable power level for various durations. These power numbers can provide training levels that address certain training objectives. One of these power levels is

(continues)

└──┘

THRESHOLD *continued*

called functional threshold power, or FTP. Your FTP is the highest level of power you can average for a 60-minute all out effort, and you can use it as your upper training threshold. Training levels based on power can then be determined as a percentage of your FTP.

One thing to keep in mind is that over an all out 60-minute effort, lactate levels will accumulate within the blood above what would be considered your MLSS. This means that using your FTP can create more training stress than using your MLSS for upper threshold workouts. For this reason, I suggest using a power level that is slightly below your FTP (5 to 15 percent less) when doing upper threshold workouts—if you haven't had your MLSS tested in a lab.

5

TRAINING ZONES

Once you've completed your fitness testing, you'll have data for determining what your training zones, or levels, will be for your base training. You need to establish these training levels so you can ride at an intensity that is appropriate for accomplishing the objectives of the workouts you'll be doing to develop your base fitness. You could just go out and ride your bike at whatever intensity suits you on a given day, and you might, over time, get faster. The problem with this approach is that you're not likely to fully develop your aerobic base, which will limit how high you can raise your fitness ceiling each year. You're also not likely to reach your highest level of fitness at the time of year that you need it most. Moreover, you might risk training too hard or too easy when your limited training time should be more focused and productive. Having zones to train within—and training within them at the right time of the year—will help you continue to build your overall fitness higher each year.

The numbers you want to use for outlining your base training levels are your CP30 average power and your upper or lower threshold heart rates. The training levels chart in Table 5.1 suggests ranges based on percentages of those parameters. A calculator may be necessary, but you can use the training levels provided in Appendix A and pencil in your zones. There are some upper training levels (5b, 5c, and maximum) that you won't be visiting very often during your base training—or at least should not be—but it's good to track the time that you do spend there and note changes in fitness that affect these zones.

Your zones may change along with your fitness, so you'll need to retest or reevaluate them about every 6 to 8 weeks to determine whether the training levels need adjusting. If you're using a power meter, you'll be able to detect changes in

TABLE 5.1: TRAINING LEVELS

LEVEL	NAME	POWER (WATTS, BASED ON CP30 TEST)	HEART RATE (BASED ON YOUR UTT)	RPE (1–10)	DESCRIPTION
1	Active recovery	< 55% of CP30 min. average power	30 BPM or more below your UTT	1–2	Very easy. Seems too slow and you feel guilty for riding this slow. This zone is used for warm-up and cool-down after and before longer or harder efforts and for recovery rides. Riding at this level also activates the fat-burning system and starts fat metabolism.
2	Endurance, lower training threshold (LTT)	55–75% of CP30 min. average power	~ 20–30 BPM below your UTT, or your LTT ± 5 beats	2–4	Moderate, all-day endurance pace. You will sense the slight increase in your breathing rate, but should be able to carry on a conversation at this effort level. You should feel as if you could ride all day at this pace if you've been training regularly ("all day" is relative to your fitness level and may mean 1–6 hours). This intensity is at your LTT. Training in this zone improves base aerobic fitness and resistance to fatigue, trains the body to burn fat, and starts to raise your VO_2max. Long rides should be based mainly in this zone, especially in the early base training phases. Exactly where this zone falls as a percentage of your CP30 will depend on how well developed your aerobic base is. It may reach as much as 75% of your CP30 near the end of your base training. This zone can be measured with a lactate step test, but it's estimated as a percentage of CP30 wattage or UTT.
3	Tempo	75–85% of CP30 min. average power	~ 10–20 BPM below your UTT	4–6	Comfortably hard, but manageable pace. You can talk at this effort level, but your breathing rate is moderately elevated and your breath will interrupt you when talking at this intensity. You should feel as if you could maintain this pace (depending on experience) up to 90 min. Focus is required to maintain this effort level, or you may find yourself slowing down. Time spent in this zone will further improve your aerobic system and develop the ability to maintain faster paces for longer durations. This zone is often referred to as "tempo" in cycling. Begin training in this zone midway through your base training and spend more time in it during the later base training phase.
4	Upper training threshold (UTT)	85–95% of CP30 min. average power	~ 5–10 BPM below, and up to, your upper threshold heart rate	5–7	Hard, upper-threshold pace. You will not feel like talking at this pace, which is at or just below your UTT pace. You're at the point where metabolic by-products are accumulating in your legs and they start to burn, but your body maintains a balance by processing the by-products just fast enough. Concentration is needed to maintain this effort level, and early in base training you will likely struggle to keep this pace for durations longer than 10–20

(continues)

		POWER (WATTS, BASED ON CP30 TEST)	HEART RATE (BASED ON YOUR UTT)	RPE (1–10)	
LEVEL	NAME				DESCRIPTION
4 (cont.)	Upper training threshold (UTT)	85–95% of CP30 min. average power	~5–10 BPM below, and up to, your upper threshold heart rate	5–7	min. Toward the end of your base training phase, you will start spending more time at this level Your level 4 heart rate will be about 8–12 beats lower than your average heart rate during a 30-min. time trial. Power level is the maximum average power you can sustain for about 60–75 min. and is just below your 40K TT pace. This is your maximum lactate steady state (MLSS), a level where blood lactate is being cleared at the maximum level possible. Going over this intensity, even slightly, will move you into the next level, 5a.
5a	CP30 power level	95–105% of CP30 min. average power	Upper threshold heart rate and up to 10–15 beats higher	6–8	Very hard, just over your upper-threshold pace. This is just above your UTT. Metabolic by-products, such as lactate and hydrogen ions, are now building up faster than your body can process them. Your legs will feel a burning sensation and want to shut down if you continue at this intensity. You will need to be very motivated and rested to maintain this level of effort. Training at this level should be limited to during the late base training phase. Heart rate will increase to several beats higher than your UTT heart rate during sustained efforts at this level.
5b	VO$_2$max	CP5–6 min.	Heart rate will lag behind actual effort at this intensity, but you should see your heart rate reach within 5 beats of your maximum during sustained efforts or intervals at this intensity	7–9	Very, very hard! You won't be able to maintain this effort level for very long—5–8 min. at the most. This is where you are during short, steep hills while racing or going all out for several min. to bridge back after being gapped. Training in this zone should be reserved for after base training is completed and limited to shorter work intervals with equal rest intervals (e.g., 30 × 30 sec. and up to 3 × 3 min.). Total effort durations for these work-outs can be 5–20 min. depending on experience. Training at this intensity improves aerobic capacity (VO$_2$max). Heart rate will lag behind and be unable to accurately reflect the effort level until about 2 min. into the effort. Power used should be your current CP5–6 min. average.
5c	Neuro-muscular power	CP5–12 sec.	N/A; your heart rate will still be rising after you complete an effort at this intensity	9–10	Maximum effort! This is when you might see your maximum heart rate. You should save maximum efforts for short moments during races or during a fitness test at the end of a recovery week. Hitting this zone frequently during regular training is a bad idea! Your heart rate will often reach within a few beats of its max during efforts at this intensity lasting more than 5–10 sec. Power is the maximum watts you can average for 5–12 sec.

TABLE 5.1: TRAINING LEVELS (continued)

fitness as you record the data from each ride and can see if you're reaching power levels more easily than you could before and at a lower heart rate and a lower rate of perceived exertion. One indication that your fitness is improving is if you're consistently seeing lower heart rates (which are backed up by perceived exertion) at the same power levels. If 175 watts now feels like an RPE of 4 rather than a 5, and your heart rate is 5 beats lower at 175 watts than it was a month ago, then your base fitness has improved.

BE FLEXIBLE

Although it's important to follow the guidelines for training intensities as outlined in the endurance chapter to ensure that you're meeting the objective of each workout, note that there is some overlap between these training levels, and it's often impractical to expect 100 percent compliance. If you have your upper or lower threshold tested in a lab and also do a CP30 test, you may see some overlap between the zones as determined by heart rate versus power. This is due, in part, to the method of testing and to the fact that test results will vary based on what kind of day you're having. If you're using a power meter, I suggest setting up the training levels based on your current CP30 average power and use heart rate and perceived exertion for additional feedback.

The purpose of training within a particular zone during base training is to stimulate certain metabolic, muscular, and neuromuscular responses, but there is some amount of physiological response overlap. The desired training effect cannot always be pinpointed to an exact heart rate or wattage but will usually fall within a given range. As the intensity of the workouts increases, the appropriate training intensity range will narrow, and using power to measure intensity becomes even more accurate than heart rate.

There will also be days when your legs are carrying some accumulated fatigue, and training at the lower end of a given range will be more appropriate than trying to struggle with maintaining the power at the upper range. At times like this, RPE can help you adjust your training intensity. When your legs are fresher, you'll find that training at the upper end of the range will be more manageable.

KEEP IT FUN

I encourage athletes to have one day per month during base training when they just go out and ride however they feel like riding on that day. Some athletes feel they're

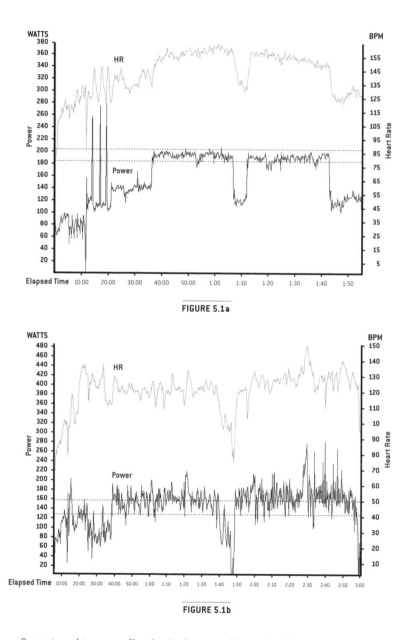

FIGURE 5.1a

FIGURE 5.1b

Comparison of two power files showing how one athlete trains within the prescribed power range, while the other is spending a high percentage of time training above the appropriate training zone. You should try to spend 90 percent of your time within the prescribed training level (noted by above dotted lines).

being lazy if they're not training hard and pushing themselves all the time. I suggest it's just the opposite and that they're actually being lazy by riding fast and hard all the time when they should be slowing down and developing their base fitness first.

Reward yourself for not being lazy by adding a fun group ride at the end of a recovery week once a month. Keep the power meter or heart rate monitor on the bike, but don't feel restricted by it. Try placing black tape over the power meter display so that you can ride guilt-free. I often see cyclists set personal best power records during these group rides. They can also take the place of a fitness test, since the group setting can increase motivation and help you crank out the watts.

During base training, aim to spend about 90 percent of the workout within the prescribed training level. This will give you the best opportunity to achieve the desired training stimulus. Keep in mind that it is also very difficult to stay exactly within a prescribed training level at all times during all rides and conditions. I have certainly witnessed athletes accomplish this, but it is usually during an indoor workout where most variables associated with riding outdoors (e.g., wind, hills, and other riders) are eliminated. These athletes also tend to be very number oriented and find the definitive structure of such workouts to be a motivating factor. It's okay to like numbers and try to hit them every time, but try not to become a slave to numbers on the bike. Do your best to stay within the prescribed intensity range, but at the same time try not to become fixated on it and demand 100 percent compliance at all times (see Figures 5.1a and 5.1b).

———————

Your training zones will serve as guidelines for your workouts, so stick to them the best you can, but keep in mind that 100 percent compliance is unrealistic and falling short of that won't be detrimental to your overall progress. Watch for signs that your fitness is changing, and make the necessary adjustments in your training zones. Tests or a fast group ride with a power meter every 6 to 8 weeks can give you data to monitor your zones.

Cut yourself some slack now and then, and make your ultimate goal improving overall fitness (including strength, endurance, and efficiency—all discussed in the next chapter) while still enjoying your workouts. Sometimes training can feel like a second job, and you lose track of some of the reasons that you ride. Remember to keep it fun and enjoy cycling!

6

FITNESS ELEMENTS

To ride your bike faster longer, you need to develop your base and advanced fitness elements. Base fitness elements include *endurance, strength,* and *efficiency;* the advanced fitness elements are *strength endurance, anaerobic endurance,* and *power.* Most cyclists will identify what is holding them back as one of the advanced elements. What they often don't realize is how all of the advanced elements are dependent on how well the base elements are developed. You still need to train the advanced fitness elements, but strength endurance development depends on both endurance and strength, anaerobic endurance development depends on both endurance and efficiency, while power development depends on both strength and efficiency. The development level of your *base fitness elements* will determine the level of development of your advanced fitness elements (see Figure 6.1).

BASE FITNESS ELEMENTS

Failing to adequately develop your base fitness will diminish your advanced fitness potential. Therefore, improving your base fitness elements is essential to raising your fitness ceiling. This is why you must set aside time each year to develop your base fitness.

Base fitness elements are the essential abilities needed to perform well in all types of cycling events. If you are new to cycling, then these elements should be your focus for the first couple of years of training. Every cyclist should return to base training each year, regardless of his or her experience. The more years of

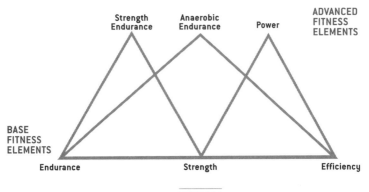

FIGURE 6.1

The base fitness elements—endurance, strength, and efficiency—support the advanced fitness elements—strength endurance, anaerobic endurance, and power. The larger and more solid your base fitness is, the higher and stronger your advanced fitness elements can be.

consistent base training you have, the shorter your base building phase needs to be each year.

Most cyclists are held back by at least one or two of the base elements and occasionally by all three. We often think of racing and riding fast in terms of the advanced elements, and we are tempted to focus our training accordingly. The error in that logic is that the advanced elements can be developed relatively quickly each year, but the base fitness elements take much longer to develop.

Endurance

Cycling is an endurance sport. Endurance is the ability to resist fatigue; it helps you finish a long ride or race. The longer the event, the more important it becomes to increase your endurance. This means that your body is able to spare carbohydrates and utilize fat for fuel efficiently through the aerobic energy system. That doesn't mean, however, that a sprinter can neglect endurance training. You have to get to the finish to be in the sprint.

Endurance is the fitness element that takes the longest to fully develop. It takes years for your body to make the adaptations needed to produce the huge aerobic engine that can make you a stronger all-around cyclist, so you need to set aside time to work on developing your endurance every year. You should see significant improvements in your endurance the first year if you make it your focus. But beware of too much intensity. I've seen athletes ultimately diminish their endurance by training too hard during their base training phase.

Strength

Strength is the ability to overcome resistance. In cycling, this involves pushing down on the pedals to overcome forces such as wind and gravity. Strength workouts are intended to improve your ability to overcome these types of challenges and, when combined with greater endurance, improve your strength endurance, which allows you to push a harder gear for longer periods. With more strength, you can actually push down on the pedals harder, enabling you to ride and climb faster.

My experience is that an appropriate strength training program provides a great advantage for cyclists. I've seen significant improvements in power output after cyclists complete a strength program during their base training. The strength program I recommend is designed to develop your core and stabilization muscles as well as your ability to apply more force on the pedals. It will also help you address possible muscular imbalances that can lead to injuries and loss of performance. Strength training can start with weight training in the gym and progress to cycling-specific workouts.

Efficiency

I use efficiency to refer to how smoothly and effectively you ride your bike. This includes your pedaling mechanics; your position on the bike; how tense or relaxed your muscles are; and your skills at cornering, climbing, drafting, descending, and sprinting. Efficiency workouts are intended to improve muscular coordination and, of course, efficiency. These workouts are usually done with light resistance and will include drills that involve high rpms that improve your pedaling mechanics and help you practice riding and relaxation skills. This aspect of base fitness can and should be improved with regular training. The idea is that by improving your efficiency, you'll be able to ride faster and longer with less energy expenditure.

Athletes with poorly developed efficiency skills are unable to use their aerobic fitness and strength to produce the power and anaerobic endurance they should be capable of. If your muscles are fighting against one another they can rob you of energy. The less energy you use riding the bike, the more energy you have available to ride hard or fast.

Think about spinning at a higher-than-normal cadence. Why does this become uncomfortable and cause you to bounce on the saddle? It's because you're not efficient at that higher rpm. The opposing muscles in the legs are not relaxing and contracting in harmony and instead are fighting one another. You are also pushing down on the pedals when you should be moving them back through the bottom of the pedaling circle. Training the muscles to work together and to move the pedals smoothly and effectively will make you more efficient. Just like anything else, it takes practice.

I also see very aerobically fit and strong riders who struggle to keep up because they lack the riding skills to draft and corner well within a pack of riders. They typically end up riding at the back of a large pack or struggle to stay close enough to the wheel in front of them. Riding in these positions forces you to work harder because you are subjected to greater air resistance than if you were staying protected within the pack and close behind the rider ahead of you. Cycling involves overcoming air resistance (and gravity, if you are going uphill), so knowing how to use the least amount of energy necessary to move the bike forward is critical.

ADVANCED FITNESS ELEMENTS

If you dedicate enough time each year to build a foundation by developing your base fitness elements, you will be able to raise your advanced fitness up higher and higher each year. When your advanced fitness elements develop, it is often referred to as developing "form." This is when you feel fast! The pedals move under you like there is no chain attached, and you start checking to make sure the power meter is reading accurately. Soon after finding their form, many cyclists begin to set personal records for the various critical power durations. It takes patience to wait until after you've put in the work on your foundation to start bringing your advanced fitness into form, but it's worth the wait if you do it correctly. Cyclists think they're being "motivated" when they are training hard all the time. In reality, they are too lazy to do the base work. It's more fun to ride hard all the time, but during the base training phase it's even more important to hold back.

Strength Endurance

Strength endurance is the ability to maintain a relatively high force load for prolonged durations. It translates into the ability to maintain a faster pace while climbing, to time trial well, and to push a harder gear while riding into the wind. It is a combination of the base fitness elements strength and endurance: you need the strength to be able to push on the pedals harder and the endurance to maintain that effort for longer durations.

Anaerobic Endurance

Anaerobic endurance is the ability to resist fatigue at very high efforts. You need this element for breaking away and staying off the front and for performing well in both fast-paced short events and long sprints. It requires both efficiency and endurance, because you must have the ability to resist fatigue and move the pedals smoothly without wasting energy.

Power

Power is the ability to apply maximum force quickly. It is important for beginning a sprint, breaking away from a group, or powering up a short, steep hill without losing momentum. Power is a blend of the base fitness elements strength and efficiency. You need the strength to push forcefully on the pedals and the efficiency to move them quickly without wasting energy.

FINDING YOUR LIMITERS: A SUBJECTIVE FITNESS ANALYSIS

So which of the fitness elements are your strengths, and which are holding you back from reaching your cycling goals? When interviewing athletes, I can usually find out what areas of fitness they need to improve, even though it's nice to have the power numbers to confirm it. It can be difficult to pinpoint your exact limiters because it is often a combination of more than one of the base fitness elements that are, to some degree, holding you back. Remember, if one of the advanced elements is holding you back, then you have to identify the base elements that support it—these will be your true limiters.

Several other things can hold you back, and these may not even have anything to do with actual fitness as we measure it on the bike. Personal limiters include such things as time available to train, nutrition, job stress, and inclement weather. You must balance your training life with your "other life." Life stress can have a big effect on your ability not only to train but also to recover from and adapt to the training. Nutrition and rest also play major roles in how your body tolerates ongoing training.

These, and other possibilities, are discussed later in the "Other Limiters" section. For now, the next sections discuss some common scenarios that can help you determine your personal strengths and limiters.

Long Rides

If you find that you can stay with your group in races or rides for a portion of the event but also find that you are unable to stay with them for the entire duration, then you most likely need a larger endurance base and perhaps greater efficiency. If your breathing rate is much higher than that of riders around you in the pack, then they probably have a higher fitness ceiling so even though you are all riding at the same pace, they are riding in a lower zone than you. You may experience this during base training, since your ceiling will be lower; but if this is happening during periods when your fitness should be at its highest, then you may be lacking the base endurance and efficiency you need to support a higher ceiling. It's common to see cyclists out riding hard during what should be their base training phase. You'll often see these cyclists reaching peak fitness or form during the holidays, but they seldom get much faster when they need to be during their competitive season. This is because they are neglecting their base fitness development. Let them ride fast and do your own workout!

Endurance plays a role in so many aspects of cycling fitness that it's almost always a limiter to some degree. If you have not been setting aside time each year and actually slowing down a bit to work on your base fitness, then you are falling behind on your endurance development. This will ultimately affect your ability to finish long events, and it will also inhibit your ability to repeat hard shorter efforts. Cycling is an endurance sport, period.

Be sure that you are using the draft of other cyclists to stay out of the wind and saving your "matches" for when you need them, because if you're not riding efficiently, then you may be wasting energy and working harder than needed. If you think this is the case, set aside time in each ride to practice the riding skills that you struggle with the most. Being able to use the draft of other cyclists effectively is crucial to cycling. If you are uncomfortable riding close to other cyclists, then you should make it a priority to practice this during your base training.

Every year I see athletes get a late start to their training, which will naturally limit their capacity for endurance. One of the biggest times for coaching inquiries is in the spring. If your important events are in the summer, then you should be setting up your training plan the prior fall. It's very common for athletes to come to me eight weeks before their most important event and want to start training for it. This does not provide the time necessary to develop the base fitness elements enough to support a high level of advanced fitness. Give yourself 8 to 24 weeks to focus on base training. The longer your events are or the newer you are to cycling, the longer your base training should be. Your fitness ceiling can be put up in about nine weeks of focusing on the advanced fitness elements—if you have your foundation well established.

Nutrition and hydration can also hold you back from finishing longer events. If you are not eating and drinking enough while riding, then you will run out of carbohydrates and have to slow down. If you get dehydrated, you will also have to slow down.

Endurance is also sport specific. I've coached cyclists who were making a move from a strong running background and still needed to develop cycling-specific endurance. They had well-developed aerobic systems, but adaptations within the muscles were specific to running. If you are training for ultraendurance events, then endurance is clearly an element that you need to focus on. Even if it's not a limiter, it's still a priority. I see athletes struggle to find enough time to train and adequately prepare for events lasting over 12 hours. In these cases, time to train is their limiter. Be realistic and set aside enough time on the weekends to gradually build your rides up to an appropriate length to adequately prepare you for your high-priority event.

Ultraendurance events are also dependent on appropriate pacing and nutrition strategies. Riders who go out too hard and don't take in enough food and water early will struggle to finish events longer than a few hours.

Climbing

If the events are hilly and you find that you are getting left behind on the hills, then it may be a combination of both endurance and strength that is holding you back.

Long Climbs

If you are falling off the back of your group on long climbs, then your strength endurance probably needs improvement. Since strength endurance depends, in part, on endurance, you must develop your endurance too. The more endurance you have, the more you can build your strength endurance.

Climbing is also affected by your power-to-weight ratio. Increasing your endurance will ultimately improve your ability to put out higher average power for the critical durations longer than a minute regardless of your weight, but endurance may just be part of what is holding you back. If you are lean but muscular and still struggle on long climbs, then endurance is most likely the main limiter.

If you are lean but very thin and lack muscle development, you may need to improve your strength as well in order to improve your strength endurance. Since climbing involves both the ability to sustain the effort and the ability to push on the pedals harder, strength may need to be improved. I see this a lot in runners who take up cycling. They have a lot of endurance but often lack muscular strength and power.

Any extra weight that you have to carry with you up the climbs can slow you down as well. Several "other" limiters are listed at the end of this chapter. One of them is body composition, and another is nutrition. These two elements are often closely connected. If one of your goals is to improve your climbing and you could also lose a few pounds of unnecessary body fat, then that should be something you focus on during base training. Be sure to read Chapter 3 on weight management.

Power output, measured in watts, can be expressed relative to your body weight in kilograms to determine your power-to-weight ratio. The higher this number is for the 12- to 30-minute critical power durations, the better you'll do on longer climbs. You can improve your power-to-weight ratio by increasing your average watts and by decreasing your body weight. If you are already lean, then raise your relative power output by first improving your base fitness elements and then increasing your strength endurance.

You may also be able to improve your climbing by using better tactics and strategies. One way to climb more successfully is to start near the front of the group. This gives you room to drop back somewhat while still remaining in contact with the main pack of riders. If you start the climb at the back of the group and lose 10 feet to them, you will be well off the back. If you start near the front, however, and lose 10 feet, you may still be within the group. I tell sprinters to get near the front, set a pace that favors them, and make the climbers find a way around.

Short, Steep Climbs

If you do better on longer climbs but struggle to keep up on shorter, steeper climbs, then you may have good strength endurance but lack power or, depending on the length of the climb, anaerobic endurance. Power requires strength and the ability to move the pedals quickly with less effort. You also need power to stand and crank up moderate rollers (short wavelike hills) while maintaining your momentum. If your muscle development is less than riders who are beating you up short, steep climbs, then strength may be holding you back. If you are muscular, then it may be that you need to work more on efficiency. This can also be an issue on longer climbs if you are wasting a lot of energy.

If the climbs are repeated frequently within the ride—like in a criterium with a short, steep hill—and the short recovery between efforts is what is blowing you up, then you may need to improve your endurance as well as your pedaling efficiency. This will help you develop better anaerobic endurance.

Riding strategies can also play a role in how well you do on short power climbs. If you are out in front of your group and riding hard as you approach the base of the climb, then you may be building up metabolic by-products in your legs and won't have the ability to step on the gas when you hit the base of the hill. Be sure that you are out of the wind and on someone else's wheel leading up to climbs. Save your "matches" for when you need them!

Short, steep hills require either power or anaerobic endurance. Both of these advanced elements are dependent on efficiency; so if you are struggling on these short, steep hills, then efficiency (smooth, effortless pedaling) is what you need to develop.

Surges

If you struggle when the pace picks up quickly for short, hard efforts on flats and can't recover in time for the next effort, then your anaerobic endurance may be your limiter. You need the benefits that come from aerobic endurance training to support your ability to perform repeated hard efforts. The stronger your aerobic base fitness, the faster you recover, and the harder you can go without being overwhelmed by an accumulation of metabolic by-products or depleting your carbohydrates. You also need to be able to move the pedals quickly and efficiently. Your pedaling skills may be holding you back here as well.

If the efforts are very short and have long recoveries between them, but they require huge amounts of power output to keep up, then it may be power that is limiting you. This is a common occurrence when accelerating out of corners. This would mean that you need more strength and efficiency. I talk with athletes who believe this is the case in criteriums because they are struggling to hang on to the back of the pack. They may have the power to keep up but they are riding inefficiently and wasting their energy. The farther back you are in a criterium, the more you get "yo-yoed" or "slinkied" off the back. Think of an elastic band that is stretched out and then has to use its energy to pull itself back. That's you using your energy to chase back on out of every corner. It may be your cornering skills or pack-riding skills that need improving here as well.

You ride strong on flats, but are dropped by the same riders on hills. If you can average 250 watts for an hour, it will take you farther on a flat route than a rider with a similar bike position who can only average 225 watts. That same 250 watts may not take you as far if you're going uphill. Athletes who can put out the most watts relative to their body weight will have the advantage going uphill. So you may have a well-developed aerobic base and strength that has helped you improve your strength endurance, but your power-to-weight ratio is what is holding you back on the climbs. So if you weigh 165 pounds and put out 250 watts for an hour, your power-to-weight ratio is 3.3 (165 ÷ 2.2 = 75kg and 250 ÷ 75 = 3.3). Another rider puts out 225 watts for an hour but weighs 143 pounds. That rider's power-to-weight ratio is better than yours at 3.4 (143 ÷ 2.2 = 65kg and 225 ÷ 65 = 3.4).

If your body composition is already appropriate, then you'll need to work on increasing your absolute power output. Absolute power output is the watts that you average for a given duration. Relative power output is your average watts divided by your body weight, or your power-to-weight ratio. Increasing absolute power comes from increasing force application to the pedals, increasing your aerobic base, and improving your pedaling mechanics. Once you have those base elements developed, you can raise your ceiling and climb at a faster pace as well as hold a higher average power output on the flats.

You climb well, finish the race, but can't keep up in the sprint. If this is you, then you are probably riding well in the pack, have good strength endurance, but are lacking absolute power and explosive power. You may want to try leaving for the sprint earlier to see if that helps, but you should also look at your 5- to 12-second power level and try to improve it. We need to race our strengths and work on improving our limiters. So you may want to try to form breaks and attacks in an attempt to use up the sprinters' legs and drop as many of them as possible early in the race.

Power is dependent on strength and form, but success in sprinting is dependent on other variables such as timing, position, reflexes, courage, confidence, and some luck. You will want to be sure you are practicing the sprinting drills and workouts I prescribe for base training. Developing your sprint starts early in base training with form development and progresses through strength and then power development. You should also practice sprinting with teammates to improve your reaction time and comfort within a bunch of riders going all out.

Time Trials

If you do well in time trials, then you probably have your strength endurance well developed. Success in time trialing also relies on an efficient position on the bike, appropriate pacing, and a strong mental capacity to tolerate the long, hard efforts. I see a lot of cyclists who can average a higher power level for 30 minutes in a road race than they can in a time trial, for a couple of reasons. For one, this difference in performance could mean that they are in a position on their time trial bike that is limiting their power output. There is a trade-off between power output and aerodynamics when setting up your time trial bike position. You will generally be able to ride at a faster speed at less wattage because of improved aerodynamics, but you need to find the position that is an ideal balance between your ability to push on the pedals effectively and aerodynamics.

Another reason you'll see lower power output in a time trial versus a road race may be that you struggle to keep yourself going hard in a time trial. During a road race, you may put out more power when you know that it means you will hold onto the main field and have other riders around you to motivate you. In a time trial, it's just you, the clock, and an ongoing internal conversation with yourself about how hard you are able or willing to ride.

It's important to realize that the mental component of the sport will affect your success as a cyclist. Fitness is necessary, but I often see athletes not able to go as hard or long as they could because they give in too early. There are a variety of reasons why we ease up when we feel maxed out, but the cyclist who can tolerate the suffering longer will have an advantage in most races or hard efforts. Being able to sustain very hard effort levels for prolonged durations is dependent on your ability to convince yourself that you can and your willingness to endure the pain required to do it. If you believe that this may be your personal limiter, begin by reading Chapter 14.

Pacing is also a major issue in time trialing. The most common mistake is going out too hard and struggling to finish. The longer the time trial, the more careful you have to be that you ease into the effort and build to the finish. Cross-country mountain bike racing is like a big time trial with a bunch of hard efforts tossed in to throw you off. You still have to pace yourself so you don't blow up early and limp to the finish. With power meters, you can better pace yourself in time trials and analyze data files after races to gain insight into how well you pace yourself (see Figures 6.2a, 6.2b, and 6.2c).

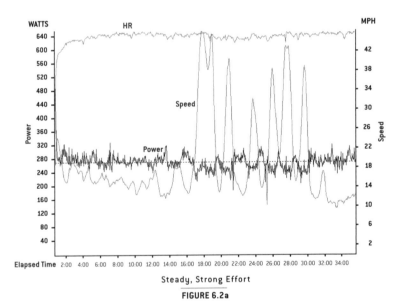

Steady, Strong Effort

FIGURE 6.2a

In each of these graphs, the dotted line represents athlete's power goal for the event. The first graph shows how an athlete does a great job of keeping his effort (measured by power) steady throughout this time trial. He eases into the effort and gradually brings his heart rate up to time trial pace over the first 7 minutes. You can see here that even though the course climbs and descends, the athlete adjusts effort level accordingly and is able to finish with a strong effort.

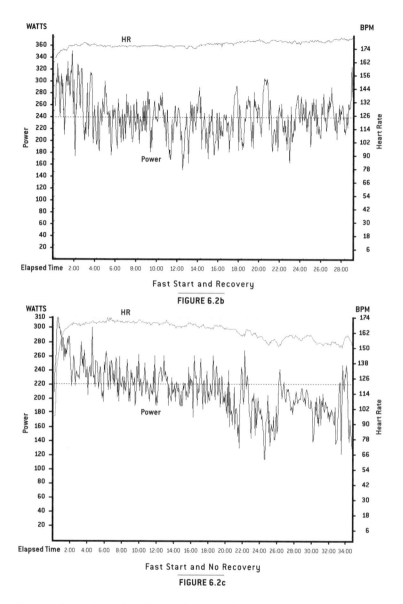

Fast Start and Recovery

FIGURE 6.2b

Fast Start and No Recovery

FIGURE 6.2c

The second graph shows the athlete starting out a bit hard. Realizing this, he backs off and is able to sustain an effort close to his goal power during the midportion of the race. He is able to recover and finish strong. The gradual, steady climb in heart rate over the duration of the race also demonstrates a good pacing strategy.

The third graph shows an athlete who goes out too hard and is unable to recover. The rapid rise in heart rate demonstrates the lack of patience. The athlete blows up, or "pops," and heart rate, power, and motivation all drop off as this cyclist struggles even to finish.

Hill Climb Time Trials

Climbing time trials come back to strength endurance, power-to-weight ratio, pacing, and mental capacity to ride hard for prolonged durations. Bike weight, especially wheels, can make some difference here, too. I subscribe to the idea that you can never have enough expensive wheels for your bicycle. Wheels make the bike. You make the bike go fast, but wheels can make it easier or harder for you. Rotating weight becomes even more relevant when you're climbing. The steeper it gets, the less of a role aerodynamics play relative to weight. If we all had an unlimited wheel budget, we could have a pair of expensive wheels for every situation.

Descending

You may or may not be able to gap everyone on the climbs, but regardless, you fall behind on the descents. This is usually skill related. Some might believe a lack of confidence is to blame, but confidence comes from knowing that you have developed the skills to control the bike. This involves cornering, braking, and what I call "seeing." You have to be looking far enough down the road or trail to give your brain enough time to process the information so you can set up accordingly. If you are looking at your front wheel, you don't have enough time to respond to upcoming obstacles or turns. You'll find exercises for descending in Chapter 13.

Lighter riders also have a disadvantage on descents, since gravity will pull a heavier rider down the hill faster. Lighter riders will have to pedal when heavier riders can be coasting and maintaining the same speed. Find a big rider, and get on his wheel so he can help pull you down the hill.

Hilly versus Flat Races

You do well in hilly road races but get dropped in criteriums. If this is you, then you probably have a good power-to-weight ratio and strength endurance but need more power and anaerobic endurance. You may also lack confidence in fast corners, so you tend to ride near the back more in criteriums. Work on your efficiency skills of pedaling and bike handling. You probably need to improve your power outputs for durations shorter than 6 minutes.

You do well in criteriums but get dropped in hilly road races. You probably have a high absolute power output and anaerobic endurance but could improve your power-to-weight ratio. You probably have great bike-handling skills and stay well protected in the pack and can take corners fast. You may need to improve your strength endurance and, if possible, your power-to-weight ratio for durations of 12 minutes and longer.

You can outsprint everyone but can't get to the finish to do it. You probably have a lot of fast-twitch type II muscle fibers and can put out a lot of power for short durations. You may also have good anaerobic endurance if you can win longer sprints as well. What you probably need is more endurance training so that you can develop enough carbohydrate sparing so you can last to the end of a race. Spending time training at lower intensities will develop the ability of your slow-twitch muscle fiber to utilize fat. If your fast-twitch fibers are kicking in early, then you'll go through carbohydrates quickly indeed.

OTHER LIMITERS

Time

One of the biggest obstacles we face as athletes is having enough time to do the training we want to. With only so many days per week and hours per day, we have to juggle our jobs, family obligations, social activities, errands, and—for me—book-writing time. Somewhere in there, we must also find time to eat, train, shower, clean our bikes, fix flats, register for events, and shop for flattering spandex clothing.

Time may always be a limiter; but if we can at least manage time better, then we may be more successful. One way to do this is to schedule your training at the same time each day so it becomes a routine. Doing your training first thing in the morning also ensures that it gets done. I've worked with many athletes who have families and work 50 or more hours a week. Some of them get up at 4 AM and put in a couple of hours of training before their family even gets up. The key to this approach is getting to bed early so you still get enough sleep.

Since daylight hours are limited, most cyclists will have to schedule their longest rides on the weekends during winter months. If you are getting up early during the week to ride, you may have to ride indoors.

It's common to have a conversation with a category 2 cyclist who wants to be able to compete alongside professional cyclists. These category 2 riders often still have to put in 40-plus hours a week at their "other job." A lot of pros will be out training more than 20 hours a week. If you're training that much, you'll also need additional sleep every day to ensure that your body can absorb the training load. If you need to train 4 or more hours a day, plus work 8 hours, commute

1 hour, prepare and eat meals, shower, and sleep 10 hours, that will be over 24 hours in one day. You can't stack it all up on the weekends.

Be realistic when setting your goals. Understand that there are cyclists who ride their bikes for a living, and the rest of us don't. Keep a balance between training and other obligations in your life, and you'll get more out of your cycling. If you're on the verge of making the move from cycling as a hobby to racing professionally, you'll need to simplify your life outside cycling as much as possible to ensure that you can focus on your training and racing. It takes a lot of personal sacrifice to succeed as a professional athlete.

Weather Watch

If you live in a part of the world that has weather extremes, you may find that it will interfere with your training. The United States certainly has a number of places where the winters are too cold and snowy and the summers too hot to allow safe training outdoors year-round. You may need to spend more time training indoors to ensure that you are getting your base work done.

You may also want to consider scheduling a training camp somewhere warm and dry during the time of year that you need to be putting in a lot of miles and when the weather in your area is usually not favorable for that.

Mind Matters

Sometimes physical fitness is not what is holding you back. For long durations even at moderate paces, you still have to overcome the discomfort of fatigue and convince yourself to keep going. If it were possible to find several cyclists with the exact same physical fitness ability, I doubt they would be able to perform at the same level in all situations. The mental component plays a big role, and it can be holding you back.

During a very hard effort, it can take as much willpower to keep you going as pedaling power. I've worked with athletes who had enough power in watts to keep up on hills but still struggled and dropped off the pace on hard climbs when their heart rates climbed. Once they realized that the gap between them and the riders ahead of them was not a physical gap but rather a mental gap, they were able to work at keeping themselves in contact with the group.

Don't expect to reach the podium without also reaching your maximum heart rate first. If you can win a race without experiencing the severe level of suffering associated with riding at your current absolute maximum physical ability, then you need to consider upgrading to a higher category. I don't suggest looking at your heart rate during a race. If you have a downloadable heart rate monitor or power meter, you can see that heart rate after the race.

Motivation

What motivates you to get out on your bike, and what reduces your motivation? When I ask this question, I get a variety of answers. Common motivators include fitness, fun, and competition; common motivation detractors include crummy weather and lack of competitiveness.

Motivation that comes from a passion for the sport of cycling will usually be your best ally. If you enjoy the process of training as much as you do the events that you are training for, you will find it easier to stay motivated throughout the year. If you keep your training fun and varied and don't train so hard that it adversely affects the energy you need for the rest of your daily activities, you'll be able to stick with it longer.

Make a list of your cycling goals and post them where you can see them frequently. Keep posters and photos of cyclists you admire around to remind you of what you aspire to be, regardless of how far off or even unlikely that may be. Keep in mind that talent is just a starting point and even those with a lot of natural ability still have to work hard to be successful; the rest of us have to work even harder!

Family Support

I've had clients tell me that their spouses did not approve of their "obsession" with cycling. It takes a network or support group to help you keep going when you are committed to your goals. If you do not have the support of those around you, then you may feel guilty for training and racing and, therefore, spending so much time away from them.

Although most parents are great at supporting their kids' interests, I've seen juniors whose parents lacked interest in their teenagers' sport. At the other extreme, I've also seen young athletes lose interest in cycling and other sports because of pressure from parents to succeed. It's unfortunate to see either a lack of support or overinvolvement from those who are most important to us.

Starting cycling later in your life can also result in a lack of understanding from those around you for your personal passion. We all need goals and physical activity to keep us healthy. Cycling can provide this, but it can also consume a lot of your personal time. Runners usually don't get the same reaction as cyclists from spouses and family members. Bikes cost much more than running shoes, and running takes a third of the time that cycling does. I know only a few runners who will head out the door early in the morning and not return until five hours later. Be sure that those around you understand why cycling is important to you and, if possible, get them involved in the sport too.

Nutrition

Every athlete I coach benefits from making better choices regarding not only what but when they eat. Your body needs fuel just like your car (although you may not want gas in your body). Running out of carbohydrates is a fast way to fatigue. You must eat before, during, and after hard and long workouts to keep your body full of energy. Failing to do so on a daily basis will increase the time it takes your body to recover, which reduces your readiness for the next workout.

If you find that you're feeling tired a lot or getting sick often, then you may be lacking the necessary nutrients that your body needs on a daily basis. Training and racing clearly increase your body's need for nutrients. Be sure to read Chapter 3. It covers the basics of nutrition for cyclists.

Stress

Stress levels have more of an effect on many cyclists than they realize. I have seen athletes' fitness level plummet when a stressful situation comes up in their life. Moving, changing jobs, ending a relationship, and facing work-related challenges seem to have the greatest effect on athletes. There are certainly others, including financial circumstances, that can also create stress in our lives. You must be aware that stress and training can have similar effects on your body. If stress levels are getting high in your life, then you need to balance that by backing off on training. I tell athletes to use riding their bikes as an opportunity to *relieve* stress rather than add more of it when life stress is building. This usually means riding easy rather than hard.

Ideally, we would keep our lives as simple as possible so we can focus our energy on training and recovering. Unfortunately, we all have other obligations that require our time, money, and energy. Be realistic when you set your goals, and take into account the amount of time you have available to train and the obligations that you have. Whenever possible, schedule any big life changes or projects before starting your base training so you'll have them behind you, or plan them after your competitive season.

Not Knowing When to Say When

For some, being overly motivated can create bigger setbacks than being under-motivated. I see it often when a cyclist comes to me after developing an overuse injury or becoming burned out from cycling. Keep your cycling fun, and learn to listen to your body. Knowing when to say when is critical if you want to see continual improvement. You are better off doing a little less each week and avoiding the setbacks that come from getting sick, injured, or burned out than you are trying to cram into your already busy life as much training as you can.

Gradual, steady increases in fitness pay off in the long run. Try to think long term and be patient. If you are ever questioning whether you should be doing a workout, skip it. If in doubt, don't work out.

Body Composition

Much of cycling is affected by power-to-weight ratio. You are into cycling for the fitness, health, and competition. If you eat well and train your base fitness correctly, you should see improvements in your body composition. If you struggle in this area, you may benefit from nutritional counseling (also review Chapter 3).

Tactics and Strategies

I've seen athletes that have made the move from being very competitive in mountain bike racing to road events only to be beaten by cyclists that are not as strong and fit as they are. This is because the mountain bike racers had to learn road tactics—how to use the pack to their advantage and where to position themselves during the races. If you are new to cycling be sure that you focus on developing your riding skills and learn to race smarter, not harder.

Mountain bike racing is more individual and relies on good pacing strategies, whereas road cycling relies more on teamwork and staying out of the wind.

BIKE FIT

How you fit on your bike can affect your comfort, performance, and ability to resist injury. Bike fit has become a specialized "science" that has branched out into several schools of thought. Everything from a thumb to a laser beam is being used to fit cyclists. I've tried most of them and can say that all the methods out there have some merit.

If you've been riding for years and don't have aches and pains associated with riding your bike, then you may not need to make any major changes. If you're new to cycling or have never had a professional bike fit, I would suggest getting one. I've had cyclists come to me for a bike fit after riding for years with minor complaints about an ache here or there, and I find that their saddle is over an inch too low and too far forward. Not only can a poor fit put more strain on your body, but it can also reduce your ability to put out power.

You want to address bike fit issues at the beginning of or before you start your base training. If you need to make changes, you may have to ease into them over time. If, for example, you've been riding with your saddle too low for a year, your muscles are accustomed to that position and will need time to adjust to the higher saddle before you go out and ride the same distances you are now.

The basics are that you need to have your contact points lined up to suit you. The contact points are the pedals, saddle, and handlebar (see Figure 6.3). If you're contacting your bike anywhere else, you're in trouble. The saddle position should provide good but not full leg extension and also keep your knee over the pedal. The handlebars should be where you can reach them comfortably but where you can still breathe and stay out of the wind when you're on them. You shouldn't have to guess where these points are. Have someone who knows where they should be help you put them there. It takes some measuring, and it may vary based on your physiology and needs. Certain types of cycling cleats demand aligning as well.

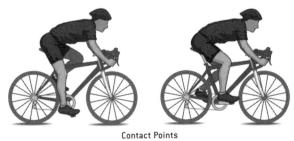

Contact Points
FIGURE 6.3

This book is not about bike fit, so I won't be telling you in detail how to set up your bike. What I am suggesting is that you take care of any bike fit issues early in your base training. Check with a local certified USA Cycling coach in your area about bike fit. Ask around at the bike shops and find out what methods and procedures they use. Ask your friends (the ones who look like they fit on their bike well) where they got their fit. You may have to try more than one fit method before you find what works best for you. I've had athletes come to me after being fitted by expert professional fitters, and I've made changes they've preferred. I've also had athletes who I've fitted later find a fit they like better elsewhere.

Once you get a fit that you feel is working well for you, mark it. Write down every measurement and place marks on your seat post and saddle rails, as well as outlining your cleats on the soles of your shoes with a permanent marker. You can use silver-colored permanent markers for writing on black soles. I've had athletes get into their late base training and suddenly develop a knee injury. After trying to figure out why, I noticed that a cleat had slipped out of place at some point. After I moved the cleat back, the knee pain went away.

If your focus will be on time trial racing, then you'll want to have your time trial bike set up so you can begin doing workouts on it during your mid base training. If you will be doing time trials only occasionally, then I suggest setting up your time trial bike so that the saddle-to-pedal relationship is very similar to your road position, so that the muscle usage is very close. This will allow a faster adjustment to the time trial position and not require you to spend as much time riding the time trial bike before a race.

There is also a trade-off between power output and aerodynamics. As your upper body gets lower or more aerodynamic, you'll find an inevitable point where your ability to put out power will drop. Finding the balance that allows you to go faster with less power is necessary to get the most from your bike fit.

———————

As your training proceeds, you need to address both base and advanced fitness elements. The base elements of endurance, strength, and efficiency provide a strong foundation and must be in place before you tackle the advanced fitness elements of strength endurance, anaerobic endurance, and power. All of the advanced elements depend on how well the base elements are developed, so take the time—well ahead of your racing season—to work on them.

PART THREE

PLANNING YOUR TRAINING YEAR

7

MEASURING TRAINING LOAD

The purpose behind training is to apply a stimulus, or challenge, to the body (which creates what is called a training load) that ultimately results in an adaptation, or increase in fitness. If you apply a training load that challenges the body's current capabilities, the body will sense a need to rebuild itself stronger to be able to better tolerate that challenge in the future. This adaptation is also called **supercompensation.** If you allow enough time and get adequate sleep and nutrition between your training sessions so your body can make the necessary adaptations, you'll continue to gain fitness. Your body needs adequate nutrition and rest to complete the recovery, or rebuilding, process that leads to these increases in fitness through adaptation.

One important message here is that the body gains fitness *as a result of* training but not *during* training. Gains in fitness occur during rest. It's not uncommon for athletes to fail to see the improvements they're training for due to a lack of recovery rather than a lack of training. An appropriate balance must be maintained between training and recovery to realize continued progress in fitness.

TRAINING BALANCE

Finding an appropriate balance between training load (accumulated fatigue and cellular damage) and recovery is important to ensure that you make continued progress in fitness without experiencing major setbacks. It's important to be aware that this balance is frequently changing and that the training and recovery may need ongoing adjustments to ensure continued success.

How quickly your body recovers and adapts to a given training load is dependent on many factors, including your age, current state of fitness and general health, the amount of sleep you get each night, what and when you eat, the amount of stress you have from your life outside cycling, and the training load itself. If you apply the correct type and quantity of training load at the appropriate times and your body is given the opportunity to make the adaptations, then you become able to ride longer and faster. If, however, any of these factors are out of balance, then the adaptation process will take longer and in some cases may not happen at all.

Failing to provide your body with the rest and nutrition it needs to recover between workouts will eventually lead to a decrease in performance because your body's ability to continue to train and adapt will be unable to keep up with the demands you're placing on it. This condition of chronic fatigue is *overtraining*. There will, however, be brief periods when performance drops off slightly during ongoing training because of fatigue accumulating in your body. This is a normal part of the process while your body is recovering and making adaptations and is called *overreaching*.

TRAINING BASICS

Progressive Overload

To see continued improvements throughout your base training, you need to add gradual increases in your training load that produce small challenges to your body's current level of fitness. If you don't do this and instead simply maintain the same training load week after week, you will remain at the level of fitness you reach after several weeks of training without any significant improvements or, if you reduce your training load, will begin to lose fitness. You can maintain your current fitness, improve it, or lose it.

If you're balancing appropriate training with adequate rest and nutrition and managing daily life stress, then your body should be able to handle a progressively higher training load over the course of your base training. This means you're getting fitter and will be able to ride longer and faster. By planning and tracking your training load, you can build in intentional, gradual increases that will place a slightly higher challenge on the body over time. How much you can increase that training load will be affected by such things as what level you start training from, how much time you have available to train, and how quickly your body is able to absorb the ongoing training load.

You may be able to structure your training load increases by adding a given percentage to your volume each week, or you may be limited by your total available training hours and will have to increase the training load by adding more time at slightly higher effort levels. Consult the annual training hours chart shown in Table 7.1 for suggested increases in weekly training hours.

We all have a limit to the amount of time we can train. Training will be limited by both time available and our personal training experience. If you've been training only five hours a week, you shouldn't start training 15 hours next week. Your body needs time to adjust to the new demands of training, so you must increase your weekly hours gradually. You may tolerate a huge increase for a week or two; but down the road, the sudden increases will catch up with you. The exception to this might be if you're a healthy 18-year-old, living at home, not working, not going to school, not in a relationship (and not looking for one), sleeping ten hours a day, and eating very well. Most of us will, however, have a limit to our available time and have to budget our training hours.

There are 168 hours in a week. If you start subtracting for working (40-plus hours), commuting (5 hours), sleeping (63 hours), preparing meals, doing laundry and housework, showering, shopping, running errands, spending social and family time (a large number if you're married with children), walking the dog, doing homework, attending meetings, cleaning your bike, shopping online for new bikes and attractive riding partners and so forth, you'll find that you'll quickly run out of hours in your week. Be sure to take all of these activities and obligations, and any others that I've left out, into consideration when you sit down and calculate how many hours you can realistically set aside for training each week.

Age

We all have a natural tendency to need more time to recover as we get older. The sad truth is that our bodies are not designed to live forever. When we're younger, our body releases more of the hormones necessary to repair the damage caused by stress, either training or life related. This means that we may need an extra day to recover from a challenging workout when we're 40 compared to when we were 20.

Learning to listen to your body and looking for clues about your rate of recovery so you can adjust your training and recovery accordingly is critical. One

TABLE 7.1: TRAINING HOURS PROGRESSION

MAX HOURS	5	6	7	8	9	10	11	12	13	14	15	16	17	18	19	20	21	22	23	24	25	26	27	28	29	30
ALL RECOVERY WEEKS	3	3	3.5	4	4.5	5	5.5	7	7.5	8	8.5	9	9.5	10	10	10	10	11	11	12	12	13	13	14	14	15
ALL PRE-BASE WEEKS	3.5	3.5	4	4.5	5	5.5	6	7	7.5	8	8.5	9	9.5	10	11	12	13	13	14	14	15	15	16	16	17	17
EARLY BASE																										
WEEK 1	3.5	4	4.5	5	5.5	6	6.5	7.5	8	9	9.5	10	10	11	12	13	14	15	16	16	16.5	17	17.5	18	18.5	19
WEEK 2	4	4.5	5	5.5	6	6.5	7	8	9	10	10	11	11	12	13	14	15	16	17	17	17.5	18.5	19	19.5	20	20.5
WEEK 3	4.5	5	5.5	6	6.5	7.5	7.5	8.5	10	11	11	12	12	13	14	15	16	17	18	18.5	19	20	20.5	21	21.5	22
MID BASE																										
WEEK 1	4	5	5.5	6	6.5	7.5	7.5	8.5	9	10	10.5	11.5	12	13	14	15	16	17	17	18	19	20	21	22	22	23
WEEK 2	4.5	5.5	6	6.5	7	8	8	9.5	10	11	11.5	12.5	13	14	15	16	17	18	18.5	19.5	20.5	21.5	22.5	23.5	23.5	24.5
WEEK 3	5	6	6.5	7	7.5	8.5	9	10.5	11	12	13	14	14	15	16	17	18	19	20	21	22	23	23.5	25	25	26
LATE BASE																										
WEEK 1	5	5.5	6.5	7	7.5	8.5	9	10	11	12	13	14	14	15	16	17	18	19	20	21	22	23	24	25	26	27
WEEK 2	5	6	7	7.5	8.5	9.5	10	11	12	13	14	15	15.5	16.5	17.5	18.5	19.5	20.5	21.5	22.5	23.5	24.5	25.5	26.5	27.5	28.5
WEEK 3	5	6	7	8	9	10	11	12	13	14	15	16	17	18	19	20	21	22	23	24	25	26	27	28	29	30
TOTAL BASE HOURS	49.5	56.5	64	70.5	77.5	87	92	106.5	115.5	126	133	143	147	157.5	166.5	175.5	184.5	196.5	204	213.5	221	232.5	239.5	250.5	255	265.5

(continues)

TABLE 7.1: TRAINING HOURS PROGRESSION (continued)

MAX HOURS	5	6	7	8	9	10	11	12	13	14	15	16	17	18	19	20	21	22	23	24	25	26	27	28	29	30
LATE BASE (cont.)																										
ALL RECOVERY WEEKS	3	3	3.5	4	4.5	5	5.5	7	7.5	8	8.5	9	9.5	10	10	10	10	11	11	12	12	13	13	14	14	15
ALL PRE-BASE WEEKS	3.5	3.5	4	4.5	5	5.5	6	7	7.5	8	8.5	9	9.5	10	11	12	13	13	14	14	15	15	16	16	17	17
EARLY ADVANCED																										
WEEK 1	4	5	6	7	8	9	9.5	11	11.5	12.5	13.5	14.5	15.5	16.5	17.5	18	19	19	20	21	22	23	24	25	26	27
WEEK 2	4	5	6	7	8	9	9.5	10.5	11.5	12.5	13.5	14.5	15.5	16.5	17.5	18	19	19	20	21	22	23	24	25	26	27
WEEK 3	4	5	6	7	8	9	9.5	10	11	12	13	14	14.5	15.5	17	17	18	18	19	20	21	22	23	24	25	26
MID ADVANCED																										
WEEK 1	4	5	6	7	8	9	9.5	10.5	11.5	12	13	14	15	16	17.5	17.5	18	19	20	21	22	23	24	25	26	27
WEEK 2	4	5	6	7	8	9	9.5	10.5	11	12	13	14	15	16	17	17	17	19	19	20	21	22	23	24	25	26
WEEK 3	4	5	6	7	8	8.5	9	10.5	11	11	12	13	14	15	16	16.5	17	18	19	20	21	22	23	24	24	25
LATE ADVANCED																										
WEEK 1	4	6	6	7	8	8.5	9	10.5	11	12	13	14	14.5	16	17	17	17	18	19	20	21	22	23	24	25	26
WEEK 2	4	5	6	6	7	8.5	9	10.5	11	11.5	12	13	14	15	16	16.5	17	18	19	20	21	21	22	23	24	25
WEEK 3	4	5	6	6	7	8	8.5	10	10.5	11	11.5	12	13	14	15	16	16	17	18	19	20	20	21	22	23	24

Use this table as a guide for selecting your training hours progression based on the highest number of hours, or maximum hours, you can train in a given week. Once you've determined what your maximum training hours will be, find that figure along the top of the chart and use the column directly underneath your maximum hours as a guide for your weekly base training hours. The chart is set up for 4-week base phases (including recovery weeks at the end of each phase of training), but you can also use 3-week phases by skipping the first week of each phase and using the hours for Week 2, Week 3, and Recovery.

of my favorite clues is how sore my legs are when I walk down the stairs in the morning. If they're noticeably sore, then I know I need another day of rest or an easy recovery ride before loading them up again with more training. This can be reaffirmed when I'm on the bike and I feel that a given wattage is more challenging to maintain than usual, or it feels like I have a flat tire when riding up the same hill I charged up comfortably the other day. Knowing when to say when, as noted in Chapter 6, is an important ability to develop and shows maturity as an athlete. Your body will tell you that it's tired and needs rest; but if you're not listening to it, you may find that your body will have to yell at you to get your attention. Getting sick, injured, or becoming overtrained is often your body yelling at you to back off. Learn to listen for the signs that you need more recovery, and remind yourself that you gain fitness during rest.

In addition to the need for more recovery days per week, older athletes may also benefit from scheduling full recovery weeks more frequently than younger athletes. A 21-year-old may be able to apply a progressive training load over three weeks before requiring a full recovery week. A 50-year-old athlete may need that recovery week after just two weeks of training. This is affected by age and also by our "other life." If the 21-year-old is working 45 hours a week and taking 25 credits at college and the 50-year-old is retired, single, has no kids, and has developed a great base foundation over the past 30 years, then the tables may be turned: the younger athlete would be the one needing more frequently scheduled recovery weeks. Seeking a balance that is appropriate for your life is more important than trying to follow the same training plan as the professional athlete living down the road. Take your unique needs into consideration, and follow your schedule.

Sleeping and Eating

If you're getting less than 8 hours of sleep a night, then you should consider keeping your training to no more than 7 to 10 hours a week. I've found that increasing your base training load over 10 hours a week requires a minimum of 8 hours of quality sleep a night. Once they reach 15 hours of training a week, most athletes will need 8 to 10 hours of quality sleep a night. The body releases growth hormones and does repair work while you're sleeping. The more repair work needed, the more quality sleep you need to get.

One way to enhance the recovery process is to eat and sleep immediately after completing a challenging or breakthrough workout. The nutrition consumed within the first 30 minutes after a workout is critical for starting the process of replenishing carbohydrate stores that become depleted during the workout. Sleeping continues the recovery process by giving the body the opportunity to go to work right away on repairing and rebuilding itself. Take a 60- to 90-minute nap after your first postworkout meal, wake up, and eat again. If you can make this your routine at least one or two times a week after a challenging workout, you will be better able to handle a greater training load on those days. Ideally, this could be your Saturday routine. If family or other obligations make it impossible to get a postworkout nap, then be sure to get the recovery nutrition started right away and plan ahead to be able to get to bed early on that day. The most common factors in overtraining are inadequate nutrition and rest, also referred to as *under-recovery.*

Health and Stress

If your body has to deal with managing an illness or injury, it will have less repairing capacity available to respond to the physiological stress caused by training. When we train, cells and tissue in the body are broken down and require rebuilding. If your body is busy repairing an injury or fighting off an illness, it will have limited resources to work on repairing damage caused by training. If you get sick or injured, back off on your training to give your body an opportunity to take care of the injury or illness. An easy "recovery" ride or a short level 2 ride might be okay if you have only a minor cold and are taking care of it through adequate nutrition and rest; but if you have a fever or any chest congestion, stop all training until these symptoms are gone.

Life stress also takes its toll on the body's ability to recover from training. I often see athletes struggle to recover from training that they would normally be able to deal with at times when work, relationship, or financial stress is higher than usual in their lives. Moving, changing jobs, and ending a relationship seem to have the most effect on athletes' ability to absorb training. My recommendation at these times is to use riding your bike as an opportunity to relieve some stress rather than adding more. This usually means riding shorter and easier than what may be on your training schedule. It's important to maintain a balance between how much stress (training, life, or environmental) you ask your body to deal with and how much recovery you can offer it. Since recovery comes in the form of sleeping and eating, you need to increase your rest when stress on your body increases.

Environmental conditions also influence your rate of recovery. When training at higher altitude, for example, your body will have more difficulty recovering than it would at sea level. Air pollution and extreme heat or cold can also slow down recovery, since these conditions can increase the relative training load. This is especially true if you're not acclimated to these conditions.

Our immune systems are also taxed and vulnerable after a challenging workout. I encourage athletes to avoid sick people right after training hard. Try not to schedule a long flight right after a hard race, either. Sitting in close quarters with that many people while your immune system is temporally weakened is asking for trouble. Don't use the airline pillows. My experience is that the airlines do not change the pillowcases between flights. The last person to use that pillow might be sick. Clean your hands frequently during cold and flu season and especially while at the gym.

TRAINING LOAD

External and Internal Loads

Training load can be classified as external and internal. External training load is the actual workout—two hours of moderate riding, for example. Even if the external load (two hours of moderate riding) remains the same every day, there is still an increase in the internal load as fatigue builds within the body from day to day. This becomes more obvious as the external load also increases. You know that riding 100 miles on Saturday creates significant fatigue. If you ride 100 miles on Sunday as well, then even though it's the same external load, you'll be able to feel the current internal load, or fatigue, left over from Saturday's century.

The external load can, to some extent, be measured as the duration, frequency, and intensity of your workouts. All of these factors also influence the level of internal training load that results from the workout. Internal load is the accumulated fatigue and damage within the body resulting from training. A 2-hour ride with high-intensity efforts is going to produce more internal load than a 2-hour ride at very low intensity, for example. Duration can be expressed as time or miles. Intensity can be measured or expressed as power, heart rate, and rate of perceived exertion (RPE). Internal load is more difficult to measure, but can be monitored through the "vital signs" discussed in Chapter 10.

Environmental stress and your "other life" can also contribute to an increased internal load. A 2-hour ride in strong winds, extreme heat or cold, air pollution, or at high altitude will have more impact on your body and, therefore, create a greater internal load than a 2-hour ride in ideal conditions. As work or life stress increases, you may also need additional recovery to absorb training to which you would otherwise easily adapt. If you're unable to eat and sleep enough, then you'll need to reduce your training load to maintain an appropriate balance and continue to benefit from training.

Training Volume

Duration and frequency combined determine the volume of your training. When starting out, measure duration as time rather than miles. Several factors can affect your training when your rides are measured as miles. If you live in a hilly or windy region, then it will take longer to cover the same distance than if you lived in a flat, calm area. You will also find that it may take longer to ride 40 miles with fatigued legs than it might with fresh legs. I frequently encounter athletes who will attempt to meet mileage goals even when elements like wind or fatigue are slowing them down. It can take all day to ride 70 miles under difficult conditions, but it takes only four hours to ride four hours.

It's also easier to schedule your training as hours, since you'll know that you'll have two hours available on Wednesday night to train, for example. As you become more familiar with your regular riding routes and know how long they take to ride, you'll be better able to estimate your weekly mileage goals.

If you record your total hours of training for the week, you can begin to develop an outline of your training volume. If, for example, you ride five times a week for two hours each time, then you could express your training volume for that week as ten hours. You can also—and should—track the mileage, but we'll be starting out by setting and monitoring your total weekly hours. Your weekly hours should also include any crosstraining and strength-training time. This is another reason that mileage tells you only part of the story. I coached a mountain bike racer who would go for a 1- to 2-hour ride every morning and would not include it in her training log. She called it "walking the dog" because she took the dog with her, but it increased her time on the bike by five to ten hours a week. Even though she was riding at a "dog's pace," she was still increasing her internal load to some degree and burning more calories each day.

Record all your activities in your daily log. Even if you don't consider an hour a day of gentle yoga as training, it still requires an hour of your time each day—

more if you have to travel to the yoga site. It all adds up when you're trying to balance your training life with your "other life." You can still break your total training hours down into time spent on the bike, crosstraining, strength training, walking the dog, and so on, to see how your training time is distributed from week to week. I checked, and even though she didn't, her dog recorded this as "crosstraining."

Total Training Load

Combine the volume and intensity of your training to get your total training load. Measuring total training load can become difficult if you're not carefully tracking the duration, frequency, and intensity of your workouts. Intensity can be measured with a power meter or estimated with a heart rate monitor or perceived exertion. If you don't currently use a power meter, you should try to estimate your training load so you'll have a way to compare your training from week to week. Even if you consistently ride ten hours every week, it may not be the same training load from week to week. If one week you spend five of the ten hours chasing down your cycling buddies, that will significantly increase the total training load for that week.

Well-structured training programs follow the guideline that as intensity goes up, volume needs to go down. Remember to keep a balance in your total training load. If intensity increases, so does the training load. To maintain a balance, you have to reduce the amount of time you're training so that you don't suddenly overload your system. This leaves more time available for recovery. You should be able to, and need to, handle a moderate increase in training load from month to month to see continued improvements, but doing it without planning and monitoring can lead to setbacks rather than continued progress. Tables 7.2 and 7.3 are examples of ways to measure training load based on time spent in HR zones.

If you are using a power meter, you can use the kilojoules feature to help measure your training load. Kilojoules are the units that measure the work being performed by the cyclist over time. On a PowerTap power meter, for instance, it is the "E," or energy measurement. Some newer software for power meters includes a "Training Stress Score" that can also be used to estimate training load of a workout. Training Stress Score may be a better estimate than kilojoules because it attempts to include the intensity of the workout, whereas kilojoules does not directly measure the relative intensity.

	TABLE 7.2: ESTIMATING TRAINING LOAD FROM TIME IN HEART RATE ZONES		
ZONE	TIME SPENT IN ZONE (min.)	VALUE/TRAINING SUM (zone × min.)	TRAINING LOAD
1	20	1 × 20 =	20
2	70	2 × 70 =	140
3	30	3 × 30 =	90
4	0	—	0
5	0	—	0
TOTAL TRAINING LOAD			250

The training load for this workout would be 250. It's not necessarily a universal measurement, but it is a number that you can use to compare one of your rides with another. If you spent more of the 2-hour ride in zone 3, then even though it was still a 2-hour ride, it would have a higher training load number because of the higher effort, or intensity, level.

You can also estimate your total training load by multiplying the time you spend in each power or heart rate zone by the number of the zone. Then add the totals together to get a number for comparison with other rides. (See Tables 7.2 and 7.3.)

If you're not currently using either heart rate or power, you can still estimate the total training load of a given workout by giving it a number based on your perceived exertion of the workout. This is much more subjective but better than nothing. Take the duration of the workout and multiply it by the perceived exertion you would give that particular workout. Rate the overall workout the same way you would a given intensity on a scale of 1 to 10. A 2-hour workout (or 120 minutes) at an RPE of 4 would be $4 \times 120 = 480$. Although this is not a precise measurement, it is still an estimate that provides a guideline for measuring and comparing your total training load from week to week.

Tracking Training Load

By comparing the weekly totals, you can see if your training load is progressing, staying the same, or falling off. Be sure to include all of your training when

TABLE 7.3: HEART RATE AND TRAINING LOAD

ZONE	TIME SPENT IN ZONE (min.)	VALUE/TRAINING SUM (zone × min.)	TRAINING LOAD
1	15	1 × 15 =	15
2	45	2 × 45 =	90
3	60	3 × 60 =	180
4	0	—	0
5	0	—	0
TOTAL TRAINING LOAD			285

You can see that the increased intensity of a 2-hour training ride, or more time spent in zone 3, increases the training load from 250 to 285. By tracking the relative training load for rides this way, you can get a weekly total for comparison throughout your base training.

calculating your total training load. This means that you'll need to give a training load rating to your crosstraining and strength workouts. One way to do this is by using a heart rate monitor that estimates your kilojoules for all activities. You can then add this into the total kilojoules from the power meter. The objective here is to get an outline of the total training load from week to week that also takes into account the intensity of the training without relying on just volume. This provides a better guide to what the actual training load is. See Figure 7.1 for an example of an appropriate training load progression.

Look for patterns in how your body responds from week to week based on the applied training load. By keeping notes in your training log on your daily life, personal stress, sleep, and nutrition, you can also see if you're maintaining a balance between training and recovery. If you experience a point during your training when you feel that your body is overloaded and not recovering as planned, take a look back through your daily logs at the total training and life stress leading up to that point. It's possible that you increased your training load faster than your

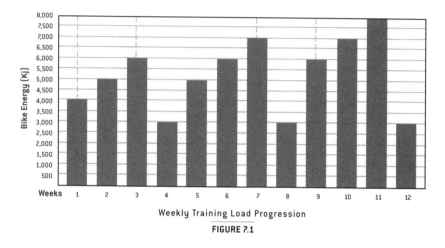

Weekly Training Load Progression
FIGURE 7.1

This graph shows examples of how gradual increases in training load progression might look. Training load progression can be measured and expressed as total kilojoules or time spent in heart rate zones, or it may be based on rate of perceived exertion. Whichever formulas you use to measure your training load, the progression should look something like this example, with each bar representing a week of training. The lower bars are recovery weeks.

life could tolerate at that time. A training schedule needs ongoing adjustments as necessary and should be considered more of a request than a demand. Be flexible, listen to your body, and learn to know when to say when. Plan ahead; and if you know you'll be having a stressful or unusually busy week, then consider backing off on your training that week to stay in balance. Keep your options open, since your body may decide that what you have on your training schedule is not going to happen regardless of how hard you try.

You'll want to determine your *personal adaptation threshold*, or how much training load your body can handle over a couple of days or weeks. You must then be sure to "unload" the accumulated internal load before applying more training stimuli. Finding this balance is important for maintaining continued progress in fitness. It can take months and years to determine your personal training load limits. Keeping accurate training logs is important if you want to know what kind of training blocks work best for you.

When I start working with a new athlete, one of the first things I ask to see is her training logs. When I review those logs, I often find points in the year when she felt run down or got sick. There is usually a sudden increase in her training load in the days or weeks leading up to this, without adequate recovery to support it, or there may be a stressful week at work or in her personal life. A training log with ample, accurate information is a great resource for analyzing how an athlete personally responds to training over time. It also provides a good starting point for what level of training load is appropriate and necessary for that athlete to see improvements. If I see that an athlete has already been training ten hours a week without struggling with recovery or setbacks, then I know that we can progress from there. If, on the other hand, there is a pattern of training 10 to 12 hours for a few weeks and then getting sick or run down and missing a bunch of training for several weeks before being able to get back on track, then I know to be cautious. Of course, the total training load is what I'm looking for here, not just the volume. I often come across training logs that include only the hours or miles and don't provide enough information regarding the intensity of those hours to make an appropriate assessment. (See Chapter 10 for more information on training logs.)

Your total training load for an entire year can provide you with a starting point for the next year's training. If your life allows it, you should increase your total yearly training load by 5 to 15 percent to see an improvement in fitness over the previous year. For base training, this usually means an increase in your training volume. If you're maxed out on total hours available to train, then you won't be able to increase your volume and will have to selectively add intensity to increase your total training load over time. For base training, this could mean more time at the upper end of level 2 early on and moving into level 3 training a bit earlier than the year before.

———•———

Training load involves accumulated fatigue and cellular damage, so it's critical to remember that rest is necessary for both recovery and progress in fitness. Strike a balance between progressive overload and recovery to ensure success.

Your body's ability to adapt to a training load and recover depends on many factors, including your age, fitness level, general health, sleep, nutrition, stress, and, of course, the nature of the training load itself. Keeping track of all your activities, not just cycling, and their cumulative training load in a daily log helps you gauge your progress and create appropriate training plans. Let's explore training plans in the next chapter.

8
TRAINING PLAN

Now that you understand the base and advanced fitness elements, you're ready to start assembling the pieces of a customized training plan. Before you start planning your base training, though, you need to outline your goals for the year.

SETTING GOALS

Why are you doing all of this training? What do you want to accomplish, and what will you have to do in order to accomplish it? It helps to have a motivating reason to get out of bed early and ride your bike for several hours on a Saturday morning when it's cold outside. Goals provide you with direction and a way to measure your progress along the way. They also help you to determine how best to set up your training.

There is a difference between dreams and goals, but dreams can become goals. A young athlete who dreams of competing in the Olympics can use that dream to help motivate himself to move through several stages of goals that will lead him closer to his dream. If you have a dream, realize that it's currently a dream and not yet a goal, but work toward it, and you may be able to make it a goal someday. The difference between a dream and a goal is that dreams take much longer than one or two seasons to accomplish. If you can realistically see yourself accomplishing it this year, then you can make it a goal.

You'll want to set both long- and short-term goals. A long-term goal could be more than a year down the road, but set some for this year, too. By having long-term goals, you're more likely to work on achieving the short-term goals.

Short-term goals are what you need to accomplish first to reach your long-term goals. Short-term goals can mean daily, weekly, or monthly goals. If your goal is to win your category on a mountain bike course that has technical sections and your skills are limiting you, then your short-term goals will need to include practicing your skills one hour every week. You can break that down into daily goals by designating 20 minutes for practicing specific skills on Tuesdays, Thursdays, and Saturdays.

Choose two or three long-term goals for the season and then start lining up short-term goals that you need to accomplish in order to reach your long-term goals. You can set up each of your long-term goals in a Goals Bracket (see Figure 8.1). There may be some overlap with short-term goals that will support more than one of your long-term goals.

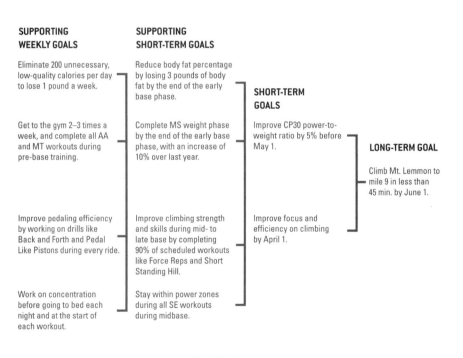

Goals Bracket

FIGURE 8.1

Goals should follow some guidelines. They should be measurable and time limited, realistic yet challenging, specific, and within your control.

Measurable and Time Limited

Climbing better is a good goal; but if you can put it in more specific terms that allow you to measure it, you'll know when you've reached your goal and can measure progress along the way. Stating it as "being able to climb Mount Lemmon to mile 9 in 45 minutes" makes it possible to know when you've reached your goal. You should also make it time limited by setting a date that you want to achieve it to help you keep your training on track. It may be necessary to adjust that time if you experience unforeseen interruptions or setbacks during your base training, but have a target date to encourage you to keep busy.

Realistic yet Challenging

Keep your goals realistic, but set goals that challenge you. If your current best time climbing Mount Lemmon is 58 minutes and you've been training regularly for several years, it may be a stretch to get up there in 45 minutes this year. However, if you can already climb to mile 9 in 46 minutes on very little training and can dedicate yourself to a lot more training this year, then 45 minutes may not be a challenging enough goal for you.

If you've been winning races in your category, then winning more races may be realistic but not challenging enough. Goals should motivate and push you to work hard and stay on track along the way to reaching them. You may want to make your goal to upgrade or improve a limiter that will help you when you do reach the next category. I've seen many talented athletes start cycling whose fitness levels allow them to move through the categories faster than their skill development could keep up. Don't neglect your skills. Make it a goal to work on them every week.

If you've never raced before, then making your goal to win your first race may be challenging but not realistic. There are certainly exceptions to this. I've seen athletes who have come from other endurance sports go out and win their first road race. They upgrade quickly and move on. But if it's your first year of racing, you may want to set a goal of finishing with the main field. There is a lot more to winning races than just fitness. Set short- and long-term performance goals that you can measure and also set goals that include developing your pack-riding skills.

A performance goal is something that you can do on your own, and measure it. It might be finishing an individual time trial in a specific time or averaging 250 watts for 30 minutes. It can also be riding in the front third of the pack in a road race rather than dangling at the back.

Within Your Control

Winning a race is a common goal to choose, but outcomes in races are something you can't personally control. You can certainly do everything you possibly can to win, and you may win; but I've seen athletes set personal records for their CP power durations during races, have a great race, and still be unable to meet their outcome goals. Their performance was up significantly, but you can't always rely on just fitness to win races. It takes a fair amount of smart riding and some luck. You can't count on, or control, what other riders are going to do either. Don't just think of a goal as which race you want to win. Look at the details of what you must do to put all the pieces in place so you have a chance to win.

Setting performance goals is a better way to measure progress than by using just outcome goals. It's okay to have as your goal to finish a race well, but how will you know if you have the fitness to do that and what skills will you need? Setting goals to reach performance objectives will not only keep the goals under control but will also increase your chances of improving your outcomes. Set out to improve with goals that address what is holding you back.

With power meters becoming more widely used, goal setting can include increasing your power output and your power-to-weight ratio. If your sprint is holding you back, then you need to improve your power for 5- and 12-second tests. If you're struggling to finish, then your longer duration power levels may be holding you back, or your limiter may be the ability to do hard efforts and recover quickly.

Setting power output goals is a good idea, but don't stop there. I've seen athletes get beat by other cyclists who are not able to put out as much power. Don't neglect your riding skills, tactics, nutrition, or mental skills, for example. A talented athlete could lose a race she might have won because she "lost it" mentally. If your mental skills are holding you back, set goals so you can work on them regularly. If you're not getting enough sleep at night, then you won't be able to train as much, so getting to bed early may be a short-term goal that's necessary to achieve your long-term goal. Look at what you do off the bike, too.

PERIODIZATION

Periodization is a well-known and commonly used method for outlining training plans for endurance athletes. Many cyclists, however, choose not to follow it. They may not be fully aware of the advantages of following a well-structured training plan based on periodization, or they just don't want to follow a structured training plan. If you go out and ride your bike a lot, you will get faster. The catch is that you're not likely to get as fast as you're capable of being, and your fitness is not likely to reach its peak when you need it most. There will be limits to how fast you can get and when you'll be fast. I've certainly seen endurance athletes do very well by just going out and training without using a well-structured periodization plan. These athletes are able to get by on natural talent and ability. When I've started coaching such athletes and put them on a periodization plan, they were able to excel even more. They could get faster by actually doing training of less volume but higher quality and with more built-in recovery. If you want to get as fast as possible each year and be fast when you most need to be, then periodization is for you.

Periodization is based on the idea that you cannot improve all aspects of fitness at the same time and that you cannot maintain peak fitness year-round. To reach your highest possible level of fitness each year, start your training by developing one aspect of fitness first. You then build through different phases of training designed to advance your fitness so you reach a very high level of fitness at a specific time. As you move through each phase, you maintain the fitness improvements you made in the previous phase while building greater fitness on top of it. Training starts out developing general fitness aspects. As you get closer to your important events, the training becomes more specific to the demands of the events you're preparing for.

Attempting to maintain a high level of fitness at all times does not work. If you could do that, then the same athlete who wins the Tour de France would simply travel to the next big race and win it, then go to the next race and win it, and then continue to win every race all year long. Athletes who excel at the exact time they need to find that excellence by following a training plan based on the concepts of periodization.

In a periodization plan, there are times of the year when your fitness ceiling, or advanced fitness, is lower and you're not as fast. Most athletes want to be fast all year. They don't want to go out and ride along with their buddies or teammates and feel slow, so they'll try to stay fast by riding hard all year. They will get faster but not as fast as they could be, their fitness will not last, and they're more likely to become overtrained and burned out than cyclists who follow a training plan based on periodization. You have to slow down during your base training to get faster each year. If you follow this plan, your slow pace will increase each year too.

For endurance athletes, the aerobic base fitness takes the longest to develop and is needed to support the advanced fitness, so it makes sense to spend time building your foundation first each year through base training.

Basic Training Concepts

The training concepts that are addressed through periodization include the following:

Timing: Reaching peak fitness at specific times of the year.

Progressive overload: Building greater fitness on top of fitness already developed.

Adaptation: Having built-in recovery to ensure ongoing adaptation.

Individuality: Providing time to improve your specific limiters.

Specificity: Breaking training into separate phases that move from general to specific.

Reversibility: Training in a regular, realistic, and flexible way so that fitness progresses and you can avoid interruption to your training program.

Timing

Since we can't maintain our highest level of fitness year-round, we want to design our training so we reach peak fitness at times of the year when events that are important to us are taking place. To peak at the right time, plan ahead and outline your training so you develop your fitness progressively and to its highest level when you need it most.

Progressive Overload

For continued improvements in fitness, you must apply an ongoing training load that provides a slightly greater challenge than what your body has become accustomed to. If you ride your bike for 25 miles every other day for a year, you will become really good at riding your bike for 25 miles. To become able to ride for 100 miles, you need to gradually increase the challenge for your body. You need to do this at a rate that allows your body time to adapt and continue to gain fitness without injury or other setbacks that can be caused by a rapid increase in training load.

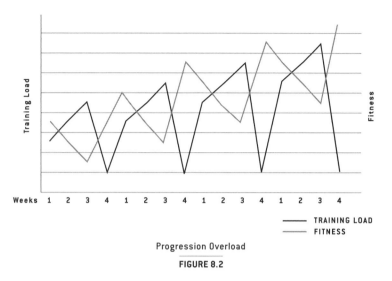

Weeks 1 2 3 4 1 2 3 4 1 2 3 4 1 2 3 4

——— TRAINING LOAD
········· FITNESS

Progression Overload

FIGURE 8.2

Fitness will actually temporarily decrease as internal training load increases until you unload the fatigue and allow enough time for adaptation to take place. This process is also referred to as supercompensation. Supercompensation is when the body makes an adaptation to a training stress, or load, and develops the ability to perform at a level higher than it could before. The adaptation requires adequate rest and nutrition after training loads are applied.

Periodization moves your training along with gradual increases in the total training load through increases in volume and intensity. These increases must match your body's ability to absorb it.

Adaptation

For your body to be able to adapt continuously, you must have rest and recovery built into your training plan. The periodization plan you'll follow will have scheduled recovery days within each week and full recovery weeks every third or fourth week. By planning ahead, you can schedule progressive increases in your training load throughout your base training to ensure that you are building fitness along the way. The built-in recovery is there to allow your body to adapt to the increases. You do need to be flexible and adjust the training plan based on your individual needs.

Individuality

Everyone has different needs and goals, and individual training plans should reflect that. The basic concepts are the same, but the specifics of the workouts and durations of the different base phases will vary from one cyclist to the next. You need to determine what fitness aspects are holding you back and what types of events you're training for, and then set your training up to meet those demands.

Specificity

Your training should prepare you for the specific demands of the events you're training for. A sprinter needs to sprint, a mountain bike racer needs to have technical skills, and a road racer has to climb. If you're preparing for a road race with 3,000 feet of climbing, you must train your body to climb. If you live in a region with no hills but the events you're training for are hilly, then you may want to schedule a cycling camp in a hilly region during your late base training phase.

The advanced fitness training phase that you move into after completing your base training more closely addresses these aspects, but how you develop your base fitness will determine how well you can develop your advanced fitness.

Reversibility

Fitness is dynamic. You're always gaining fitness, trying to maintain it, or losing it. It will rarely remain constant; and if it does, it's for a short period of time. If you stop training, you will lose fitness.

The objective is to schedule your training in a way that is realistic but challenging, takes into account your personal life obligations, and provides some flexibility for unforeseen events. A continued increase in fitness that is slightly below what may be the maximum possible is better than pushing yourself too hard and having setbacks from injury, illness, and burnout. Keep moving forward rather than getting ahead and then falling behind (going in reverse, so to speak).

DESIGNING YOUR BASE TRAINING PLAN

Building a Strong Foundation First

Base training is all about laying down a large foundation of fitness that will support more advanced fitness down the road. With each phase of base training, you develop your base fitness elements so you'll be able to raise your fitness ceiling. How high you can raise it and how long it stays up depends on the size of the base fitness foundation you lay down each year.

Although I was not actually there when they built them, it seems that in order to build the great pyramids in Egypt, a bunch of stones would have had to be placed to cover an area large enough to support the remainder of the structure before adding the next layer of stones. With each layer placed on top of the previous layer, the pyramid grew higher. Without the huge foundation that they put in place first, each pyramid could not have been built as high and could not have stayed up as long as it has. Think about that when you're outlining your base training plan. The bigger the base fitness foundation you lay down each year, the higher you can raise your fitness ceiling and the longer it will stay up.

I'm also guessing that there was a plan laid out before the Egyptians started building the pyramids so they would know where to place the first stones that would support the other stones all the way to the top. The cyclist who goes out and rides too hard too frequently during her base training is trying to build her fitness from somewhere other than the foundation up. Building your foundation first will lead to fitness that will last and won't crumble before your competitive season ends.

Guidelines for Base Duration

Advanced cyclists should schedule 10 to 12 weeks for base training; intermediate cyclists, 12 to 14; and beginners, 14 to 16 (see Table 8.1 for example base training outlines). In addition, add 6 to 8 weeks for your pre-base training. Advanced cyclists need enough time in the pre-base training to complete the anatomical adaptation (AA) and maximum strength transition (MT) phases (covered in Chapter 12). Beginner and intermediate cyclists can start their early base training phase while still in the AA strength phase, since they'll be skipping the maximum strength phase.

Each of the three base training phases (early, mid, and late) is designed to address and build on specific fitness aspects. You can adjust your base training phases based on your specific needs.

If your goals include losing weight, then you should extend your early base phase. If your goals are improving your time trialing, then you could increase your mid and late base phases. If your goals include improving your climbing ability, then you should increase your late base phase. Do not increase your mid or late base phase by shortening your early or mid base training, however. If you

TABLE 8.1: SUGGESTED DURATION OF BASE TRAINING

ATHLETE	PRE-BASE WEEKS	EARLY BASE WEEKS	MID-BASE WEEKS	LATE BASE WEEKS	EARLY ADVANCED WEEKS	MID-ADVANCED WEEKS	LATE ADVANCED WEEKS	TOTAL WEEKS
NEW	6	8	4	4	3	3	2	30
INTERMEDIATE	6	6	4	4	4	3	3	30
ADVANCED	8	4	4	4	4	4	4	32
ULTRA-ENDURANCE	6	6	6	6	3	3	3	33
CLIMBING LIMITED	6	4	4	6	4	3	3	30
TIME TRIAL LIMITED	6	4	5	5	4	3	3	30
WEIGHT LOSS	6	8	4	4	3	3	3	31
INJURY RECOVERY	8	6	4	3	3	3	3	30
ABBREVIATED WITH PRIOR EASY TO MODERATE TRAINING	0	0	3	3	3	3	0	12
ABBREVIATED WITH PRIOR HIGH-INTENSITY RIDING	0	3	3	0	3	3	0	12
ABBREVIATED PREPARING FOR ULTRA-ENDURANCE	0	6	3	3	0	0	0	12

need more time to prepare for the advanced maximum strength phase, then you should extend your pre-base phase as necessary. If you're recovering from an injury, you may want to extend your pre-base phase until the injury is healed.

If you're training for ultraendurance events, you would benefit from extending the overall duration of your base training and extending late base training into your advanced training. You can also extend the phase that best addresses your individual needs or the challenges of the course you're training to race on. If this is your first year attempting a solo 24-hour event, I would suggest extending your early base phase.

Abbreviated Base Training

I don't recommend this, but if you've picked up this book two months before your important event and want to set up a base training program, then you can do an abbreviated version for now and set up a full base training program after that. If you have been riding but not following a structured program, you could start out in the mid base phase. If your training has included a lot of strength work and climbing already, you could start out in the late base phase. If you've been riding hard and fast all year and you're training for a long event, you may be better off doing 4 to 6 weeks of early base training to give your aerobic system a boost. If your training has been a good mix of moderate rides with only occasional hard efforts, you could take the base phases outlined in the endurance chapter and compress them into six weeks.

If the event you're training for is a self-paced ultraendurance event and you've been spending more than 20 percent of your training time above zone 3 over the past couple of months, then I suggest completing six weeks of early base training and progressing into mid base before your event.

Where to Start

The trick is knowing when to start your base training or, more likely, when you want to have it completed so you can move on to race-specific advanced training. You need to have your base training completed 9 to 12 weeks before your most important race or event. To set this up, you need to know when, or at least approximately when, this event is going to take place. So the first thing you need to do is choose your highest-priority events. You may be able to maintain your peak fitness for 4 to 6 weeks, so there could be several races within that period for which you expect to have your fitness ceiling up. After completing that first competition phase, you'll need to shift your training back to the late base or early advanced phase and build back up for about 8 weeks to a second peak, or competition phase. If you have done your base work, you should be able to bring your fitness ceiling back up a second or third time before having to go back and rebuild your foundation. One guideline for when to drop back down and start building back up is when your CP30 average power starts dropping off.

It's not hard to find events that you want to do well in. The problem is narrowing it down to few. Find a specific event or two to four events that are clustered together within about a 4-week period, and aim for reaching your peak fitness then. This is your first peak. If you're peaking for a race, you'll want to have four to six races before the peak event to use as workouts and to tune up your fitness, skills, and tactics. It also helps to have a few races behind you before your most important event to reduce the anxiety that is usually highest at your first race of the year. You will not come into these earlier races with your fitness at its highest, but will use them to help build your advance fitness. Schedule these races into your advanced fitness phases as lower-priority races but high-priority breakthrough workouts.

Once you've established when you want your fitness ceiling the highest, you can then take the calendar and count backward. Block out the 12 weeks back from there, and that is the week by when you want to have your base training completed. These 12 weeks between the end of your base training phase and high-priority events include a week for tapering and a week or two for adjustments that may be necessary if you have minor setbacks in your base training (e.g., getting the flu).

From the point that you want to have your base training completed, count back the number of weeks that your base training will cover, and that's the point that it should begin. If you find that you don't have enough weeks between now and your first priority event, then you'll need to compress some of the training phases as outlined earlier.

Pencil It In

Once you have selected your peak event and added up the weeks of your base and advanced training, you can use the outline from Table 8.2. Start by marking in your peak event at the appropriate week. If you will be doing 12 weeks of base, 6 weeks of pre-base, and 12 weeks for advanced training, then you'll put your peak event at week 30 (12 + 6 + 12 = 30). Week 18 would be the last week of your base phase. Week 1 would be the first week of your pre-base training. Break up the base weeks according to Table 8.2 or based on your specific needs.

Weekly Training Hours

You'll need to determine how many total hours you can train each week. Add up how many hours you have available on the weekends and on weekdays. Be conservative, keeping in mind all other obligations in your life. Leave yourself enough space to keep a balance. Your training should not seem like it's interfering with your life, or the other way around. If your schedule gets so hectic that you're rushing to get your workouts done, then the productivity will diminish, and you may be better off doing shorter or fewer workouts. What you're looking for are the maximum hours you can realistically set aside for training during your biggest training weeks.

Your training will progress in total weekly hours as you move through your base phases, and you'll have the greatest amount of training hours during your late base phase. Plan ahead so you'll be able to spend more time training during those weeks. During your pre-base and into your early base training, the total weekly hours will be less, so use that "extra" time to catch up on projects that you may not have time to do once you reach your late base training.

Refer to the training hours chart from Chapter 7 (Table 7.1), and find along the top row the hours that you've decided that you can allocate to training during the late base phase. Down that row are suggested hours that you could use for all the training phases. Use this as a guideline and adjust it if necessary. Note the reduced hours suggested for all your recovery weeks.

Tables 8.2, 8.3, and 8.4 are examples of beginner, intermediate, and advanced cyclist training plans. You'll see that the hours column has been left blank for you to fill in your appropriate training hours.

———•———

Goals set the direction for your training plan, ranging from completing a century or losing 10 pounds to finishing in the top 10 at a national championship. Whether short- or long-term, goals should be measurable and time limited, realistic yet challenging, specific, and within your control.

Periodization is the guiding principle of a sound base training plan. This well-known method takes into account timing, progressive overload, adaptability, individuality, specificity, and reversibility. Proper rest is essential for improving fitness, so plan for recovery days and weeks throughout your training.

Build a sound base foundation of 10 to 16 weeks, depending on your fitness level, so you'll be able to realize greater fitness down the road. Count backward from your highest-priority event to know where to begin your more structured training, and then pencil in a conservative estimate of the hours you can dedicate to your training every week. Your training will progress in total weekly hours as you move through your base phases, with the most training hours during the late base phase. In the next chapter, we'll look more closely at how to consider your training plan in terms of blocks of time.

TABLE 8.2: BEGINNER TRAINING PLAN

ATHLETE'S EXPERIENCE: FIRST YEAR OF TRAINING

Year:

Goals:

1.

2.

3.

WEEK	SUBPHASE	PHASE	HOURS	STRENGTH PHASE	EVENT
1	Pre	Base		AA	Fitness test: CP30 or 30-min. time trial
2	Pre	Base		AA	
3	Pre	Base		AA	
4	Pre	Base		AA	
5	Pre	Base		AA	
6	Pre	Base		AA	
7	Pre	Base		AA	
8 R	Pre	Base		AA	Fitness test: CP30 or 30-min. time trial
9	Early	Base		AA	
10	Early	Base		AA	
11	Early	Base		AA	
12 R	Early	Base		AA	Fitness test: CP30 or 30-min. time trial
13	Mid	Base		AA	
14	Mid	Base		AA	
15	Mid	Base		SM	
16 R	Mid	Base		SM	Fitness test: 30-min. time trial
17	Late	Base		SM	

(continues)

TABLE 8.2: BEGINNER TRAINING PLAN (continued)

WEEK	SUBPHASE	PHASE	HOURS	STRENGTH PHASE	EVENT
18	Late	Base		SM	
19	Late	Base		SM	
20 R	Late	Base		SM	Fitness test: 6-min. time trial
21	Early	Advanced		SM	
22	Early	Advanced		SM	
23 R	Early	Advanced		SM	Fitness test: 30-min. time trial
24	Mid	Advanced		SM	
25	Mid	Advanced		SM	
26 R	Mid	Advanced		SM	Fitness test: 6-min. time trial
27	Late	Advanced		SM	
28	Late	Advanced		SM	
29	Late	Advanced			
30 R	Taper	Compete			Peak event
31		Compete			
32		Compete			
33		Compete			
34		Compete			

TABLE 8.3: INTERMEDIATE TRAINING PLAN

ATHLETE'S EXPERIENCE: 2 TO 3 YEARS OF TRAINING

Year:

Goals:

1.

2.

3.

WEEK	SUBPHASE	PHASE	HOURS	STRENGTH PHASE	EVENT
1	Pre	Base		AA	Fitness test: CP30 or 30-min. time trial
2	Pre	Base		AA	
3	Pre	Base		AA	
4	Pre	Base		AA	
5	Pre	Base		AA	
6 R	Pre	Base		AA	Fitness test: 30-min. time trial
7	Early	Base		AA	
8	Early	Base		AA	
9 R	Early	Base		MT	Fitness test: CP30 min. and CP12 sec. or 30-min. time trial
10	Early	Base		MT	
11	Early	Base		MT	
12 R	Early	Base		MT	Fitness test: 12-min. time trial
13	Mid	Base		SM	
14	Mid	Base		SM	
15	Mid	Base		SM	
16 R	Mid	Base		SM	Fitness test: 30-min. time trial
17	Late	Base		SM	

(continues)

TABLE 8.3: INTERMEDIATE TRAINING PLAN (continued)

WEEK	SUBPHASE	PHASE	HOURS	STRENGTH PHASE	EVENT
18	Late	Base		SM	
19	Late	Base		SM	
20 R	Late	Base		SM	Fitness test: 6-min. 12 sec. test
21	Early	Advanced		SM	
22	Early	Advanced		SM	
23 R	Early	Advanced		SM	Fitness test: 30-min. time trial
24	Mid	Advanced		SM	
25	Mid	Advanced		SM	
26 R	Mid	Advanced		SM	Fitness test: 6-min. time trial
27	Late	Advanced		SM	
28	Late	Advanced		SM	
29	Late	Advanced			
30	Taper	Compete			Peak event
31		Compete			
32		Compete			
33		Compete			
34		Compete			

TABLE 8.4: ADVANCED TRAINING PLAN

ATHLETE'S EXPERIENCE: 3 OR MORE YEARS OF TRAINING AND RACING

Year:

Goals:

1.

2.

3.

WEEK	SUBPHASE	PHASE	HOURS	STRENGTH PHASE	EVENT
1	Pre	Base		AA	Fitness test: CP30 or 30-min. time trial
2	Pre	Base		AA	
3	Pre	Base		AA	
4	Pre	Base		AA	Fitness test: CP6 and CP12 min.
5	Pre	Base		MT	
6	Pre	Base		MT	
7	Pre	Base		MT	
8 R	Pre	Base		MT	Fitness test: CP30 min. and CP12 sec. or 30-min. time trial
9	Early	Base		MS	
10	Early	Base		MS	
11	Early	Base		MS	
12 R	Early	Base		MS	Fitness test: CP6 and CP12 min.
13	Mid	Base		SM	
14	Mid	Base		SM	
15	Mid	Base		SM	
16 R	Mid	Base		SM	Fitness test: CP30 min. and 12 sec. time trial
17	Late	Base		SM	

(continues)

WEEK	SUBPHASE	PHASE	HOURS	STRENGTH PHASE	EVENT
18	Late	Base		SM	
19	Late	Base		SM	
20 R	Late	Base		SM	Fitness test: CP6 and CP12 min. time trial
21	Early	Advanced		SM	
22	Early	Advanced		SM	
23	Early	Advanced		SM	
24 R	Early	Advanced		SM	Fitness test: CP30 min. and CP12 sec. or 30-min. time trial
25	Mid	Advanced		SM	
26	Mid	Advanced		SM	
27	Mid	Advanced		SM	
28 R	Mid	Advanced		SM	Fitness test: 6-min. time trial
29	Late	Advanced			
30	Late	Advanced			
31	Late	Advanced			
32	Peak	Advanced			
33		Compete			Peak event
34		Compete			

TABLE 8.4: ADVANCED TRAINING PLAN (continued)

9
TRAINING BLOCKS

How you set up your weekly and monthly training makes a difference in how your body is able to absorb the training load and make continued adaptations. You may have a very flexible life schedule that allows you to set up your training any way you want, or you may be limited by obligations outside cycling that will dictate when you can train. I have coached athletes who get up at 4 AM and train for several hours because that is the only time of day they have free of kids, work, or other obligations. I have also coached athletes who can leave work early on Wednesday afternoons to get in a long ride. You will have to set up your training to fit your life and needs.

WEEKLY TRAINING BLOCKS

I've seen the most success when athletes train for two to three days and then have one or two recovery days or complete days off. This works well for most cyclists who are working Monday through Friday because they will be doing a large part of their training over the weekend and can have Monday and Friday as rest days. This way, they have two training days (Saturday and Sunday), a rest day (Monday), followed by three training days (Tuesday, Wednesday, and Thursday), a recovery day (Friday), and then two training days over the weekend again. One of the ideas behind this is that you're more likely to get your largest training load over the weekend because you'll have the most time available then to train and rest. Having a rest day leading into the weekend gives the body some rest before loading it up for two days. Then, on Monday, you give the body a day to rest before loading it up again for three days. During the week, your training time is more likely to be limited and you'll be placing less load on your body each day and should be able to tolerate a few days of training before requiring a rest day again.

This outline also allows for some adjustments. If, for example, you have a higher than usual training load over the weekend, you can use both Monday and Tuesday as rest or recovery days to balance it out. If you load up on Tuesday and Wednesday, then you can start resting up for the weekend's training load on Thursday rather than waiting until Friday. Remember, fitness happens because of training but takes place during rest. The more training load you apply, the more rest or recovery you will need to gain a benefit from that training.

Here, in basic terms, is how a regular training week might look:

Monday: Rest day

Tuesday: Training day, or rest

Wednesday: Training day

Thursday: Training day, or rest

Friday: Rest day

Saturday: Training day

Sunday: Training day

If you're able to follow a weekly block like the one described, then make Saturday and Wednesday your most challenging training days during base training. We call workouts that most challenge your current fitness "breakthrough" workouts. This schedule gives you the most time between these workouts to recover before the next one arrives.

If you can't do this because other life obligations won't allow for a longer workout during the week, then you may want to do your most challenging workouts on Saturday and Sunday and schedule recovery on both Monday and Tuesday to ensure that your body has a chance to absorb the training load. If your life is relatively low stress and you have few other obligations, then you may be able to do challenging workouts three times a week. A good pattern for this would be to have the challenging workouts on Tuesday, Thursday, and Saturday or on Saturday, Sunday, and Wednesday, since this allows for some recovery between them.

Adaptation Threshold

During these 2- and 3-day "training blocks," your body is placed in a state known as overreaching. Overreaching is the result of an ongoing applied training load and can be described as a point of accumulated fatigue and cellular damage within the body. This condition is necessary to place a challenge on the body to make an adaptation, or what is called supercompensation.

Be careful, however: there is a fine line between overreaching and overtraining. We all have a personal adaptation threshold or limit to the amount of internal training load we can tolerate without overwhelming our body's ability to keep up and adapt. Your body should be able to recover from overreaching after a day or two, or sometimes up to 7 to 10 days of rest, depending on the amount of the accumulated training load. If you apply too much training load too quickly and without an adequate recovery balance, you can go beyond overreaching and into overtraining. Although the exact physiological cause or specific markers of overtraining are not definitively defined, it is a physiological state that can cause serious setbacks. An athlete who becomes overtrained may be unable to fully recover for months, so be careful when approaching your personal training load limits. (See the sidebar "Symptoms of Overtraining.")

Athletes who reach an overtrained condition have usually accumulated more internal load than their body can tolerate, through either an overly aggressive training schedule or high levels of personal life stress, and they have not been eating and sleeping enough to maintain a training load balance. I suggest just dipping your toe in a few times rather than diving in head-first. Get a sense of how your body responds to a given training load before increasing it, and make conservative increases from there. The potential setbacks associated with going beyond your personal adaptation threshold are not worth the possible benefits of the additional training. Sometimes "less is more." As Joe Friel puts it, the best approach to training is to do the least amount of the most appropriate training at the right times, resulting in a continued improvement.

It's best to realize gradual, continued increases in fitness. You're much better off lining up at the start of an important event being slightly undertrained than overtrained. You'll do better feeling like fresh juice than feeling like burnt toast. I've seen athletes who have had to miss training because of other life obligations still be able to combine high levels of motivation and available energy into a great performance. I've also seen athletes who try to do too much show up at races that they should do well in, but they struggle to even finish. Trying to do too much too soon may create short-term gains in fitness, but a setback can result in a loss of all that fitness and the reality of having to start your base training over. One way to avoid this potential downfall is to ensure that you're maintaining an appropriate balance between internal load and adaptation. You do this by including recovery days and weeks in your training schedule.

Your adaptation threshold is also affected by your overall life demands. A professional cyclist who does not have an additional 40-plus-hour work week obligation can handle more training load because he can also balance it with more rest time. As your training load increases, you have to include more recovery to ensure that your body is able to absorb the training load and create an adaptation.

One common mistake is to start piling on a large amount of training too quickly. I meet cyclists who start out by training 15 or more hours a week during their first year of training while still trying to manage a full-time job, school, and family life. They may start off realizing some rapid gains in fitness, but inevitably they reach a point when life catches up with them, and they will get sick, injured, overtrained, or burned out.

I've seen some strong athletes who have tried to reach their full potential as a cyclist in their first year of training and racing by riding hard all the time during base training. Their logic is that you have to ride fast to get fast. They tend to start off with a strong season but plateau quickly, have short-lived success, and often fade away quickly before midseason. This is one of the pitfalls of failing to be patient and develop your base fitness first. Give yourself time to build to your potential. It takes the body years to fully develop, or, as the saying goes, "It takes five years to build a champion." For the athlete who attempts to reach her full potential in just one season it may take even longer, because she'll be a year behind on her base development and might suffer setbacks like injuries, illness, and burnout.

MONTHLY TRAINING BLOCKS

Follow a similar training block outline for multiple weeks as you do for training days. In other words, just as you take a rest or recovery day every third or fourth day, you should take a full recovery week every third or fourth week (see Figures 9.1a and 9.1b). Even though a training week has rest days built into it, you will not

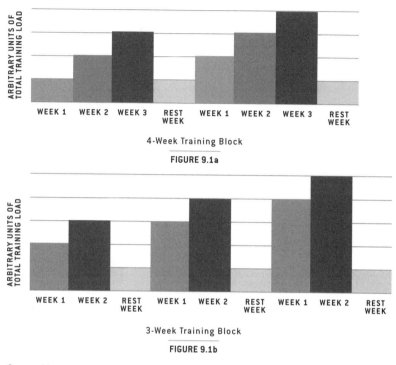

4-Week Training Block

FIGURE 9.1a

3-Week Training Block

FIGURE 9.1b

Some athletes can manage three weeks of training before needing a recovery week while others will need a week of rest every third week. These are examples of how those weeks might look with regard to training load progression.

likely be able to fully recover from two or three days of training in just one day. This means that you'll still be carrying some internal training load, or fatigue, into the next 2- or 3-day training block. After a few weeks of this, the internal load will have increased to a point that will require a recovery period longer than a day or two. This is when you start a full recovery week.

Recovery Weeks

At the end of a full recovery week, your legs should feel like most of the accumulated training load has been unloaded and your body has made the adaptations necessary and is ready to take on more training.

A recovery week will not have any breakthrough or challenging workouts. The format for a recovery week should include at least one extra day of full rest and a

SYMPTOMS OF OVERTRAINING

At this time, the specific physiology associated with overtraining syndrome (OTS) is still not completely understood, but there are several common causes and symptoms to watch for. Overtraining is most common among very ambitious and highly motivated athletes who struggle with the idea of taking a day off now and then. An overtrained condition is also closely associated with consuming a diet that is low in nutrients or calories.

You might be at risk for overtraining if . . .

- You keep exercising even when you get sick or injured.
- You refuse to take a day off from training even when your legs are screaming at you to stop the madness.
- Your daily diet consists mostly of coffee and donuts.
- You get less than eight hours of quality sleep per night.
- You have an enormous amount of job and life stress.
- You ride as hard as you can every day you ride.

You might be overtrained if . . .

- You bump into walls or have a general loss of coordination.
- You're grumpier than usual (check with your friends or spouse on this one).
- You feel depressed (and it's not even raining) and lack your usual motivation.
- You have a sudden loss in body weight and/or appetite.
- You are unable to sleep well for several days.
- Your legs are sore, and even after several days of rest they're still sore.
- You keep getting sick or injured.
- Your power output or performance keeps dropping, and training no longer feels productive.
- You push down on the pedals, and they seem to be pushing back.

If you have some of these symptoms and suspect that you might be overtrained, try taking three to five days completely off (meaning no exercise at all) and see if you feel better on the bike after that. If you do, then you were likely just overreached more than usual and had to dig yourself out of a recovery deficit. This is common after a stage race, where it can take a full 10 to 14 days of recovery before getting your legs back and realizing any new fitness. If you still struggle after taking a few days off, try taking another full week off. If, after this time off, you're still not getting your legs back, then you'll have to try taking more time off and should visit a

[continues]

sports medicine doctor. You may have some underlying illness going on as well. I've seen thyroid disease, mononucleosis, and anemia cause symptoms similar to those of overtraining.

One important thing to check for is iron levels. If they're low, then it will be difficult for your body to tolerate training and gain fitness. I've known many struggling athletes who finally discover that their iron levels are low. After getting treated, they're able to train again and feel much better. Some research shows that if you're in what is considered the normal range for iron levels but are at the low end of that range, you may still struggle as an endurance athlete. Finding a doctor who understands the needs of endurance athletes is important. I encourage my athletes to have baseline blood tests done when they're feeling great so that we have a reference if they start to feel run-down.

Another trouble for athletes is allergies. Several athletes I've worked with have displayed patterns of struggling with training and recovery at certain times of the year. We've been able to trace it to allergies that, once treated, no longer created a problem. Allergies can also trigger asthma in some individuals.

One of the most common issues that can lead to overtraining is poor nutrition. Food is not only fuel but is also necessary for supporting the immune system and for repairing the body from training and daily life. Eating well is important for good health and increased fitness (see Chapter 3). If you feel that you struggle in this area, consider working with a registered dietitian.

---

significant reduction of total training load. You should reach a point where you feel guilty that you're not doing enough during a recovery week.

Highly motivated athletes tend to resist the idea of a full recovery week. I recall reviewing the training log of a very talented triathlete and was unable to find a single recovery week during a 6-month period. A few times he had cut back on the training load, but it was because he got sick. This athlete also put lead weights in his saddle bag and sand in his tires to make riding harder! He was already doing well but started doing much better once I structured his training to include more recovery and took the lead out of his saddle bag.

A good time to perform a fitness test is after you've completed a full recovery week. You should be well rested and able to at least match your last test performance. If your weekly training load is modest and you seem to be managing it well from week to week, you can try scheduling your fitness test on the Sunday at the end of the recovery week. If you've accumulated a large amount of training load and will need more time to complete the recovery process, then wait and do the test as your first workout of the next week on Tuesday. Remember, testing is training, especially when doing critical power testing with a power meter.

If testing during the week is difficult because of other daily obligations, then you may find that you'll perform better on a weekend. You can wait and schedule a test for the first Saturday at the end of your first week of regular training after the recovery week. Be sure to go easy on Thursday and Friday before testing.

If your test results are less than expected and you can't explain the lower performance on some other variable (like stress, weather, poor warm-up, less sleep than usual, or someone putting sand in your tires), then you may need a few more days of recovery before beginning your next load of training.

Here is one sample of how to structure training weeks (refer back to Figures 9.1a and 9.1b for examples of 4- and 3-week training blocks, respectively):

Week 1: Regular training load.

Week 2: Slight increase in training load.

Week 3: Either a slight increase over week 2 or the start of a recovery week with a reduction of training load below week 1.

Week 4: Start of the next 3-week training block or a full recovery week if using 4-week training blocks.

———•———

For regular improvement, the best approach to training is to do the least amount of the most appropriate training at the right times. Weekly and monthly training blocks should have challenging training days and recovery, including complete time off, built in. Ongoing training leads naturally to overreaching, which is the point of accumulated fatigue and cellular damage within the body. This condition is necessary to challenge your body to adapt in the process known as supercompensation. The trick is to recognize your adaptation threshold so you don't start showing symptoms of overtraining, such as less coordination, sleep disturbances, sore legs even after rest, a tendency to get injured or sick, lack of motivation, and mood swings. A daily training log, discussed in the next chapter, can help you recognize such troubles before they derail your training plan altogether.

10
DAILY TRAINING LOG

It's not enough to have a training schedule. You need to keep track of what you actually do. How much time you spend on the bike may differ from what is planned from week to week. You also need to measure intensity by recording how much time was spent in each training level. Your training log is one of your most valuable possessions because it can tell you when your training was working and when it wasn't.

A training log is somewhat like power files. You may not personally know what to look for in reviewing your training log, but a coach does. If you ever have questions about your training that you can't answer, your training log is usually the first thing a coach wants to see.

If you don't have accurate records of your actual training, finding ways to improve on what you've been doing can be difficult. If you don't know how many total hours or miles your rode last year, for example, and you want to increase your base training load, you'll have to guess.

Your daily log also provides insight into how your body is tolerating the training load and how your daily life stress affects that. Over time, you'll be able to identify training and recovery patterns that provide an outline of what works for you and what does not. It's easy to look back to the weeks before an athlete begins to feel run-down or get sick and see what level of training and life stress he was trying to absorb. This record gives insight into his personal limits. You can also look back at the weeks leading up to a point when you realized a jump in fitness and see what an appropriate training and recovery balance looks like for you.

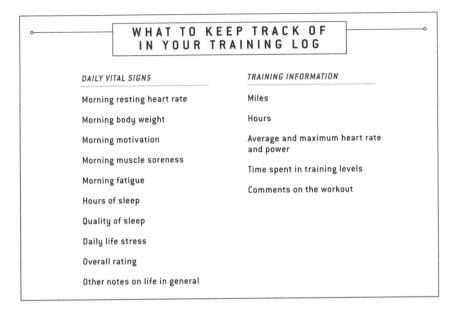

WHAT TO KEEP TRACK OF
IN YOUR TRAINING LOG

DAILY VITAL SIGNS	TRAINING INFORMATION
Morning resting heart rate	Miles
Morning body weight	Hours
Morning motivation	Average and maximum heart rate and power
Morning muscle soreness	
Morning fatigue	Time spent in training levels
Hours of sleep	Comments on the workout
Quality of sleep	
Daily life stress	
Overall rating	
Other notes on life in general	

VITAL SIGNS

Morning Resting Heart Rate

Resting heart rate should be taken when you first awake and while still in bed. It can be used to monitor your state of recovery and improvements in fitness. Be consistent in how you test this so you have an accurate comparison from day to day. I suggest that you place your watch on the stand next to your alarm clock. When the alarm goes off, tap the snooze button and pick up your watch. (Use a snooze button because you may fall back asleep while checking your pulse.) After resting for about a minute, place two fingers on your wrist and use your watch to count your heartbeats for a minute. Do this before the alarm goes off again because the alarm will startle you and raise your heart rate.

I'll often see a rise in morning resting heart rate a day or two before I realize I have a cold. I have also seen distinct patterns from an athlete's logs showing that her resting heart rate was climbing just before she got sick. A high morning heart rate can also mean that you're dehydrated. You'll see higher heart rates during exercise as well when you're dehydrated. Be sure to weigh yourself consistently to rule out dehydration.

A slightly higher than usual morning resting heart rate can also be caused by a night of poor sleep or ongoing stress in your life. Certain medications can also affect your resting heart rate, as can caffeine.

A gradual drop in resting heart rate over the course of a few months is a sign that your heart is able to pump more blood with each stroke. A sudden change in your resting heart rate over the course of a few days could mean that your body is in a state of overreaching and needs rest.

Morning Body Weight

Weighing yourself each morning just after using the bathroom is a consistent way to monitor your state of hydration. If you lose a full pound over a 24-hour period, it's not from dropping a pound of body fat but from water loss. There will be a natural fluctuation from day to day of one to three pounds. By weighing yourself daily, you can track patterns in your weight and compare that to how you feel on the bike. If your heart rate is higher than normal and your weight is not down, then it means that the higher heart rate is not being caused by dehydration.

Morning Motivation

How do you feel today? Each morning, give yourself a rating on a scale from 1 to 5 to reflect factors such as motivation, soreness, sleep, and fatigue. If you jump out of bed and can't wait to get on your bike even though it's raining, that's a 1. If you have a long argument with the snooze alarm and you win, that's probably a 4 or a 5.

Your motivation can be influenced by how well you sleep, how late you went to bed, how much work and life stress you're dealing with, and how bad the weather is. The level of training load you're carrying in your legs can also be a factor. As you get overloaded, you may begin to lose your motivation. Tracking this can give you insight into whether you should train that day or not. If, for example, you sleep well and your body weight is normal but your resting heart rate and motivation are not normal, you may want to play it safe and take a rest day.

Morning Muscle Soreness

Your muscles will be sore after you break them down with training. You'll often find that they are more sore two days after a tough workout, especially weight training. I gauge muscle soreness by how the muscles feel when I'm walking down the stairs in the morning or by how they feel when I get up out of a chair. You can also push on your muscles to see if they are tender. If they are, then they're still working on repairing themselves.

Be careful if you score your soreness as 3 or higher. Give your legs the time they need to repair themselves before tearing them down again.

Morning Fatigue

As your internal training load increases, your overall fatigue level will climb as well. You'll feel tired or sleepy and might need more coffee than usual to carry on a conversation. Make a note of this in your daily log.

Fatigue can also be caused by things other than training such as daily life stress, lack of quality sleep, poor nutrition, and sickness. If you feel fine around the house but when you get on the bike your legs feel fatigued and you struggle to keep the pedals moving, make a note of this in the daily log. You should also consider cutting your ride short that day and staying away from intensity until your legs are back to feeling normal.

Hours of Sleep

Write down how many hours of sleep you get each night. Look for patterns in how your body responds to more or less sleep. It's common to have difficulty sleeping at night if you do a hard workout in the evening. If you notice this pattern, you'll need to make adjustments in your training schedule to account for that.

Quality of Sleep

Don't write down that you got 10 hours of sleep if you laid in bed for 8 hours tossing and turning. That's not sleeping. Your body needs deep, sound sleep. If you have a pattern of struggling to get sound sleep, you might want to check with a sleep specialist. Although certain conditions can cause poor sleep, like sleep apnea, poor sleep itself can lead to fatigue, slow recovery, and overtraining.

Daily Life Stress

What happens throughout our day has a big effect on how much of a training load our body can handle. Record how much daily stress you are dealing with each day. This can provide insight into how well your body can tolerate it. I've seen the power output of athletes plummet during weeks of high stress. Don't underestimate the effect stress can have.

Daily stress can come in many forms, including financial, work, family, or just plain life. The life stressors I've seen have the biggest effect on an athlete are related to moving, relationships, and money, not necessarily in that order. Watch out for the additional stress that comes with these life situations, and adjust your training load as needed.

Overall Rating

Here is your chance to sum it up. How do you feel today about life, training, the weather, the whole deal? For some people, this is the most important of the subjective numbers. It tells a story about where you're at right now. You can then look back at the other subjective ratings and try to pin down what is most influencing the way you feel.

If your overall rating is poor and you have not been sleeping well, then you need to focus on improving there. If muscle soreness and fatigue are high, they may be affecting how you feel. If your overall rating is up, your resting heart rate is low, the legs feel great, and you're sleeping well, then your training and recovery are well balanced, and you might even be able to handle a slight increase that week or the next.

Other Factors

Record anything else that might have an effect on your training and recovery. Did you get fired? Are your allergies acting up? Did you just find out that the company you bought your $2,000 wheel set from is coming out with a lighter-weight version?

By making notes of what is going on in your life from day to day, you'll be better able to determine what causes such things as fatigue, poor sleep, loss of motivation, and poor recovery from workouts. It may not be just the training that is making you tired.

Good things happen, too, so note them as well. I see athletes' motivation increase when the sun is out or they get a new bike. Having things going well in your life can help your motivation, too. Not everyone is swayed by all things the same way, so keeping track of what affects you and how is helpful.

If in Doubt, Don't Work Out

I've asked you to track nine vital signs. There certainly can be more, but these are the most critical. If you find that three or more of your subjective vital signs are higher than 3, then you should consider taking a day off or doing an easy recovery ride instead of suffering through a challenging workout. If you have a couple of higher than usual subjective numbers but otherwise feel fine, it may be okay to start a challenging workout but with the understanding that if everything doesn't line up as it should, you'll "shut it down" and rest instead.

Say, for example, you wake up and discover that your resting heart rate is high but your body weight is normal. You also have legs that are sore and fatigued; you rate them as 3. You begin warming up for your breakthrough workout and everything seems fine, heart rate is a little lower than usual, legs are stiff but coming around, and RPE matches power. You finish your warm-up and start your first level 4 interval, and you can't get your heart rate up to match the level of power and RPE. So you push a little harder on the pedals, yet your heart rate still refuses to climb. This is when you shut it down. A suppressed heart rate during exercise is often a sign that you're carrying a lot of fatigue and are overreached. If anything feels "off" during your workouts and you have a few indications from your vital signs that your body needs rest, then rest.

If your resting heart rate is five beats higher or lower than normal and your body weight is normal, then you should be careful with your training that day, too. If you can't explain your unusual resting heart rate as stress or dehydration, then you might be getting sick or your body is in a state of overreaching. It's always better to err on the side of caution. Missing one day of training will not determine your season. Missing a week or two because you get sick is a bigger setback.

TRAINING INFORMATION

Miles and Hours

Also in your daily log, record how many miles you rode and how many hours it took. You'll want to also track this on a weekly basis to help you monitor your total training load. Keep track of your other training, too, such as weight training and crosstraining. You can break it into separate categories, but don't leave anything out.

Heart Rate and Power Data

If you're not already using a downloadable training device and don't have a system for tracking those files, then you'll want to record the data in your daily log manually. Some of the most important information to track is how much time you spend in each of your training levels during your rides. This provides insight into your total training load and tells you if you're meeting the objectives of the workouts. Some heart rate monitors will provide this information. If you're doing sprints on that day, then maximum power should be recorded. When you do your lower training threshold ride, you should record your average heart rate and average power for each of the aerobic intervals that you do.

Comments on the Workout

Here is what it comes down to: How did the workout or race go? Did you have trouble hitting your power-level targets? Did your heart rate respond normally to today's efforts? Did your legs have some snap in them, or did it feel like the chain weighed 50 pounds? Was the weather a factor, and did you eat and drink enough? Who did you ride with and what route did you take? All this and more can give you something to look at and assess the progress of your training, fitness, and recovery.

Power tests tell us something but not the whole story. Why are you getting faster or slower? If you're continually training when your legs are heavy and tired, then you may be training when you need more rest. If your legs feel great every day, then maybe you can handle a bit more of a training load.

———•———

If workouts are not going well, you feel unproductive, and your training is not progressing as it should, then your daily log can help you determine what is causing this and how you can make changes. If you have no records of what you actually did and what may be affecting the quality of your training and recovery, then you'll be unable to make informed decisions on how to proceed. An accurate, detailed training log is a invaluable tool that can help you get more out of your training by providing insight into how effective it is, how your body is responding to it, and how things outside of the actual training affect it. That is why I call indicators like morning heart rate, motivation, and sleep the vital signs—they are vital to your success.

PART FOUR

BUILDING A STRONGER ENGINE

11
ENDURANCE

Developing your aerobic system through ongoing endurance training is essential for success in all cycling activities. Your aerobic system needs time to make adaptations. If you don't spend enough time each year focusing on improving your endurance, then you won't be able to reach your fitness potential. A weak aerobic system will mean that you won't be able to raise your fitness ceiling as high, and it won't stay up as long.

BUILD FROM THE GROUND UP

Build your endurance foundation from the ground up. This translates into starting most of your training in levels 1 and 2, increasing the amount of time spent in level 2, then adding some time in level 3, increasing the time you spend in level 3, adding some time in level 4, and then increasing the time you spend in level 4. There will be times you wander into level 5 zones, but keep these visits short.

Also, even though you're adding and increasing time in the next level up as you progress through your base training, it doesn't mean that you are greatly reducing your level 2 rides (see Figure 11.1). You will continue to ride at your lower training threshold (LTT) throughout your base training and will use these rides for aerobic system maintenance after your base training is completed and you begin your specific race preparation or advanced fitness training. As you progress through your base training, your total training volume (duration plus frequency) will be increasing as well. You may reach your maximum volume before late base training if your training time is limited.

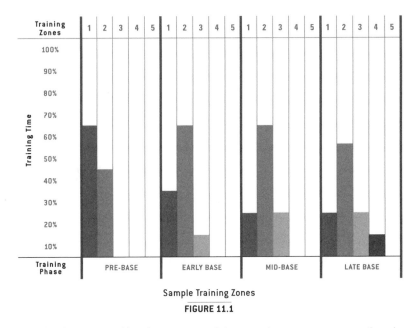

Sample Training Zones
FIGURE 11.1

Training time, measured here by percentage of time spent in a zone, can progress through the training zones, but as you move from the early base phase to the late base phase, you will gradually spend more time in zones 3 and 4, and less time in zones 1 and 2.

The exact form that your endurance workouts take in late base training depends on the type of events you're training for. If your focus is on shorter races like criteriums or track racing, which require more attention to anaerobic endurance and power development, then you'll move in late base training toward shorter workouts that include level 4 efforts but still emphasize a high percentage of aerobic system contribution. If your focus is on ultraendurance events, then you'll want to continue to fine-tune your nutrition and pacing strategies and keep your training volume higher to improve your ability to resist fatigue longer. Once you've completed your base training, your workouts will become more and more like the demands of your highest-priority events.

For mountain bike racers, I suggest doing your pre-, early, and some of your mid-base training either on a road bike or with slicks on your mountain bike, on paved roads or flat hard-packed trails. You can maintain steady aerobic efforts more easily this way. Riding off-road on technical trails makes it more difficult to keep the effort steady and stay aerobic. Once your aerobic base development is under way, you'll be able to move your endurance rides off-road in late base training. The exception to this is when you're working on your technical skills.

The objectives of endurance workouts include:

- Developing aerobic ability and strength of the type I and type IIa muscle fibers
- Improving carbohydrate conservation and training muscles to burn fat
- Enhancing the oxygen delivery and utilization systems
- Preparing the body for more challenging workouts down the road
- Developing resistance to fatigue
- Improving on-bike nutrition strategies
- Improving pedaling mechanics
- Improving the strength and resiliency of connective tissue
- Burning fat and losing unnecessary body fat
- Setting the foundation that will support a higher fitness ceiling

Endurance workouts will start out with easy effort levels at your LTT. These rides are used for base aerobic system development and maintenance. Training rides will gradually build to longer rides, on-bike strength development, faster aerobic effort levels, and strength endurance rides.

Pre- and Early Base: Ease into Training

During early base training, your endurance workouts should be limited to low strength requirements, moderate hills only with higher cadences (above 80 rpms), and lower heart rates and power levels. Strength development during pre- and early base phases is accomplished through weight training in the gym, while aerobic system development is being addressed on the bike and through crosstraining.

Pre- and early base is also the time to focus on the skills and drills outlined in Chapter 13 to improve your efficiency on the bike.

Mid-Base: Bring it All Together

Strength development progresses to on-bike strength workouts when the mid-base phase begins. Some of the cycling workouts will increase to moderate efforts in level 3. As you move into your mid-base training, you will have finished your strength development in the weight room, and you can now add strength-specific workouts on the bike. You'll continue to improve your cycling skills and do strength maintenance work in the gym. If you live in a relatively flat region and are training for events that are hilly, or you are a sprinter, you may need to extend your strength development in the gym further into your mid-base training.

Late Base: Rise to the Challenge

In late base training, your endurance workouts will include gradually steeper and longer hills and increasing durations at intensities that are close to but still below your upper training threshold (UTT).

During late base, you'll be combining strength and endurance through strength endurance workouts on the bike and spending more time riding just below your UTT. Late base will see the introduction of level 4 efforts on the bike. Once you've completed your late base training, you'll have the aerobic base fitness needed to move into the advanced training that most simulates the actual demands of your most important events.

CONSIDERATIONS FOR ENDURANCE TRAINING

Ride Duration

If you develop your aerobic endurance gradually and appropriately, you are also improving your body's ability to avoid injury. Cyclists commonly become injured through overuse. Pedaling a bicycle is a repetitive motion that not only takes its toll on our rear ends but also wears on muscles, tendons, and joints. If you try to pedal too many miles or with too much intensity before your body is prepared for the repetitive motion and the increases in force (i.e., how hard you push the pedals), then you'll be more susceptible to developing an overuse injury. You must start your endurance training early enough each year to allow time to build your base foundation large enough to support a higher ceiling when you need it most.

Ride Pace

During the early base training phase, cyclists often choose to ride with a group that requires them to maintain a pace too hard to be considered aerobic. This is a mistake you should avoid. It will not help you develop your aerobic endurance and can actually have just the opposite effect by teaching your body to rely on, or prefer, carbohydrates to fat. You will also be recruiting a higher percentage of type IIb muscle fibers and creating a lot of training load stress that requires more recovery. One objective of base training is to train the type IIa muscle fibers to prefer fat over carbohydrates by placing aerobic rather than anaerobic demands on them.

It's not easy to grasp the concept that riding slower can make you faster down the road, but I've seen it work for many athletes once they accept the idea and commit to it. You're better off finding a slower group to ride with or, even better, choosing to ride on your own most days. The occasional harder effort is okay during later base development, but making it your regular training ride is a bad idea.

Remember to do your own workout and not get caught up in the group mentality. Check your ego at the door when you head out for your ride. Remind yourself that the focus is aerobic system development, so if the group becomes competitive and the pace pulls you above your appropriate training level, drop off and finish the ride on your own. This also means that if you're "just riding along" and another rider blows by, you will maintain your discipline and do your workout, not hers. In other words, do not jump on the other rider's wheel, and do not attack her on the hill—just let her go.

I've had athletes tell me, "It will take all day to ride for two hours at a slow pace." The logic behind that remark is clearly flawed but common. Two hours is still two hours regardless of how fast you're riding. I've also seen cyclists unable to keep their heart rate low enough on moderate climbs during base training because they're trying to ride in harder gears and keep up with faster, more developed riders. Do your base work first. You won't keep getting faster if you always ride hard.

Compact Cranks

If you live in a hilly region, it can be difficult to find training routes that allow you to stay aerobic. One approach is to install a set of compact cranks on your bike and use a cog set that has a 27- or 29-tooth cog on it (see Figures 11.2 and 11.3). Compact cranks are not shorter crank arms, but they have smaller chainrings. I often hear from athletes that using a triple front chainring set up on their road bike is something they want to avoid. The double compact rings are a good alternative.

Look for crank sets with 50/34 or 50/36 tooth rings set up rather than the standard 53/39. The easier gears will allow you to spin up hills at slower speeds

Compact Cranks

FIGURE 11.2

Full Speed Ahead has used its extensive experience making high-performance cycling components to create aluminum and carbon-fiber compact cranks that offer a lightweight alternative to the standard triple chainring setup.

so that you can train on them aerobically. It will still take an hour to ride an hour, however.

Selected Cadence

We all have a preferred speed, or revolutions per minute (rpms), that we'll select for turning the pedals around. This is your cadence. To find what your "selected" cadence is, you'll need to look at the training files from your long endurance rides and track your most frequently used cadence or rpm range. You'll have a self-selected or most frequently used cadence that you prefer. It may show up as your average cadence for a ride, but you'll need to know if the device calculating this is averaging in the zeros when you're coasting. If it includes the zeros, then it will give you a lower number.

You can also take your average cadence for your 30-minute power or individual time trial testing as your selected range, since you won't be coasting during either of these efforts. Keep in mind that if you do the test on a climb, you'll most likely use a slightly lower cadence than you would when riding on flats.

If you don't have a cadence-measuring device on your bike, you can estimate it by manually counting while riding along at what feels like your selected rpm range. By counting how many times one knee comes up for 15 seconds and multiplying it by 4, you'll have your cadence, or rpm. So, if you count your knee 25 times in 15 seconds, you'll have a cadence of 100 rpms, since $4 \times 25 = 100$.

Cadence Building

Early base is the time to begin developing or improving your ability to spin the pedals smoothly at higher cadences. Use the pedaling drills outlined in Chapter 13 to help you with this. Include the leg speed and endurance spinning drills

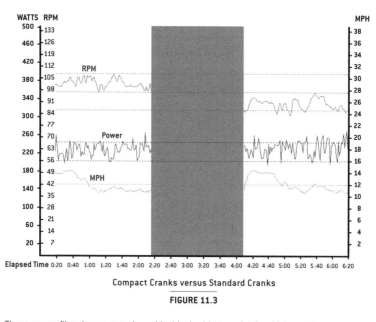

Compact Cranks versus Standard Cranks

FIGURE 11.3

These power files demonstrate how this rider is able to maintain a higher cadence on a steep grade by using compact cranks with 50/34 chainrings versus standard cranks with 53/39 chainrings.

in every workout. If your muscles are relaxed enough to spin smoothly at 100 rpms, you're better off than if you struggle at 90 rpms. By being able to ride comfortably in a larger range of rpms, you'll be better prepared for a variety of riding conditions.

I find that when athletes are able to ride comfortably at higher rpms, they can ride longer with less muscular fatigue. Sprinting also requires being able to spin at high cadences with more relaxed muscles. By training the muscles to cooperate with each other better at higher rpms, you'll become smoother and more efficient. If you find that your selected cadence is below 90 rpms, make it your goal to improve it.

Breakthrough Workouts

Rides that place a greater challenge on your body than what you are accustomed to are called breakthrough workouts. These workouts can result in an increase in your fitness, or they can create setbacks. You must go into them rested enough that your body can handle the higher training load and follow good recovery processes afterward to gain fitness from them.

The challenge of these workouts may come in the form of more duration, intensity, or some combination of both as compared to what you've previously been doing. You should also consider how the additional training load from a breakthrough workout affects your overall weekly training load. If, for instance, you add more rides to your week but none of the rides are longer or harder than what you're accustomed to, you're still increasing your training load and placing a greater demand on your body through an increase in volume without a specific breakthrough workout. By including breakthrough workouts, you're adding additional training stress that needs to be balanced with additional rest and nutrition. A common mistake is adding too much volume and intensity during the same week. Remember that both will increase the training load.

Start out with adding one breakthrough workout per week, and then, once you're certain that the balance is being maintained, try adding a second. By the end of the late base training, you may be doing up to three breakthrough workouts per week.

Remember, breakthrough doesn't have to mean more intensity. If your longest ride has been two hours for the past several weeks and you go out and ride three hours, then you'll create an overload that will challenge your body. That is a breakthrough workout.

Interval Training

The term interval is often associated with high-intensity efforts. This is not what the word means or should imply. Sometimes your intervals may be high in intensity, but an interval is merely the combination of changing between a work, or harder effort portion, and a recovery portion for prescribed durations.

Intervals are usually expressed in a series of three numbers: the first number indicates how many work efforts to do, the second number describes the duration of each of those work efforts, and the third number represents the rest period between each of the efforts. For example, an aerobic interval might be expressed as $2 \times 30 \times 5$. This means you will do two work efforts that are each 30 minutes long, with 5 minutes of rest between them. (Table 11.1 also describes a couple of sample interval workouts.)

TABLE 11.1: READING EXPRESSIONS OF INTERVALS

INTERVAL	NUMBER OF EFFORTS	WORK INTERVAL (MIN.)	REST INTERVAL (MIN.)	TOTAL WORK TIME (MIN.)	EXPLANATION
2 × 30 × 5	2	30	5	60	Do 2 efforts that are each 30 min. long with 5 min. of rest between each effort.
5 × 3 × 3	5	3	3	15	Do 5 efforts that are 3 min. long with 3 min. of rest between the efforts.

Here are a few different ways to make intervals more challenging:

- Increase the duration of the work portion (e.g., 20 minutes rather than 15).
- Increase the intensity of the work portion (e.g., level 3 rather than level 2).
- Reduce the duration of the rest portion (e.g., from 10 minutes down to 5).

PRE-BASE TRAINING

Before starting your early base training, you'll need to have a few things completed. This is why planning your training year is important. You need to have all your training outlined in advance so you'll be certain to finish your base training with enough time left to complete specific advanced training before your first important event.

Many athletes find themselves forced to cut their base training short because they have not planned far enough ahead and realize that their important event is only 12 weeks away.

A high percentage of the inquiries I receive from cyclists happen in the three months before their first important event. Some cyclists have already begun their season before they seek out a coach. It makes more sense when athletes contact me six or more months before their important events so that the most important part of their training, their base training, can be structured and completed without having to rush or compromise it.

⚬ ─┤ **PRE-BASE CHECKLIST** ├─ ⚬

Here are the achievements you should complete during pre-base:

☐ **Postcompetitive season recovery transition phase completed (2–4 weeks).** You need to be certain that you are physically and mentally ready for several months of ongoing training that starts with your early base phase. Take some time to unload the previous year's training from your legs, and get your life organized by making sure big projects are off your plate (e.g., get the house painted before starting your base training). You can, and should, exercise during your transition and pre-base phase, but keep it fun.

☐ **Anatomical adaptation and, if applicable, maximum strength transition weight training completed.** Advanced cyclists need to begin their maximum strength training phase in the gym at the same time they start their early base training. You must have your anatomical adaptation and maximum strength transition phases completed before beginning your maximum strength phase. (See Chapter 12 for more information on strength phases.)

☐ **Training plan outline completed.** You need to know when your competitive season will begin in order to work the schedule backwards to complete all your base training.

☐ **Cycling-related injury treatments completed or progressed to the point that training will not interfere with their complete recovery.** It doesn't make sense to start training if it will cause a setback rather than advance your fitness. Trying to "train through" an injury is a common way athletes end up having to start their base training over or having regular interruptions in their training progression. You may be able to move into your early base if the injury is healing. Use crosstraining to build fitness during the final stages of healing.

☐ **Begin consulting with a coach.** If you're going to be working with a coach, have him or her on the job before you start your base training. The coach will help you with the structure and can take the work out of designing your training plan and schedule. This is also a good time to assess your relationship with your coach and, if necessary, try a different one.

EARLY BASE TRAINING

Start your early base training with 2 to 4 rides per week. If you're crosstraining, then you'll ride 2 or 3 times a week and can crosstrain 2 or 3 times per week. You'll also be in the gym a few times a week during this phase.

Strength training is addressed in the weight room during the early base phase. Advanced cyclists who have completed their anatomical adaptation and maximum strength transition phase will begin their maximum strength phase. You need to have the maximum strength phase completed before moving on to mid-base training. Cyclists in their first year of strength training will continue with the anatomical adaptation phase through their early base and will move to strength maintenance at mid-base. Cyclists who have at least a full year of strength training experience and no issues with injuries in their legs will move to the maximum strength transition phase during early base and to strength maintenance in mid-base. See Chapter 12 for more details.

Early Base Endurance Workouts

Lower Threshold Ride
One of the most frequent workouts you'll do throughout your base training will be riding at your LTT. This is why it's important to understand where this point is. The longer the events you're training for, the longer the steady durations you spend riding in your level 2 will need to be.

Do the lower threshold ride at an intensity and duration that you can maintain without any increase in heart rate or perceived exertion. The duration at which you can maintain this steady low-end aerobic effort may range from 15 to 20 minutes for cyclists new to training to several hours for advanced cyclists. You should be able to ride at this effort level several times a week without creating significant fatigue in your legs.

Another way to look at it is that you should be able to "back it up" every day by riding at that intensity again without having it feel noticeably harder than it did the day before. If it does, then you may not be ready to ride at that intensity that long, or it's higher than your current LTT. If your endurance base is limited, then you may be able to ride at your LTT for only 15 to 20 minutes at a time without having your heart rate, perceived exertion, and even your blood lactate levels rise. As your endurance increases, you'll be able to sustain longer durations at your LTT without significant increases in your heart rate and perceived exertion. Your LTT should also begin to rise as you progress through your base training, so you should check or retest it about every 6 to 8 weeks.

Lower threshold rides should be done during early base with low strength requirements and at the high end of your comfortable cadence. This requires

---

━│ EARLY BASE CHECKLIST │━

Early base training is a time of easy effort levels. Specifically, the focus during this phase is on the following:

☐ **Develop your cycling-specific aerobic system pathways through easy rides at your LTT.**

☐ **Either begin your maximum strength phase or build on your anatomical adaptation strength.** The maximum strength phase is done only after completing a full year or two of anatomical adaptation strength work.

☐ **Crosstrain to enhance your central aerobic system (heart and lungs) adaptations, and allow any cycling-related injuries to have a chance to heal.**

☐ **Develop your cycling-specific skills.**

☐ **Establish baseline fitness through testing.**

☐ **Begin to examine your nutritional program and assess your needs.**

☐ **Address issues such as bike fit, and begin to adjust to the new position.**

☐ **Get into the habit of following a training schedule, and establish good patterns of rest, life balance, and filling out your daily training log.**

☐ **Begin to prepare the body for more challenging training loads.**

---

choosing routes with only very moderate hills of less than 5 percent grade. Depending on the terrain in your region, this may or may not be easy to accomplish. Using compact cranks and larger cassette cogs (e.g., 27- or 29-tooth) will help you keep your cadence higher during these rides so that you're focusing on aerobic system adaptations rather than strength. During early base training, you'll be focusing on strength training in the gym and beginning to ramp up the loads there. If you include high strength requirements on your rides (steep and long hills or riding at low cadences in big gears) while you're increasing the loads in the gym, you risk overloading yourself with strength workouts and you will be more susceptible to overuse injuries and excessive fatigue. Wait until you're done with your maximum strength phase in the gym or your early base phase before adding strength workouts on the bike. Once you've completed your early base weight phase in the gym, you can move to the mid-base training phase and add cycling-specific strength workouts.

I recommend focusing your riding at this level for at least the first 4 to 6 weeks of your initial base training, regardless of your cycling experience. At that point, more advanced riders (cyclists with three or more years of solid base training) can move into the mid-base training rides while still including the lower threshold rides a couple of times per week. If you're in your first few years of cycling, then you'll want to continue to focus on the rides for 6 to 8 weeks. If this is your first year of consistent training, then focus on the lower threshold rides for up to 10 weeks while completing a longer anatomical adaptation strength phase, and then add the more advanced rides of the mid- to late base training more gradually.

During the early base training, you will also be working on efficiency drills, including leg speed drills and perhaps form sprints. These drills will take your power and effort above your LTT for very short durations. I've had incredibly disciplined riders send me power files from indoor workouts where they spent exactly one hour within 5 watts of their prescribed level 2. It's great to see such compliance, and I think there is a benefit from accomplishing that, but you also need to ride the way the real world is built. Aim for 90 percent compliance in these rides. So, even though the workout calls for level 1 and 2 riding and you spend a few minutes above level 2 but it's less than 10 percent of the total ride time, you'll still receive a passing grade. A new rider will spend 15 to 30 minutes in level 2, with the remainder of the ride actually just below that intensity. An advanced rider may warm up for 20 minutes in level 1 and then ride for a couple of hours in level 2.

Remember, your LTT, or level 2, is at the point where you see the first rise in your blood lactate levels over your baseline. It can also be estimated through perceived exertion (RPE 2–4 on the 1–10 scale) and as 55 to 75 percent of your CP30 average power, depending on the strength of your base aerobic fitness.

Tables 11.2, 11.3, and 11.4 provide examples of lower threshold rides for beginner, intermediate, and advanced cyclists, respectively.

TABLE 11.2: BEGINNER LTR RIDE

PURPOSE	ZONE	DRILLS	DESCRIPTION	TOTAL TIME
Warm-up, efficiency	1	Back and forth, leg speed, and form sprints	20 min.	20
Efficiency	2	Endurance spinning	$2 \times 5 \times 5$	15
LTR	2	Back and forth	$2 \times 20 \times 5$	45
Cool-down	1	Breathing drills	10 min.	10
TOTAL RIDE (hr.:min.)				1:30

TABLE 11.3: INTERMEDIATE LTR RIDE

PURPOSE	ZONE	DRILLS	DESCRIPTION	TOTAL TIME
Warm-up, efficiency	1	3–5 leg speed or form sprints	20 min.	20
Efficiency	2	Endurance spinning	$3 \times 5 \times 5$	25
LTR	2	Back and forth	$2 \times 40 \times 5$	85
Cool-down	1	Breathing	10 min.	10
TOTAL RIDE (hr.:min.)				2:20

TABLE 11.4: ADVANCED LTR RIDE				
PURPOSE	**ZONE**	**DRILLS**	**DESCRIPTION**	**TOTAL TIME**
Warm-up, efficiency	1	3–5 leg speed or form sprints drills	20 min.	20
Efficiency	2	Endurance spinning	4 × 5 × 5 min.	35
LTR	2	Back and forth	2 × 60 × 5	125
Cool-down	1	Breathing drills	10 min.	10
TOTAL RIDE (hr.:min.)				3:10

Form Sprints

If you'll be racing in events that have a sprint at the end or would just like to improve your sprint, include form sprints during your early base. Include three to five form sprints throughout your rides. Find slight downhill sections on your regular routes that allow you to jump and sprint in an easy gear safely. There should be no cross streets, driveways, intersections, or traffic to contend with. If training indoors on a trainer, don't attempt sprinting, but do leg speed drills instead. More skilled cyclists can practice sprinting indoors on rollers, but be sure of your ability before attempting this. Chapter 13, "Efficiency," describes sprint workouts.

Crosstraining

Develop your endurance early in your base training by crosstraining. Sometimes it's a good idea to get away from the bike a bit to regain your enthusiasm for cycling. Crosstraining is also a way to activate and develop muscles that are not normally used in cycling.

Crosstraining can include aerobic activities other than cycling that develop central aerobic adaptations (heart and lung function). Running, cross-country skiing, snowshoeing, and swimming are common forms of crosstraining that I recommend. Swimming can be used if you're recovering from any injuries in the lower extremities that make cycling and activities that load the legs inappropriate. It's also possible to run in a pool with a flotation device around your waist.

Running

My first recommendation for crosstraining is running, because cycling does not provide the load bearing necessary for the body to develop stronger bones. Research has shown that even younger cyclists can have very low bone density. We need to put mild stress on our bones on a regular basis in order for them to become and remain strong. Each time you run, your bones are actually broken down and have to repair themselves. If adequate time and nutrients are available, the bones will rebuild themselves stronger than they were before.

If you're new to running or have not been running for over a month, you should ease back into it. Your cycling fitness will tempt you to run faster and farther than your body is ready for. Allow your body some time to adjust to running, or you may wind up injured and unable to even walk. It can take a couple of months of consistently running up to three times a week before you will start to feel the running become easier and comfortable.

Don't run on consecutive days. Give your bones a minimum of 48 hours to recover before you pound on them again. You can also use running as a warm-up for weight training sessions or to enhance your metabolism by running in the morning if you cycle in the evening.

If you race cyclo-cross, I suggest maintaining your running all year by running easy for 30 minutes twice a week. Doing so will allow you to ramp it up much faster and include harder efforts when you begin preparing for your 'cross season.

Table 11.5 outlines a running program from the ground up. Start your running by walking (yes, walking), alternating between the two for about 3 to 5 minutes each. This approach will lead to fewer injuries, which will keep you running longer. Begin by walking 5 minutes for the first several weeks, and split the run up with walking as well. This will help keep your heart rate down and your lactate from building up.

Keep your running paces slow for the first eight weeks. Your heart rate should be no more than about 10 beats above your cycling lower threshold. It may seem painfully slow to run at this pace, but it's better than the pain of developing an injury. Remember that you are trying to develop your aerobic system.

TABLE 11.5: BEGINNING RUNNING OUTLINE								
WEEK	1	2	3	4	5	6	7	8
TIMES PER WEEK	2	2	2	3	3	3	2	3
DURATION (MIN.)	20	25	30	2 × 20 1 × 30	2 × 20 1 × 30	2 × 30 1 × 20	20	30
FORMAT (MIN.)	Walk 5; run 3–5; walk 5; run 5	Walk 5; run 5; walk 5; run 10	Walk 5; run 10; walk 5; run 10	Walk 5; run remainder	Walk 5; run remainder	Walk 5; run remainder	Walk 5; run remainder	Run entire duration
EFFORT LEVEL BY HEART RATE	10 beats above LTT	10 beats above LTT	10 beats above LTT	10 beats above LTT	10 beats above LTT	10 beats above LTT	10 beats above LTT	10 beats above LTT

Be sure to start out with new, high-quality running shoes. Find a running store in your area that specializes in fitting runners with the correct shoes. This is not just an issue of size and comfort; it concerns your specific running mechanics. Shoes are offered in many designs that address certain biomechanics that are specific to your running technique. If you just grab a pair of shoes off the shelf and wear them because "the shoe fits," you may be buying a pair of shoes designed to support high arches and to correct supination when you have flat feet and overpronate, for example. These terms refer to how your feet "roll" over when you land on them while running. If the shoe store experts don't watch you run in the shoes, then they're not going to be able to help you get the correct shoes. Many quality running shoe stores now offer slow-motion video analysis of you running on a treadmill to help fit you.

When you run, try to land near the middle, or ball, of your foot rather than on your heel. Also, try to keep your feet underneath your body rather than extending them out in front of you. Take short, rapid strides and count them. Aim for 85 to 95 foot strikes per minute if counting one foot. Run on soft surfaces like trails and parks whenever possible.

Cross-Country Skiing

Cross-country skiing is very technique dependent. This means that if you don't have good technique, you'll be working much harder to keep yourself moving. This can make the workout much higher in intensity than it should be for developing base fitness. If you don't already have your technique developed, I suggest taking some lessons. Try to learn the skating method, since it involves pushing off more with your legs rather than just gliding along. You should be able to rent all your equipment to try it out first.

Cross-country skiing can be a nice break from cycling and is a great whole-body exercise. It has little impact, so there is not much stress placed on the joints, and it gets you out into the fresh air away from the city. You can cross-country ski two or three times a week during early base training, but you will want to cut it back to two times, and then once as you progress into more and more cycling-specific training. Once you get into your late base training, you will want to stop your crosstraining altogether and focus your training time on your cycling.

As with running, don't overdo it the first time you go. It will be fun and feel great until the next day, when your sore muscles will tell you that they are not accustomed to being used that way. Try to keep your heart rate no more than 20 beats above your lower cycling threshold when cross-country skiing.

Snowshoeing

Snowshoeing can be a fun way to get an aerobic workout. You can rent snowshoes to try them out. If you get lightweight snowshoes, you can also run in them. If the snow is deep or the terrain is hilly, you will also be incorporating strength work into your snowshoe workout, so be careful not to overdo it, since you'll be working on strength development in the gym during early base training. Wait until you're done with your maximum strength phase in the gym before adding hills and deep snow to your workouts. Try to keep your heart rate no more than 10 beats higher than your lower cycling threshold.

Swimming

Swimming is also very technique driven. If you don't have your swimming technique dialed in, then you'll be working very hard just to swim the length of the pool and you may even be at risk of injuring your shoulders. Take a few private lessons and find a masters group to swim with. Stay away from groups that focus on high intensity. This does not agree with your goals of base building.

Heart rates during swimming are generally lower than cycling heart rate zones. This means that you need to keep your heart rate below your cycling lower threshold while swimming. If your technique is poor, you'll find it difficult to keep your heart rate low and still get across the pool. Water is about 1,000 times more resistant to move through than air, and you'll feel the resistance without good swimming form.

Putting It All Together

You can begin developing your aerobic engine by planning out your weekly training and incorporating all of the components of early base training. Table 11.6 shows a sample training week. Use it to begin developing your aerobic engine.

MID-BASE TRAINING

Once you've completed your maximum strength phase (advanced riders), maximum strength transition (intermediate riders), or extended anatomical adaptation phase (beginning riders) in the weight room and have completed 6 to 10 weeks of LTT base riding, you can move on to your mid-base training. Mid-base is a time of easy to moderate efforts. It introduces strength work on the bike and is when crosstraining starts to phase out. (The exception to this is for cyclo-cross racers, who will continue to run two times a week. If you're building up for your 'cross season, then you'll want to maintain your running fitness and gradually build up to a 45- to 60-minute run at the end of your mid-base training. Near the end of your mid-base training, you can introduce moderate hills into your running and then more challenging hills during late base training.)

Strength Training

Begin strength workouts on the bike and move to the strength maintenance phase in the gym (discussed in detail in Chapter 12). It's important to maintain some leg strength as well as core and upper body strength throughout base training.

If you find yourself behind on your strength training progression, don't rush it. It's all right, and sometimes necessary, to overlap your gym and bike training and still be finishing up your maximum strength transition or maximum strength phase when you start your mid-base training. Wait before starting your on-bike strength workouts until your strength transition or maximum strength phase

TABLE 11.6: SAMPLE BASE TRAINING WEEKS

Here are examples of possible outlines for early, mid, and late base training weeks. Hours and specific workouts will vary depending on your personal training hours and experience.

Bike Workouts
FR = Force Reps
LHR = Long Hill Ride
LR = Long Ride
LTR = Lower Training Threshold Ride
LTT = Lower Training Threshold
MGR = Moderate Group Ride
RR = Recovery Ride
SE = Strength Endurance

PS = Power Sprints
X-train = Crosstraining

Strength Workouts
AA = Anatomical Adaptation
MT = Maximum Strength Transition
MS = Maximum Strength
SM = Strength Maintenance

MON.	TUES.	WED.	THURS.	FRI.	SAT.	SUN.
			BEGINNER EARLY BASE			
Day off	Workout 1: X-train LTT in levels 1–2; Workout 2: Strength AA	Workout 1: Bike LTR, include form sprints and drills	Workout 1: Strength AA	Day off	Workout 1: Bike LTR, include form sprints and drills	Workout 1: X-train LTT in levels 1–2
			INTERMEDIATE EARLY BASE			
Day off	Workout 1: X-train LTT in levels 1–2; Workout 2: Strength MT	Workout 1: Bike LTR, include form sprints and drills	Workout 1: X-train LTT in levels 1–2; Workout 2: Strength MT	Day off	Workout 1: Bike LTR, include form sprints and drills	Workout 1: Bike LTR, include form sprints and drills; **Workout 2:** Strength core, after warm up, do 4-way hip exercises and 15 min. of abs, lower back work, and stretching of your choice
			ADVANCED EARLY BASE			
Day off	Workout 1: X-train LTT in levels 1–2; Workout 2: Strength MS	Workout 1: Bike LTR, include form sprints and drills	Workout 1: X-train LTT in levels 1–2; Workout 2: Strength MS	Day off	Workout 1: Bike LTR, include form sprints and drills	Workout 1: Bike LTR, include form sprints and drills; **Workout 2:** Strength core, after warm up, do 4-way hip exercises and 15 min. of abs, lower back work, and stretching of your choice
			BEGINNER MID-BASE			
Day off	Workout 1: Bike FR, warm up and do strength sprints and FR; Workout 2: Strength SM	Workout 1: Bike LTR, include form sprints and drills	Workout 1: X-Train LTT in levels 1–2; Workout 2: Strength SM	Day off	Workout 1: Bike LTR, aerobic hill ride	Workout 1: Bike LTR, include form sprints and drills; **Workout 2:** Strength core, warm-up and do 4-way hip exercises (1 set each of 20 reps) and 15 min. of abs, lower back work, and stretching of your choice

(continues)

TABLE 11.6: SAMPLE BASE TRAINING WEEKS (continued)

MON.	TUES.	WED.	THURS.	FRI.	SAT.	SUN.
INTERMEDIATE MID-BASE						
Day off	Workout 1: Bike FR, warm up and do strength sprints and force reps; Workout 2: Strength SM	Workout 1: Bike LTR, include form sprints and drills	Workout 1: X-Train LTT in levels 1–2; Workout 2: Strength SM	Day off	Workout 1: Bike LTR, aerobic hill ride or Bike MGR	Workout 1: Bike LTR, include form sprints and drills; Workout 2: Strength core, warm up and do 4-way hip exercises (1 set each of 20 reps) and 15 min. of abs, lower back work, and stretching of your choice
ADVANCED MID-BASE						
Day off	Workout 1: Bike FR, warm up and do strength sprints and force reps; Workout 2: Strength SM	Workout 1: Bike LTR, include form sprints and drills	Workout 1: Bike SE; Workout 2: Strength SM	Day off	Workout 1: Bike LHR, aerobic hill ride or Bike MGR	Workout 1: Bike LTR, include form sprints and drills; Workout 2: Strength core, warm up and do 4-way hip exercises (1 set each of 20 reps) and 15 min. of abs, lower back work, and stretching of your choice
BEGINNER LATE BASE						
Day off	Workout 1: Bike PS; Workout 2: Strength SM	Workout 1: Bike LTR, include form sprints and drills	Workout 1: Bike SE, including standing starts or strength sprints and intervals; Workout 2: Strength SM	Day off	Workout 1: Bike LHR or Bike MGR	Workout 1: Bike LTR, include form sprints and drills; Workout 2: Strength core, warm up and do 4-way hip exercises (1 set each of 20 reps) and 15 min. of abs, lower back work, and stretching of your choice
INTERMEDIATE LATE BASE						
Day off	Workout 1: Bike PS; Workout 2: Strength SM	Workout 1: Bike LTR, include form sprints and drills	Workout 1: Bike SE, including standing starts or strength sprints and intervals; Workout 2: Strength SM	Day off or Bike RR	Workout 1: Bike LTR or Bike MGR	Workout 1: Bike LTR, include form sprints and drills; Workout 2: Strength core, warm up and do 4-way hip exercises (1 set each of 20 reps) and 15 min. of abs, lower back work, and stretching of your choice
ADVANCED LATE BASE						
Day off	Workout 1: Bike PS; Workout 2: Strength SM	Workout 1: Bike LTR, include form sprints and drills	Workout 1: Bike SE, including standing starts or strength sprints and intervals; Workout 2: Strength SM	Day off or Bike RR	Workout 1: Bike LHR or Bike MGR	Workout 1: Bike LR or Bike MGR

has been completed. If you live in a flat region, I recommend that you extend your anatomical adaptation phase deeper into your early base and schedule your strength transition or maximum strength phase for your mid-base.

Mid-Base Strength Workouts

Force Reps

Most types of cycling events demand an ability to produce power output at very low cadences. These include riding very steep grades, accelerating out of a corner, climbing steep and technical off-road sections, and starting a sprint on the track. Being able to produce power at these lower cadences can give you an advantage in these situations.

If you are free of knee injuries, then you can add force reps to your schedule in mid-base. These are done after a long warm-up and can be included early in a long ride that otherwise has low strength requirements (i.e., flat routes). Stop doing force reps if you experience any knee discomfort.

The workout consists of doing work efforts lasting between 1 and 5 minutes at 50 to 60 rpms, with rest periods between them at 80 to 100 rpms. Your heart rate can climb up to level 4 during these efforts, but you should back off if it gets any higher; power can be in the upper range of level 5a. Advanced riders who have completed power testing at different durations can use their CP12 power level for these efforts. Choose a hill that is a steady, steep grade that takes a few minutes to climb at 50 to 60 rpms at your CP30 to CP12 power level. Start out with 1- to 3-minute work intervals with equal recovery intervals for a total of 3 to 6 minutes of work time—or 5 × 1 × 1, for example. Build up to 12 to 20 total minutes of effort time over six to eight weeks. You can increase the total training load by increasing the length of the work portion or reducing the rest portion. Table 11.7 has examples of what an appropriate progression would look like.

The progression you follow will depend on how your body is responding to the workouts. If you're struggling with these, allow yourself more time to develop and progress more gradually. Advanced riders may be able to start out with 3-minute work efforts and build to 4 × 5 × 5; but if you're new at this, start out with 1-minute efforts and gradually add time.

You want to keep your core region (abdominals and lower back) firm, but keep your upper body relaxed while doing force reps. Loosen your grip on the bars and

---

╾┤ MID-BASE CHECKLIST ├╼

At this stage of your training, focus on the following elements:

☐ **Add on-bike strength workouts and aerobic hill climbing.** You'll have completed your maximum strength phase (or anatomical adaptation phase for first-year cyclists) and will be transferring those strength gains to the bike.

☐ **Begin the strength maintenance phase in the weight room.**

☐ **Continue to improve your cycling-specific aerobic system pathways through progressively longer rides in level 2.**

☐ **Phase out crosstraining.** Cyclo-cross racers and those who have bone density concerns, however, should continue to run once or twice per week.

☐ **Continue developing and fine-tuning your cycling skills.** You should also begin practicing more advanced skills.

☐ **Recheck training levels through fitness testing.**

☐ **Reassess your nutritional program and body composition progress.**

☐ **Monitor life balance and recovery closely as training loads increase.**

☐ **Introduce level 3 training rides.**

☐ **Develop on-bike nutrition strategies for rides longer than two hours.**

☐ **Include a well-disciplined monthly group ride.** You should only do this if you are an advanced rider.

☐ **Introduce strength sprints.**

---

drop your elbows and shoulders. Focus on deep, comfortable, diaphragmatic breathing. Be sure to start your power stroke early by pushing the pedal up over the top of the stroke and down the front side forcefully (quadrants 1 and 2; see Chapter 13).

It works well to climb up the hill for the work portion and then coast back down to the bottom, spin easy at the bottom until the rest portion is completed, and head up the hill for the next work portion. You can do these once or twice per week, but don't do this workout more than twice a week.

Long Hill Ride

Mid-base is also the time to introduce longer steady hill climbing in a long hill ride. The trick is finding a hill that is long enough yet still gradual enough that it allows you to remain within training levels 2 and 3 while keeping your rpms above 80. Something around a 3 to 5 percent grade will work for most cyclists, but you'll need to see what grade will work for you. (This is when compact cranks and larger cogs are a benefit.) You'll want to find a hill that will take more than 10 minutes to climb at your level 2 or 3 effort. Depending on the events you're training for, it may be necessary to build up to 30 to 60 minutes of steady aerobic climbing.

On your long hill ride day, warm up and then climb steadily for 10 to 60 minutes in upper level 2 and low to mid-level 3. If your region necessitates it, you can repeat a shorter hill several times to reach a greater total amount of climbing.

When climbing, focus on upper body relaxation, breathing technique, and lifting your knee and pushing over the top (quadrants 4 and 1). Stand periodically to stretch out and relieve pressure. When you stand, your elbows should be slightly bent, and your hips should be over the cranks. Don't lock your elbows or place your weight on the bars. The bars don't move the bike—the pedals do. Also, when standing, remember to lift the leg coming up the backside of the pedaling circle and drive the knee up over the top. Gently rock your body from side to side and drive the pedals up, over, and down. You should be moving your body weight over and down onto the pedals as they cross over the top quadrant. Stay relaxed and keep your cadence above 75 rpms when you stand. Ease back down into the saddle smoothly. You may find it necessary to shift into the next harder gear just before you stand so that the pedals don't "fall out from under you." You can use slight increases in the grade to help with this by standing at those points without shifting and trying to keep your cadence up as high as you comfortably can while standing.

If you live in the flatlands, you may have to ride into a strong headwind or do your strength work on an indoor trainer with the resistance cranked up. You can also raise the front wheel about six inches to help simulate your climbing position.

The climbing portion of a long hill ride is done in upper level 2 and into your level 3. Try to avoid going into level 4 for more than a minute here or there. Save steady efforts in upper level 3 and into level 4 for your late base training.

TABLE 11.7: FORCE REPS WORKOUT PROGRESSION
(in minutes)

WEEK	TIMES PER WEEK	BEGINNER (TOTAL MIN. WORK PORTION)	INTERMEDIATE (TOTAL MIN. WORK PORTION)	ADVANCED (TOTAL MIN. WORK PORTION)
1	1	3 × 1 × 1 (3)	3 × 2 × 2 (6)	2 × 3 × 3 (6)
2	1	4 × 1 × 1 (4)	4 × 2 × 2 (8)	3 × 3 × 3 (9)
3	1–2	3 × 2 × 2 (6)	3 × 3 × 3 (9)	3 × 4 × 4 (12)
4	1–2	4 × 2 × 2 (8)	4 × 3 × 3 (12)	4 × 4 × 4 (16)
5	1–2	3 × 3 × 3 (9)	3 × 4 × 4 (12)	3 × 5 × 5 (15)
6	1–2	4 × 3 × 3 (12)	4 × 4 × 4 (16)	4 × 5 × 5 (20)
7	1–2	5 × 3 × 3 (15)	3 × 5 × 5 (15)	4 × 5 × 4 (20)
8	1–2	5 × 3 × 2 (15)	4 × 5 × 5 (20)	4 × 5 × 3 (20)

Note: For each week, the drills should focus on breathing, upper-body relaxation and upper-quadrant pedaling.

Moderate Group Ride

Okay, here is your chance to go out and ride with your buddies. Don't commit to doing this ride more than once a month during your mid-base training. Chances are, you'll be riding a bit harder than you should be for base training, and doing it more than once a month may interfere with the progression of your aerobic development. This is a strength endurance type of ride, about which we'll learn more when we discuss late base training.

Try to find riders who are mature enough to understand the concept of setting goals and riding in a progressive format that builds base first before you start riding superhard. Every city has the "weekly race" or "shootout." This is where everyone rides as hard as they can every time they ride together. If you have 10 years of consecutive base training behind you, then you may not be working as hard as everyone else in these rides. Fitness is relative. A top professional cyclist's level 2 pace can be a beginner's level 5c pace. In general find a group ride that allows you to ride mostly in levels 2 and 3 with no more than 10 to 20 percent of the ride above level 3.

Group rides have cyclists of so many different levels of athletic progression that one rider may be riding in their level 2 while the rider next to them is in his level 5 at the same pace. I've been on group rides where I'm riding along having a conversation with the person next to me and the rider on the other side of us is breathing so hard we can hardly hear ourselves talking. I've also been the one having to breathe so hard I can't talk. I learned to drop off and ride on my own when the group is not riding at a pace that is appropriate for my aerobic development. Find a group that rides aerobically during your base development. Not everyone is in base training at the same time of the year.

I coached a cyclist who complained that her teammates always had to wait for her at the top of the climbs because I was making her ride too easy. But I convinced her to stick with the plan, and she went on to win more than 10 races that year, including her state road race championships, and she finished in the top five at the U.S. Pro/Elite National Criterium Championships that year. She was riding more easily than her teammates during their base training and was faster than they were during the race season. Moral of the story: do your base work first.

This is a good time to check your ego at the door before heading out for your group ride. If you don't know the route the group is taking, carry a map and cell phone in case you have to drop off because the pace is too fast.

Use group rides to keep you motivated in bad weather, to meet other riders, and as an opportunity to practice your pack-riding skills. This is another reason to keep the intensity and pace lower, since it will provide a more comfortable environment for you to practice moving around in the pack and drafting. When you max out your muscles and feel the suffering, your skills begin to suffer, too. We lose coordination when our muscles become fatigued.

Strength Sprints

If the events you're training for involve sprinting, then you'll want to add strength sprints to your training during mid-base (these are explained in Chapter 13). Start by including strength sprints once a week and then adding them on a second day after a couple of weeks. Do them early in the ride but after warming up well. Start with three of them per ride and build to five. Continue to include form sprints two times per week.

Recovery Ride

With the introduction of more demanding rides in mid-base training, you'll benefit from adding recovery rides to your schedule. Remember, fitness happens during rest or recovery, so you don't want to challenge your body every day. Repeat after me: fitness happens during rest, fitness happens during rest, fitness happens during rest. . . .

The recovery ride is intended to loosen up the legs, enhance circulation, burn some fat, and encourage the body to release some growth hormones. Ride in your small or middle chainring, and keep the ride very easy and short. Avoid riding on hills.

Recovery rides should not reach the level that would be considered training for either duration or intensity. Intensity should be level 1, and durations should be 30 to 90 minutes. You should ride slowly enough to make you feel guilty. I don't recommend attempting a recovery ride with your closet cycling rival. And if a rider passes by you, just let him go and do your own workout.

A good rule of thumb is for your recovery ride to be about a quarter the duration of your current long ride. So, if your long ride is currently four hours, then your recovery ride can be one hour.

Keep the route flat and fun. Use this ride to relieve some daily stress and enjoy riding your bike without any structure other than keeping the intensity low. Ride to the coffee shop, get a tasty beverage, say hi to your favorite barista, and ride home.

Use recovery rides on one or two days during a normal training week and two or three days during a recovery week. Placing a recovery ride or a complete day off the day after a challenging or breakthrough workout may expedite the recovery process.

LATE BASE TRAINING

Late base training includes comfortably hard efforts. The focus areas of the late base training phase involve the items in the "Late Base Checklist" sidebar. Continue strength maintenance and core workouts in the weight room as described in Chapter 12.

Strength Endurance Workouts

It's time to start combining the endurance you've been developing with the strength you've built up into what is called **strength endurance** or **muscular endurance.** The objective is to be able to turn over a bigger gear for longer durations. This is what endurance cycling is all about. Increasing your strength endurance means that you can climb faster and longer, take on the wind with confidence, and ride at faster paces for longer durations.

These workouts are very challenging, and you need to be sure that you're maintaining a balance with your personal life demands and keeping your nutritional intake up to adequate levels around these workouts. These are breakthrough workouts.

You'll be adding three strength endurance (SE) workouts to your base training. The first one will have you riding in level 3 at a lower cadence. The second

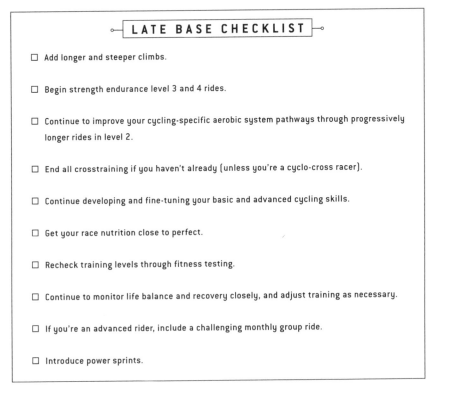

LATE BASE CHECKLIST

☐ Add longer and steeper climbs.

☐ Begin strength endurance level 3 and 4 rides.

☐ Continue to improve your cycling-specific aerobic system pathways through progressively longer rides in level 2.

☐ End all crosstraining if you haven't already (unless you're a cyclo-cross racer).

☐ Continue developing and fine-tuning your basic and advanced cycling skills.

☐ Get your race nutrition close to perfect.

☐ Recheck training levels through fitness testing.

☐ Continue to monitor life balance and recovery closely, and adjust training as necessary.

☐ If you're an advanced rider, include a challenging monthly group ride.

☐ Introduce power sprints.

TABLE 11.8: DETERMINING YOUR CADENCE FOR SE INTERVAL TRAINING (in RPM)			
SELECTED CADENCE	SE-1	SE-2	SE-3
100–110	70–80	110–120	100–110
90–100	70–80	100–110	90–100
80–90	70–80	90–100	80–90
70–80	70–80	80–90	80–90
< 70*	70–80	80–90	70–80

* If your selected cadence is below 70 rpm, then first focus your training on increasing it.

is riding in level 3 at slightly higher than your selected cadence. The third is riding in level 3 at your selected cadence (see Table 11.8).

SE-1 Intervals

Warm up for at least 20 to 40 minutes. Include level 2 and some short (1- to 3-min.) level 3 efforts in your warm-up.

For the first strength endurance workout, you'll be riding at 70 to 80 rpms on a flat to slightly rolling course. Choose a gear in which you can maintain your level 3 intensity for steady durations starting at 10 minutes. If you find that your heart rate and RPE increase to what you would consider your level 4, then use a power or effort level at the bottom end of your level 3 until they remain below your level 4 for the duration of the work interval.

Pedaling drills to include during SE-1 are the Back and Forth and Pedal Like Pistons (see Chapter 13), but add others that address your personal limiters. See Table 11.9 for some suggested progressions. Adjust the durations and progression as needed to fit your life and adaptation ability. Listen to your body.

SE-2 Intervals

You can begin your SE-2 intervals at the same time as your SE-1. In this workout, you'll be riding at slightly higher rpms than your selected cadence on a flat to

TABLE 11.9: PLANNING YOUR SE-1 AND SE-2 WORKOUTS
(in minutes)

WEEK	TIMES PER WEEK	BEGINNER (TOTAL MIN. WORK PORTION)	INTERMEDIATE (TOTAL MIN. WORK PORTION)	ADVANCED (TOTAL MIN. WORK PORTION)	DRILLS
1	1	3 × 5 × 5 (15)	3 × 10 × 5 (30)	2 × 20 × 5 (40)	Back and Forth, Pedal Like Pistons
2	1	4 × 5 × 5 (20)	3 × 10 × 5 (30)	2 × 20 × 5 (40)	Back and Forth, Pedal Like Pistons
3	1–2	2 × 10 × 5 (20)	3 × 15 × 5 (45)	3 × 20 × 5 (60)	Back and Forth, Pedal Like Pistons
4	1–2	3 × 10 × 5 (30)	4 × 15 × 5 (60)	2 × 30 × 5 (60)	Back and Forth, Pedal Like Pistons
5	1–2	2 × 15 × 5 (30)	3 × 20 × 5 (60)	2 × 30 × 5 (60)	Back and Forth, Pedal Like Pistons
6	1–2	3 × 15 × 5 (30)	2 × 30 × 5 (60)	3 × 30 × 5 (90)	Back and Forth, Pedal Like Pistons

slightly rolling course. This workout can also be done on a long gradual climb with a mostly steady grade.

You can do them separately or combine them with your SE-1 workouts by doing an SE-1 work interval, an SE-2, and then another SE-1, for example. So, if you're doing 3 × 10 × 5, the first 10-minute work interval would be an SE-1 effort, the second 10 minutes an SE-2, and the last interval an SE-1 (see Table 11.9). Pick the strength endurance workout that addresses your personal limiter best. If you normally ride at a lower cadence, do more SE-2 work, and if you normally ride at a higher cadence, then include more of the SE-1 work. Otherwise, follow the instructions for SE-1 intervals.

SE-3 Intervals

You can begin your SE-3 intervals after you've completed two weeks of SE-1 and SE-2 workouts, but keep them as a separate workout.

In this workout, you'll be riding at your selected cadence, but in level 4. If climbing is a personal limiter, then do this workout on a long gradual climb with a mostly steady grade. If time trialing is your priority or is a limiter, then do these on a flat to rolling course on your time trial bike. Include level 2 and some

		BEGINNER (TOTAL MIN. WORK PORTION)	INTERMEDIATE (TOTAL MIN. WORK PORTION)	ADVANCED (TOTAL MIN. WORK PORTION)	
WEEK	TIMES PER WEEK	BEGINNER (TOTAL MIN. WORK PORTION)	INTERMEDIATE (TOTAL MIN. WORK PORTION)	ADVANCED (TOTAL MIN. WORK PORTION)	DRILLS
1	1	3 × 5 × 5 (15)	3 × 10 × 5 (30)	3 × 15 × 5 (45)	Back and Forth, Pedal Like Pistons
2	1	4 × 5 × 5 (20)	3 × 10 × 5 (30)	3 × 15 × 5 (45)	Back and Forth, Pedal Like Pistons
3	1–2	2 × 10 × 5 (20)	3 × 15 × 5 (45)	4 × 15 × 5 (60)	Back and Forth, Pedal Like Pistons
ADVANCED TRAINING PHASES					
4	1–2	3 × 10 × 5 (30)	4 × 15 × 5 (60)	4 × 15 × 5 (60)	Back and Forth, Pedal Like Pistons
5	1–2	2 × 15 × 5 (30)	3 × 20 × 5 (60)	3 × 20 × 5 (60)	Back and Forth, Pedal Like Pistons
6	1–2	3 × 15 × 5 (30)	2 × 30 × 5 (60)	3 × 20 × 5 (90)	Back and Forth, Pedal Like Pistons

TABLE 11.10: PLANNING YOUR SE-3 WORKOUTS (in minutes)

short (3- to 5-min.) level 3 efforts in your warm-up. See SE-1 intervals for other instructions (also review Table 11.10).

Short Standing Hill Ride

The short hill ride is done on a slightly steeper hill and is an extension of the force reps workout. Find a hill that takes 4 to 10 minutes to climb at your level 4 or 5a intensity. After warming up well, climb by starting out seated, and shift into the next harder gear and stand every minute for 20 pedal strokes (counting both legs). When you stand, keep your elbows bent and your hips centered over the cranks. Use your upper body to gently rock yourself from side to side along with your pedaling. Rock your body, not the bike, but keep your upper body relaxed while doing this. Don't sprint when you stand; just keep your pace steady and work on standing climbing form. Vary the cadence from one climbing interval to the next by starting out in a different gear each time to fit the outline in Table 11.11.

You'll do three work efforts. The first one will be done at 60 rpms, the second at 80 rpms, and the third at 100 rpms. Being able to stand and climb at a cadence of 100 rpms may be the most challenging for you. Keep working on it.

TABLE 11.11 SHORT HILL RIDE WORKOUT PROGRESSION
(in minutes)

WEEK	TIMES PER WEEK	BEGINNER INTENSITY, LEVEL 4	TOTAL MIN. WORK PORTION	INTERMEDIATE INTENSITY LEVEL 4–5A	TOTAL MIN. WORK PORTION	ADVANCED INTENSITY, LEVELS 4–5A	TOTAL MIN. WORK PORTION	DRILLS
1	1	3 x 4 x 4 RPM for each work effort is 60, 80, 100	12	3 x 5 x 5 RPM for each work effort is 60, 80, 100	15	3 x 7 x 5 RPM for each work effort is 60, 80, 100	21	Back and Forth, Pedal Like Pistons
2	1	3 x 4 x 2	12	3 x 5 x 3	15	3 x 7 x 3	21	Back and Forth, Pedal Like Pistons
3	1	3 x 6 x 6	18	3 x 7 x 7	21	3 x 9 x 6	27	Back and Forth, Pedal Like Pistons
4	1	3 x 6 x 4	18	3 x 7 x 5	21	3 x 9 x 4	27	Back and Forth, Pedal Like Pistons

Note: Adjust as needed.

If you're training for events with long climbs, you can extend the duration of these efforts but will need to decrease the intensity to your level 3.

Power Sprints

If you've been progressing with your form and strength sprints, then you can introduce power sprints to your training during late base. Start by including power sprints once a week, and then add them on a second day. Do them early in the ride but after warming up well. Start with three power sprints and build to doing five.

Power sprints require 3 to 5 minutes of rest between sprints, so that you're focusing on power development. It also helps to have a power meter for these, since you can see whether your power is dropping off. If it is, then you should stop the power sprints for that day. Continue to include form sprints twice a week and strength sprints once a week. (See Chapter 13.)

Fast Endurance—Upper Threshold

This can be a moderate-paced group ride with some challenging sections or a ride that includes a total of 10 to 60 minutes in upper level 3 to mid-level 4 training. This should not be an all-out effort, however. Save the most challenging group rides for after completing your base training and the all-out efforts for races. Don't do all 60 minutes of the level 3 and 4 efforts at once. Break it up into 5- to 20-minute efforts with level 1 or 2 efforts in between.

If you've found a group ride that you can sit in on and stay in your level 2, you can now start taking some turns up at the front, breaking the wind. Spend some time in levels 3 and 4, and then get back into the draft to recover. This is a way of combining the strength endurance workouts into a group ride.

Advanced riders can include this ride once a week. Beginner and intermediate riders should not do it more frequently than every second or third week.

Long Ride

The longer the events you're training for, the longer you need to ride to prepare for them. If you're training for 24-hour mountain bike races, your long ride won't need to reach 24 hours, but you will be doing more hours of riding over consecutive days than someone who is training to race in a one-hour criterium. (See the next section on ultraendurance training.) You'll start out in the early base training at shorter durations that match your experience and current training level ability and build to longer durations throughout base training. All but ultraendurance athletes will reach their longest durations during late base training. Ultraendurance athletes will continue to increase their ride durations after base training.

The long ride is what most cyclists do on their weekends. I've encouraged many serious cyclists to arrange to leave work early midweek so that they can also get a long ride in on Wednesday, for example. This isn't always possible; but if you can arrange it, you'll be able to space your long rides apart better. The idea is for you to get a quality long ride in, have a few days of shorter rides and recovery, ride long again over the weekend, rest a bit, and then be able to ride long again midweek.

During the long ride, you'll be challenging your mental and physical abilities to resist fatigue and improve your fat-burning capability. You'll want to increase the duration of your long rides gradually to ensure that you're allowing enough time for your body to adapt to the challenge. One way of doing this is by increasing the duration of your long ride by about 15 minutes per week starting in the early base phase.

As a general guideline, your long ride should reach 3 to 5 hours. I feel that even if you're training for track and criterium racing, your long ride should reach 3 hours.

I've seen the best improvements in aerobic system development and fat burning when cyclists ride for at least 3 hours. If you're preparing for a century, your long ride should reach 4 to 5 hours. If you're preparing for road races, you should build your long ride to cover at least the distance of those races.

Once you build to your longest duration, you'll repeat that duration one to three times per week. The duration of your long ride may be limited by your experience or your personal life schedule, and you may reach its full duration during mid-base.

Ride in levels 1–3 for your long ride, with no more than 20 percent of the ride being above level 2 in late base and only 10 percent above level 2 in mid-base. It should stay in level 2 during early base. Use this ride to practice your on-bike nutrition and include a variety of pedaling drills throughout the ride.

Ultraendurance Training

As you near the end of your base training, you're getting prepared to move into advanced training. Advanced training takes you into the realm of the specific challenges of the events you are training for. If your events are road races, track, or criteriums, then your specific training will include anaerobic endurance and power training during shorter, faster rides. If your events are ultraendurance events like 24-hour mountain bike races, multiday stage races, or bike tours, then you'll need to prepare for them by developing your training to address the demands that these events pose. In addition to being able to sit on a bike and pedal it around all day and night, these events also require appropriate nutritional and pacing strategies.

Late base is when you should be getting your ultraendurance training strategies dialed in so that you can fine-tune it in the 6 to 9 weeks between the end of your base training and your important event. Begin to add duration to them, and practice your fuel intake and pacing to see what is manageable. You'll be doing long weekends of training starting in your advanced training phases.

NUTRITION NEEDS DURING ENDURANCE TRAINING

On-Bike Nutrition

As your rides grow to longer than 90 minutes, you'll need to look at taking in some nutrition while on the bike. You should be drinking about 20 to 30 ounces an hour of water during rides of all durations and adding calories when riding longer than 90 minutes. If you'll be racing for durations longer than 1 to 2 hours, then you'll need to get your body accustomed to taking in energy while riding and trying different mixes and concentrations to see what agrees with you. Use your base training to develop this.

If you show up for a long race without your nutrition program perfected, you'll be taking a guess at what might work and may find that you'll have trouble getting in enough calories and fluids. This can be a major setback, creating stomach discomfort, dehydration, and bonking. Since your body needs an ongoing supply of energy to feed the muscles and you have limited stores of carbohydrates, you need to be able to take in as many calories as possible in events longer than an hour. If you don't, and you run out of carbohydrate stores before the end of the race, you'll have to slow down considerably to continue on to the finish. Remember, carbohydrates must be present to burn fat. If you run out of carbohydrate stores, your body may begin breaking down protein and converting it to carbohydrates. This is a lengthy process, and since the body doesn't actually store protein, it means that it's having to break down "body parts" like muscle to accomplish this.

The longer the events you're training for, the more calories an hour you'll need to be able to consume. This can balance itself out because as the length of the event increases, the intensity will decrease. You can usually tolerate more caloric and fluid intake at lower intensities. You could take an easy ride along a flat bike path after consuming half of the Sunday brunch buffet, but you probably wouldn't be able to ride very fast until you had a chance to digest all that food.

Be sure to dilute the calories you consume with enough water to allow your body to digest them. If you don't, your body will have to move fluids (i.e., blood) into your gut to aid in processing the calories. This leads to *peripheral dehydration* because you won't have as much blood available for supporting the muscle activity and for moving blood to the skin, which helps keep the blood and body's core temperature down. Stomach cramps and bloating are often caused by taking in too many calories and not enough fluids to allow your digestive system to do its job. If your events will be less than three hours long and are not "self-paced," you may also find that the intensity will not allow you to take in more than 100 to 200 calories an hour. Do your experimenting during training, not during racing.

Although there are formulas available to determine the exact concentration, or *osmolality*, of your drink mix, a good general guideline is to include at least

10 ounces of water with every 70 to 100 calories. In this case, osmolality refers to how many calories are in a full water bottle. Other factors affect osmolality, such as the source of the calories, but the general idea is that too many calories in too little fluid is too difficult for your stomach to tolerate. The body has semipermeable membranes that allow "stuff" to pass through them. The "thicker" or higher the concentration of that stuff, the less likely it will be able to pass through. In this case, the stuff we're concerned about is the calories within the fluid that we want to be able to permeate through our digestive system.

As the intensity of your riding increases, the concentration, or calories-to-fluid ratio, needs to decrease, and you need to move to more liquid sources for your caloric intake. Calories consumed in a liquid form are easier for the body to process than solid foods. At slower paces, you can add solid food, but chewing it up thoroughly will help your body process it faster. I've also found that in events over 5 hours, most athletes need to add some solid food to their intake to help offset hunger and feel more satisfied. Break the food into small chunks and chew it well. Avoid foods high in fiber (and thus digestive troubles) before and during races.

Start out consuming 200 to 300 calories an hour, along with 24 to 40 ounces of water. Lighter riders can start at 200. Riders over 150 pounds can start at 250; over 175 pounds, 300 an hour. If you're training for events that will last less than 4 to 5 hours, this may be enough for you. If, however, your events will be longer than 5 hours or up to 24 hours, you'll need to work on increasing your total hourly calorie intake. Try gradually increasing your intake or concentration and see how your body responds.

If your events are longer than 5 hours, you may also benefit from including a small amount of protein in your caloric intake. The research is mixed on this recommendation, and some athletes will find that adding protein creates digestive problems for them. The ratio of carbohydrates to protein usually recommended is about 5:1. Some research suggests that this protein should include the branch chain amino acids (L-leucine, L-isoleucine, and L-valine) and the amino acid L-glutamine, so check to see if your energy drink contains them.

For ultraendurance events, nutrition and pacing become even more critical to your success. Mid-base is the time to start working on both of these strategies so that you'll have it close to dialed in before the end of your base training and can fine-tune it during practice races and race simulation training. During the late base training, you'll be able to practice this in the ultraendurance rides (discussed in Chapter 15). Ultraendurance athletes I've coached have been successful in winning 24-hour solo events by consuming 400 to 600 calories an hour.

After-Bike Recovery Nutrition

As your rides become longer than 2 to 3 hours or include more level 3 and 4 efforts, you'll need to be sure that you're taking in calories immediately after you complete your ride. The first 30 minutes after a ride is when the body can most easily replace carbohydrate stores within the muscles. Since it's nearly impossible to replace your carbohydrate stores as fast as your body can use them while riding, it is necessary to start your recovery nutrition right after a challenging workout, so that you'll have your energy stores back up to full strength before the next one.

Take in 3.5 to 3.75 times your body weight (in pounds) of calories within the first 30 minutes after finishing your workout (see Table 11.12). Break those calories down as three times your body weight of carbohydrates and the remainder in protein. Research indicates that including protein during the recovery period right after completing a workout can enhance carbohydrate replenishment. So, for example, a 150-pound athlete would need to consume 525 to 563 calories:

150 lbs. × 3.5 = 525 and 150 lbs. × 3.75 = 562.5

These calories would include 450 from carbohydrates (150 lbs. × 3 = 450), with the remainder coming from protein.

Hyponatremia

If the events you'll be training for dictate that you'll be riding longer than 4 to 5 hours, you'll also want to consume sodium with your energy drinks. *Hyponatremia* is a condition that can start by taking in a lot of water while sweating out a lot of fluid that contains sodium. As you lose the sodium from your body through your sweat and replace body fluids with sodium-free water, you start to dilute the sodium concentration within your body tissues. This can lead to a very serious condition that can cause coma and death.

If you'll be out exercising for more than 5 hours, make sure that the energy drink you're consuming also includes sodium. If you notice that you are a "salty sweater" and have a white residue on your skin and clothing (or it looks like

	TABLE 11.12: MINIMUM REQUIREMENT OF CALORIES DURING FIRST 30 MINUTES AFTER EXERCISE		
WEIGHT (LBS.)	CALORIES FROM CARBOHYDRATES	CALORIES FROM PROTEIN	TOTAL CALORIES
100	300	50–75	350–375
110	330	55–83	385–413
120	360	60–90	420–450
130	390	65–98	455–488
140	420	70–95	490–525
150	450	75–113	525–563
160	480	80–120	560–600
170	510	85–128	595–638
180	540	90–135	630–675
190	570	95–143	665–713
200	600	100–150	700–750
210	630	105–158	735–788
220	660	110–165	770–825

you're wearing a sweater made of salt) after a long ride, you could benefit from consuming 400 to 800 milligrams of sodium an hour with your energy drink.

One of the issues with hyponatremia is overhydration. This means that you're replacing fluids faster than you're losing them through sweat and your breath. Weighing yourself before and after your workouts can help you determine your sweat rate.

The Weigh-In

During your base training, get into the habit of weighing yourself before and after your long rides for insight into your fluid intake needs. The weigh-in should be done naked and dry just before you head out on your ride. Then, after your ride, weigh yourself the same way. For every pound of weight you've lost, there is a pint (16 ounces) of fluid less in you than when you left. If you are a pound heavier, then you drank a pint more than you lost. This means that you need to adjust your fluid intake up or down to balance this out, with the goal being to weigh the same when you return as when you started out.

Your rate of fluid loss will vary based on the intensity that you're riding at as well as the temperature and humidity on that day. You'll also lose more fluids climbing, since your body will have to sweat more to provide better cooling when you're working hard but at a speed that is slower and doesn't provide cooling from air passing over you. On dry, windy days, you may not think you're sweating because your skin is dry, but when you weigh yourself after the ride, you'll see that you did in fact lose fluid. Keep in mind, too, that on cool days, you're still losing fluids through your breath. By getting your fluid intake dialed in during your base training, you'll be able to have more productive races and events down the road.

———•———

During your base training, efforts will progress through your training levels. Early base starts out focusing on level 2 training on the bike while building strength in the gym. Complete any advanced strength training you'll be doing in the gym before moving on to your mid-base. In mid-base, strength workouts take place on the bike, while core strength is maintained in the gym. Crosstraining is phased out in mid-base, and level 3 is introduced to bike workouts. As you progress into late base, time in level 3 is increased, and level 4 efforts are introduced. Skills, nutrition, and pacing should all be addressed and developed throughout the base training phases so that you'll be ready to move to advanced training.

12
STRENGTH

Although some people still debate the value of strength training for endurance athletes, I've personally found there to be a great benefit for cyclists I've coached. This is especially true for those cyclists who have strength as a limiter or live in relatively flat regions. The key is in how you approach your strength training program. The standard gym or body-building routine will not result in the best possible benefit for a cyclist. Key elements to a successful strength program for cyclists include the following:

- *Focus on the recruitment and firing patterns of the cycling-specific muscle groups* (called ***prime movers***). For cycling, these are your legs and include the quadriceps, hamstrings, and gluteus muscles—or the muscles that you work during the leg press, for example.
- *Use exercises that involve multiple joints.* The leg press, for example, involves the ankle, knee, and hip joints. Arm curls isolate just the bicep muscles and include only one joint, the elbow. The exception here is the leg curl and extension. These are used to address possible muscle imbalances or specific weaknesses in the cycling muscle group.
- *Improve strength without adding unneeded muscle bulk.* Since cycling ability is influenced by your power-to-weight ratio, you want to build force production capability of the muscles that will help you the most in cycling without increasing the size of those muscles any more than necessary.
- *Develop the stabilizer muscles of the hips and core* (hip stabilizers, abdominal and lower back). When you push down on the pedals forcefully and for long

durations, you are dependent on the muscles of your hips and core that stabilize your legs. Neglecting to develop these muscles will reduce your ability to put out power and resist fatigue and may make you more susceptible to injury.

- *Do not lift until failure.* Body-building programs increase the size of the muscle fibers by frequently pushing the muscles to, and beyond, the point that they can no longer lift the weight. An assistant will help move the weight through a couple of more reps so that the person can go beyond failure. It's not necessary for you to go to failure to realize the benefits of strength training. I recommend that you stop when you reach the point when you can do only two more repetitions. Although it is rare in cycling, a *hypertrophy* strength phase (a period of strength training dedicated to gaining muscle mass) can be used by a cyclist who is lacking the necessary muscle mass in his upper legs and gluteus muscles. For such a cyclist, the additional strength gains offset the resulting additional body weight. Even if you need to "bulk up" muscle mass in your legs, you can accomplish that without lifting to complete failure.

- *Be conservative.* You will gain strength from weight training, but trying to do too much too quickly can lead to potential setbacks caused by an injury. Cyclists who attempt to lift too much too soon face a greater risk of knee injuries. Back, shoulder, and groin injuries can also occur when you overdo it in the gym. Use strength training to complement your bike training, not complicate it.

- *Use good form.* Sloppy form can lead to injuries as well and often will result in not training the muscles in the desired way. If you need help with this, consider working with a qualified coach or trainer until you're confident that your form is correct.

- *Address muscle imbalances.* Your pre- and early base training is the time to detect and work to correct any muscle imbalances you might have. By doing single leg presses, step-ups and step-downs, leg extensions, and leg curls, you'll be able to find whether you have one leg that is stronger than the other. You'll want to do 10 percent more with the weaker leg until it catches up.

- *Model the exercises after cycling as much as possible.* This means that the positions and range of motions that you use in the gym should be similar to those you would use on the bike.

A strength program for cyclists should focus on the ability to produce more force to the pedals for longer durations. This means developing the firing patterns, or recruitment and synchronization, of the cycling-specific muscles and the muscles that stabilize them. Strength gains made in the gym must also be directly transferred to cycling-specific strength to realize the full benefit of the strength program. This is accomplished by developing strength in the gym first and then reinforcing it with strength workouts on the bike.

PHASES OF STRENGTH TRAINING

The strength training program should be kept simple, and you should be able to get through it in an hour or less, one to three times per week. The strength phases that I recommend are anatomical adaptation (AA), maximum strength transition (MT), maximum strength (MS), and strength maintenance (SM). Table 12.1 explains which phases should be incorporated in your training based on your goals and your experience.

Each phase has a specific objective and an appropriate time to be implemented. If this is your first year of strength training or you have been out of the gym for several years, then I suggest extending the AA phase and skipping the MT and MS phases. I've seen significant strength gains made by cyclists who have done just

TABLE 12.1: STRENGTH PHASES			
PHASE	ATHLETE CATEGORY	DURATION (WEEKS)	PURPOSE
I: Anatomical adaptation (AA)	All cyclists	6–12	Develop foundation for future phases and on bike structural integrity
II: Maximum strength transition (MT)	Intermediate (1–2 years of AA phase completed); advanced (2 or more years of strength training experience)	4	Increase loads on leg press in preparation for MS phase
III: Maximum strength (MS)	Advanced only (2 years minimum strength training experience)	4–6	Increase total muscle fiber recruitment in cycling-specific prime movers
IV: Strength maintenance (SM)	All cyclists	Most other weeks of the season	Maintain strength gains made in gym and core muscle group development throughout year

this. After you have successfully completed an extended AA strength phase during one season, then you can move on to adding the MT phase the following season.

If strength training has been a regular part of your training for more than two years, then you should prepare for and include the MS phase this year. I suggest a minimum of six weeks of AA for the cyclist with a lot of experience with strength training and at least eight weeks of AA if you've strength trained before but this is the first year you'll be including the MS phase. It's not uncommon for overly ambitious athletes to make errors in the MS phase that create setbacks and long-term chronic injuries. These mistakes are not worth the potential gains. Caution and adequate preparation are critical for success in the MS phase.

Some athletes will benefit from strength training year-round and may stop lifting only during periods of heavy racing. Among these athletes are masters, females, strength-limited athletes (especially those living in flatter regions), and sprinters.

You'll realize increases in strength quickly once you start strength training. You will be tempted to increase the load quickly as well. As you begin to place greater demands on the muscles, they'll recruit, or activate, a greater number of muscle fibers to perform the task that you are demanding of them. The more muscle fibers activated, the greater the strength production. The problem is that the connective tissue that attaches the muscles to the bones, called tendons, adapts to the stresses from strength training at a slower rate than the muscles. Therefore, it is important to give the tendons enough time to strengthen before increasing the loads or demands that you place on them. A good guideline is not to increase the loads more frequently than about every fifth workout during the AA phase. This is not the time to try to make big gains in a short period.

During strength training, you'll be working on training the whole body and increasing the strength of the core muscles (hip stabilizers, abdomen, and lower back). A strong core muscle group is needed to stabilize the body on the bike so that power can be delivered through the legs. Remember, you are only as strong as your weakest link. Power output begins, and ends, with the core muscle group. This is why some of the exercises that I recommend for upper body muscle development will be done while standing, or while balancing on a large gym ball so that the core muscles are activated to assist in stabilizing the body.

You may wonder why, then, I don't recommend squats over the leg press. Squats are a great exercise, but they also carry a higher risk of injury than the leg press. The leg press is easier to perform in the correct form, allows you to do heavier loads more safely than squats, and lets you do single-leg presses.

Keep records of the weight that you lift for all strength phases, especially the leg press during the MS phase. Knowing how much you lift throughout the year will give you a target range for the next base-building phase. You can use the Strength Training Log provided in the Appendix A to track your weight training.

During your pre- and early base phases, you should include moderate to long endurance training rides to offset reduced capillary density resulting from increased muscle fiber surface area.

Phase I: Anatomical Adaptation (AA)

The purposes of the AA phase are to learn and practice correct form, to begin to develop better muscle fiber recruitment patterns and strength gains in the cycling muscles (prime movers), and to develop a stronger core region to support your cycling activities. The AA phase is also used to prepare the tendons for the upcoming increases in the strength loads during the MT and MS phases and for greater loads in the mid- and late base phases on the bike. All cyclists will be in this strength phase during the pre-base training. Start the AA phase shortly after one cycling season ends and at least 6 weeks before your early base phase begins.

Movements in the AA phase and all phases to follow should be slow to moderate. You want to keep the weight under control at all times and focus on your form. Don't throw the weight or make any sudden stops or changes in direction. Keep it smooth. Rest periods between sets in the AA phase should be 1 to 1.5 minutes. (You can use the rest period to stretch the muscles you are training.)

Aim for 18 to 20 reps, stopping before failure (i.e., when you can't perform another rep). Select a weight with which you can comfortably perform more than 20 repetitions, but stop when you reach 20.

Do this routine a few times per week with a day or two between workouts— Monday, Wednesday, maybe Friday, or Tuesday, Thursday, and maybe Saturday, for example (see Table 12.2).

Phase II: Maximum Strength Transition (MT)

If you have strength trained consistently for at least one full year and you have completed 6 to 8 consecutive weeks of the AA phase, you can move on to the MT phase. If this is your first year of strength training, skip this phase and continue

TABLE 12.2: AA PHASE

Loads	Able to do at least 20–25 reps
Reps	18–20
Sets	1–3, depending on exercise
Rest intervals	90 sec. between sets
Sessions per week	2–3

Progression of Exercises	Sets
Step-ups	1–2
Step-downs	1–3
4-way hip extension	1
Standing bent-over cable row	3
Lat pull-down	3
Bridging	3
Lower trunk rotation	3
Leg press	3–5
Chest press	3
Ab curl	3
Opposing limb bridge	3
Standing upright cable row	2–3
Calf raise	2–3
Hamstring curl	1–2
Leg extension	1–2
Upper trunk rotation	3
Leg raise	3

Note: The AA phase is the foundation for all of the strength phases. You will follow this same progression for the other strength phases; however, in some of the phases the number of sets will change for specific exercises. These exceptions are noted in the corresponding tables.

with more weeks of the AA phase. You can still make gradual increases in the loads, but keep the number of reps higher.

The objective of the MT phase is either to bridge up to the loads that you'll be using during the MS phase on the leg press or to increase the loads on the leg press to advance your strength before moving on to bike strength workouts.

Sprinters can also benefit from applying the MT and MS phases to the bent-over row. You'll continue with all the same exercises as in the AA phase. Only the leg press and perhaps the bent-over row follow the MT and MS phase guidelines. See Table 12.3 for the guidelines for these two exercises during the MT phase. All other exercises follow the AA outline.

Rest intervals should be extended on the MT exercises to 3 minutes (see Table 12.3). Loads should still be increased conservatively, and movements should remain slow and controlled. Any increases will show progress, but attempting to be too aggressive can lead to injury or strain of a muscle or tendon. Remember that your main objective during base building is consistency: improvements without major setbacks. It's better to see progress that may be only 95 percent of what is possible than to push too far and end up losing fitness.

Phase III: Maximum Strength (MS)

The objective of the MS phase is to recruit and activate the maximum number of muscle fibers possible in the cycling-specific prime movers. Again, caution is

TABLE 12.3: MT PHASE*	
Loads	Able to do 15 reps
Reps	10–13
Sets	3
Rest intervals	3 min. for leg press and bent-over rows
Sessions per week	2–3
Number of weeks	4–6

Increase the load so that you can do only 10–15 reps. As in the AA phase, stop 1 or 2 repetitions before failure. So, if you can lift 200 pounds using both legs on the leg press sled a maximum of 15 times, then you should stop at 13 reps. You can increase the weight again after the third workout. Use single-leg press as warm-up sets for the MT leg press sets, but don't try to do heavy loads with single-leg press because it increases your risk of injury.

*Applies to leg press and bent-over rows only. For all other exercise, continue to follow the AA outline.

important. The greatest potential for injury occurs in this phase. Limit your risk of injury by making gradual, conservative increases in the loads and moving the weight in a slow, controlled manner. The MS phase applies to the leg press only. Follow the specific instructions in Table 12.4. Do not attempt to do the MS phase with single-leg presses.

You will be making a jump in the amount of weight you're lifting when you transition from the MT to the MS phase. Use the first MS training session to sneak up on the load you'll be using by starting at the weight you finished with in the MT phase, and add a small amount of weight for each set until you reach the point at which you think you can do only 8 to 10 repetitions. This will be the weight you'll use for the first two weeks of the MS phase. If, after 3 to 5 sets, you can still do more than 8 to 10 reps, then start out at that weight on your next strength day and move up from there until you reach a weight that you can lift for only 10 reps. You'll stop at 6 to 8 reps during this phase (see Table 12.4). During the MS phase, you'll increase the rest interval between sets on the leg press to 5 minutes. All other exercises follow the same pattern as the AA phase.

A guideline I use for total weight lifted on the leg press is no more than 2.5 to 3 times my body weight. There are exceptions to this, of course. Some athletes will not reach this much weight, and others may go slightly over it. Avoid using much more than triple your body weight. If you reach the point that you can manage to lift this much, you should increase the loads by doing more reps and/or more sets, rather than adding more weight. As you increase the amount of weight over triple your body weight, you are increasing the risk of injury and development of muscle imbalances. Finish the MS strength workout with 10 to 20 minutes of easy spinning on your bike or a stationary bike at the gym. This will remind the muscles what we're training them to do.

Phase IV: Strength Maintenance (SM)

The objective of the SM phase is to keep the strength that you've developed in the gym throughout the training year. This is especially important for the upper body and stabilizer muscles that are not worked as much on the bike.

After warming up, run through all the exercises as if you were doing the AA phase (see Table 12.5). After completing all of the exercises, do one heavy set on the leg press. Try to keep this set at about 80 to 90 percent of the maximum

TABLE 12.4: MS PHASE	
Loads	Able to do 8–10 reps
Reps	6–8
Sets	3–6 (do only 3–4 until loads increase to 3 times your body weight, and then add more sets)
Rest intervals	5 min.
Sessions per week	2–3
Number of weeks	4–6 depending on experience

Note: A thorough warm-up is important before doing your MS leg presses. Use single-leg presses and lighter sets with legs together as part of the warm-up. Once your legs are well warmed up and you're ready to begin your MS sets, focus on your legs and on producing the most force possible. Use your focus to attempt to activate every muscle fiber in your legs and push the leg sled with a powerful, forceful, and smooth movement. The transition from extending your legs to bringing them back down should be smooth and deliberate.

weight you reached during the MS phase. If you stay out of the gym for too long, you should not attempt this much weight and will have to build back up to it gradually. Be consistent with your SM by getting into the gym at least once each week, and two times if possible.

As your bike training becomes more demanding, you can cut your total number of sets back during the SM phase and focus on getting the leg press, step-ups, step-downs, 4-way hip, standing bent-over row, bench press, and core exercises done one or two times every week. You should be able to do this routine in 30 minutes.

If you're in your first years of strength training and you skipped the MT or MS phases, then continue with the AA phase one or two times a week.

STRENGTH EXERCISES

Warm up before all strength workouts with 20 to 30 minutes of easy aerobic exercise and stretching. You'll do the same exercises during each of the strength phases,

TABLE 12.5: SM PHASE	
Loads	Able to do 20+ reps
Reps	18–20
Sets	1–3 depending on exercise and available time
Rest intervals	2 min.
Sessions per week	1–2
Add	Leg press; do one heavy set at 80–90% of MS weight achieved
Number of weeks	Remainder of season; can stop during hard racing weeks

Note: Applies to all exercises.

only changing the number of repetitions and sets and the amount of weight used on certain exercises. The strength exercises described are presented in the progression that your workout should follow. Be sure that you are breathing with each repetition. Exhale during exertion and inhale during the recovery movement. You can also stretch between sets.

Step-Ups

Use a stable box or platform. You should be able to place your foot on the platform without bending your knee at a 90-degree angle (see Figure 12.1). Start using just your body weight and use the leg on the box to lift yourself straight up toward the ceiling. Do not push off with the foot that is starting on the floor. This is cheating.

Activate your glutes and keep your core firm and strong, chest out and shoulders back, and head up. Keep your working knee—and your weight—over the ball of your foot. Don't allow your knee to move from side to side or in front of your toes. Raise and lower yourself smoothly and with steady control.

When you can do two sets of 20 without fatiguing or compromising your form, you can add a small amount of resistance by holding light weights (5 to 10 pounds), but don't add more than this. Step-ups will improve your knee and hip stabilization.

Step-Downs

Using the same box or platform you used for the step-ups, stand with one foot along the edge and the other suspended. Lower your body weight about 6 inches below the platform. Do not drop your foot to touch the ground. Keep your weight and your knee over the ball of your foot and dip like you're sitting down on a chair, so that your knee does not move in front of your toes (see Figure 12.2).

FIGURE 12.1

You'll find these to be a bit more challenging at first. Start out with one set per leg and build to two or three sets. Don't add any weight to this exercise; use just your body weight. This exercise is intended to improve the muscles that stabilize the knee and hips.

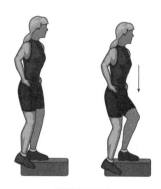

FIGURE 12.2

4-Way Hip Extension

Use light resistance for the 4-way hip extension exercise. You might want to start out using an exercise band for this exercise. If so, firmly anchor one end of the band around a chair or a table leg and the other around your working leg. You can also use a low cable pulley if you have an ankle strap, but only if it allows you to set very light weights.

There are four exercises, including hip adduction, abduction, flexion, and extension. Keep the supporting leg slightly bent to activate the stabilizing muscles during all four exercises; this is important. Do one set of each of the following exercises for each leg. There are four exercises per leg, making for a total of eight

FIGURE 12.3

FIGURE 12.4

FIGURE 12.5

FIGURE 12.6

sets. You should be able to do at least 20 repetitions for each exercise.

Hip extension: Begin by facing the fixed point of the exercise band or low cable pulley, with your working leg extended (the heel of your working leg should be positioned just ahead of your supporting foot). Pull the band or cable back past your supporting leg until your toe is even with the heel of your supporting leg. Return to starting position with a slow, smooth movement (see Figure 12.3).

Hip flexion: Turn so that your back is to the fixed point or pulley. The toe of your working leg should be just behind the heel of your supporting leg. Pull the working leg forward until your heel is just in front of the supporting toe. Slowly return to starting position (see Figure 12.4).

Hip abduction: Stand perpendicular to the fixed point or pulley and place the band or cable around your working (outside) leg. Standing with your feet together, begin pulling the working leg away from the center of your body. Return slowly to resting position (see Figure 12.5).

Hip adduction: Turn in the opposite direction, still standing perpendicular to the fixed point or pulley, and place the band or cable around the working (inside) leg. Your working leg should be extended in the starting position. Pull the working leg toward your supporting leg and slowly return to starting position (see Figure 12.6).

The range of motion for these exercises is small, as shown in Figures 12.3–12.6. Keep in mind that straightening the supporting leg will take those muscles out of the activity and you won't gain the benefit this exercise is intended to provide. You'll find that it makes the exercise harder if you keep the supporting leg slightly bent. This is how you can be sure you're doing it right. These exercises will strengthen your stabilizer muscles.

Standing Bent-Over Cable Row

Do this exercise standing with a low pulley. Bend your knees slightly and bend at the waist to hold a 90-degree angle, keeping your back flat. Your arms should be positioned at a 90-degree angle to your upper body, and your feet should be parallel to each other and about shoulder width apart. Pull the weight up to your chest while pointing your elbows out (see Figure 12.7).

FIGURE 12.7

Move the weight in a slow and controlled movement, and use your abdominals and lower back to stabilize your spine. You should be able to move through the entire range of motion smoothly. If you struggle, then reduce the weight. Keep your head up while doing these. Use a bar that is as close to your handlebar position as possible. Mountain bikers should use a flat bar, and roadies should use a bar that places the hands as if on the hoods or in the drops.

Lat Pull-Down

Do this exercise in a seated position on a large gym exercise ball, if possible. Sitting below a high cable pulley, start with your arms stretched up to the bar. Pull the bar down in front of your body to just below your neck and slowly return to the starting position (see Figure 12.8). Activate your abdominals and lower back to stabilize yourself on the ball.

FIGURE 12.8

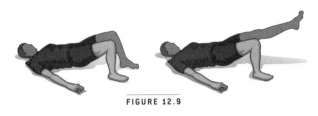

Bridging

Lie on your back with your knees bent and your feet flat on the floor. Raise your hips up off the floor so that your body forms a straight line from your shoulders to your knees (see Figure 12.9). Press one foot into the floor while lifting the other leg until it is aligned with your body. Do not allow your hips to drop—keep that "bridge" strong and straight. Hold this position for as long as you can and then switch legs. Do three repetitions with each leg.

FIGURE 12.9

Lower Trunk Rotation

Lie on your back with your arms out to your sides. Grip an exercise ball between your calves and raise your legs to be perpendicular to the floor. Slowly lower the ball to one side (see Figure 12.10). Stop just before reaching the floor and lift the ball back up, then slowly lower it to the opposite side. Keep your lower back pushed against the floor throughout this exercise.

FIGURE 12.10

Leg Press

For this exercise, use a sled-type leg press, if possible. The range of motion for the leg press begins with your knees positioned at slightly greater than a 90-degree angle. Your feet should be about pedal or shoulder width apart, with your toes pointing straight or slightly out. Focus on keeping your knees over the balls of your feet.

Extend your legs in a slow, controlled motion until they are near full extension, but do not lock your knees (see Figure 12.11). Smoothly transition from extension of the legs to lowering the sled back toward you. Be sure not to bend your knees more than 90 degrees; doing so can place the knees at higher risk for injury.

Avoid making sudden or jerky movements, and keep your feet high enough on the platform that when it slides toward you, your knees stay below your toes and fall in line with, or over, the balls of your feet. Don't

FIGURE 12.11

let your knees drift to the inside or outside during the exercise. Think about pushing with a forceful, intentional motion.

To start, do two sets of single-leg presses with little or no weight on the sled. If you find that one leg is stronger than the other, then do an extra set with the weaker leg. Then do three to six sets with both legs (depending on which strength phase you're in).

Chest Press

Use an exercise ball and dumbbells for this exercise. Position your upper back and shoulders on the ball, with your feet flat on the floor, about shoulder width apart. Hold your hips up parallel to the floor. Start with your elbows out and upper arms about level with

FIGURE 12.12

the ground. Lift the dumbbells in an upward arc that brings your hands closer together and over your chest when your arms are fully extended (see Figure 12.12). Bring the weights back down to the starting position slowly and begin the next repetition.

Ab Curl

Begin this exercise in push-up position, with your arms fully extended. Place an exercise ball underneath your lower legs. Supporting yourself with your hands, begin to bend your knees as you use your legs to roll the ball up under your hips (see Figure 12.13). Extend your legs back to the starting position and repeat until fatigue. You will feel your core working to keep your movements steady and balanced throughout this exercise.

FIGURE 12.13

Opposing Arm Bridge

Lie facedown with an exercise ball under your waist. Use your left hand and the toe of your right foot to balance yourself as you raise your right arm and left leg. Raise your arm and leg just to the point where they are aligned with your hips (see Figure 12.14). Slowly lower your arm and leg. Alternate, using the opposite leg and arm, and repeat until fatigued.

FIGURE 12.14

FIGURE 12.15

Standing Upright Cable Row

Using the low pulley, stand with your feet shoulder width apart and your knees slightly bent. Grasp a flat bar with your arms extended toward the floor. Pull the bar up to your chest while pointing your elbows out. Move the weight in a slow and controlled movement and use your abdominals and lower back to stabilize your spine. You should be able to move through the entire range of motion smoothly. If you struggle, reduce the weight (see Figure 12.15).

Calf Raise

You can use body weight for these to start and then add a dumbbell in your hands as needed. Stand on the edge of a low box or platform. You can support yourself by placing your hand on a wall or post if needed. Position the ball of your working foot on the edge of the platform, taking your weight off your resting foot. Rise up onto your toes in a slow, controlled motion (see

FIGURE 12.16

Figure 12.16). Lower yourself back down and place a mild stretch on the calf (by lowering the heel slightly lower than the platform) before rising up again.

Hamstring Curls

Use a machine for this exercise. Lie facedown on the machine and slowly curl the weight bar toward your glutes (see Figure 12.17). It's important that you be able to move the weight through the entire range of motion without having to "throw it" toward the end of the movement. If you struggle to complete the motion, reduce the weight. Focus on a smooth, full range of motion rather than on lifting more weight.

FIGURE 12.17

Leg Extension

This exercise also requires that you use a machine that isolates the quadriceps, but for this exercise limit the range of motion to the last 20 to 25 degrees of extension.

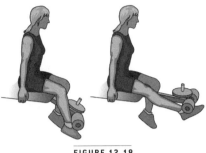

FIGURE 12.18

By working each leg separately, you can be sure your weaker leg is benefiting equally.

Point your toe slightly out and slowly extend your leg. Bring it back in a controlled movement, stopping well before you reach a 90-degree bend at the knee (see Figure 12.18). The shorter range of motion helps to protect the knee from injury. This is an exercise that can easily be overdone, so be conservative and use light weights to start.

Upper Trunk Rotation

Position your shoulders on an exercise ball, with your feet flat on the floor and your hips level. Extend your arms to the ceiling, holding your hands together. Rotate your

FIGURE 12.19

upper body as you move your arms first to the right, back to center, and then over to the left (see Figure 12.19). With each rotation your arms should be parallel to the floor. Move slowly, keeping your balance on the ball and your hips up.

Leg Raise

Lie facedown with an exercise ball positioned under your waist. Support yourself by placing your forearms on the floor. With your feet together slowly raise your legs so they are aligned with your body (see Figure 12.20). Do not lift your legs past the point of alignment. Do as many repetitions as you can.

FIGURE 12.20

STRETCHING EXERCISES

Stretching can help keep muscles loose and relaxed and may reduce the risk of injury. Stretch every day if tight muscles are a personal limiter, or several times a week for maintenance. Good times to stretch are after your rides and between strength training sets. You can also include stretching while you're doing your core work in front of the television.

Stretches should be mild and gentle. Try to hold each stretch for 10 to 90 seconds. A good goal is 10 minutes of total stretching per session.

Here are some basic stretches to get you started.

Hamstring Stretch

Lie flat on your back with one leg extended. Wrap a strap or towel around the arch of the other foot and raise that leg up as high as you can comfortably. Keep a slight bend in the knee and gently pull the leg toward you with the strap until you feel a light stretch. Keep your lower back and the extended leg flat on the floor (see Figure 12.21). Hold the stretch for at least 10 seconds, then relax it for a few seconds, and repeat the stretch.

FIGURE 12.21

You can alternate legs or relax and stretch the same leg again. You should feel the stretch in the back of your thigh, both just below your glutes and also behind the knee. Try alternating between straightening and bending the knee on the stretched leg. Straightening your leg will stretch the muscles behind your knee, while bending your leg slightly will stretch the muscle group just below your glutes.

Glute Stretch

Lie flat on your back as you did for the hamstring stretch. With your right hand pull your right thigh across your body, and move your knee toward the opposite shoulder (see Figure 12.22). You should feel the stretch in your

FIGURE 12.22

glutes and along the side of the leg you're pulling across your body. For more stretch, gently use your left hand to pull the leg across your body while slightly rotating your hip toward the center of your body.

Quadriceps Stretch

Stand while supporting yourself against a wall or doorway. Grasp your foot with the same hand (i.e., right hand supporting right foot). Use your hand to support the leg being stretched, but do not pull back with your hand. To increase the stretch, push the front of your hip forward while keeping the upper legs aligned (see Figure 12.23). Think of it as moving your pelvis forward. You should feel the stretch in the upper thigh. Maintain good posture, and do not bend forward at the waist.

FIGURE 12.23

Calf Stretch

Stand as shown in Figure 12.24 while supporting yourself against a wall. Bend the forward leg so that you can drop your hips down lower to allow you to stretch the leg out behind you. Push the heel of the leg behind you onto the floor while bending that same knee until you feel a slight stretch just above the heel (see Figure 12.24). Alternate between dipping the knee down and straightening the leg being stretched. You should feel the stretch move from above the heel to behind the knee while doing this. Hold the stretch position.

FIGURE 12.24

Neck Stretch

Stand upright and tilt your head to one side. With the arm on the opposite side that you tip your head to reach your hand toward the floor (see Figure 12.25). You should feel the stretch along the side of your neck.

Shoulder Stretch

Cross one arm over the front of your body. Place the other hand just above the elbow of the arm across your body and gently pull the arm in toward your chest and across your body (see Figure 12.26). You should feel the stretch in the front and outside of the shoulder.

FIGURE 12.25

———•———

Strength training plays a valuable and important role in every cyclist's training, especially for those who live in flatter areas or those who have identified strength as a limiter. Developing your core strength (hips, lower back, and abdominals) is important for ensuring high force production and resistance to fatigue during cycling. The four phases of a strength training program—anatomical adaptation, maximum strength transition, maximum strength, and strength maintenance—will help you maximize your strength training. Remember that if you are just getting started, it is more important to allow your body to adapt before adding weight. Get a year or two of training under your belt before you attempt the more aggressive strength training phases.

FIGURE 12.26

13

EFFICIENCY

During base building, you should be working on developing your cycling efficiency. The advantage of being more efficient is that you use less energy to produce the same results. Even the development of explosive power is dependent on the ability to accelerate the pedals quickly and with less effort. Increasing your skill level allows you to ride more relaxed and with more confidence. Confidence comes from competence, which means that just as having greater fitness increases your confidence, so does having better skills.

One way to develop efficiency is through drills designed to improve the coordination and synchronization of the muscles used in cycling. You can accomplish this by practicing correct pedaling techniques, riding skills, relaxation, and breathing drills.

To become more efficient, you have to practice. As with any new motor skill being learned, you'll find that it may take more energy at first to perform the movements until your body develops the neurological pathways and muscle memory of the improved movements. I'm using the term *muscle memory* to describe that point when a movement becomes automatic. When you walk into a room in your house, you can reach for and hit the light switch without having to look for it or think about it. That's muscle memory. I want you to be able to move the pedals on the bike and direct the bike down a curvy road or tight criterium course efficiently without having to think about it. That's why you want to develop your skills during base training and then keep practicing them all year.

Efficiency drills can be incorporated into your training schedule and included in every ride. I'll start with introducing pedaling drills and then move to drills intended to improve your riding, relaxation, and even your breathing skills.

PEDALING DRILLS

Pedaling drills are intended to help you learn to move the pedals more effectively. Understanding some of the objectives will create more meaning when you're doing the drills. You are the engine that moves the bike. Moving the pedals around moves the crank, and the more effectively you move the cranks, the less energy you expend to move the bike.

Outline of Pedaling Mechanics

Some people may tell you that consciously practicing your pedaling mechanics is not necessary and that you should "just ride your bike" and you'll improve. This is true to a point, but these are the same people who might play tennis but never take lessons. Sure, they'll get better at hitting the ball around, but without knowing what to practice and actually practicing it, they are limiting their potential.

Start with a sturdy platform. Your pedals and shoes should transfer power to the cranks, not take it away. A large pedal surface to push against and a stiff shoe work better than a small pedal that allows your foot to rock back and forth or shoes that flex under pedaling loads. Excessive float can create problems for some people, too. Think about doing squats while standing on blocks of ice.

The downstroke is the most important relative to power output because that is the point where power is being applied to the pedals. If you find that your knees are not tracking over the balls of your feet (or over the pedals) on the downstroke, then you may need to adjust your bike fit.

You may also need to work on the muscles that stabilize your hips and knees. Be sure to do the strength exercises covered in Chapter 12 that address this area. Make a conscious effort to move your legs up and down like pistons rather than like flags waving in the wind.

Apply force in a direction that is 90 degrees to the crank arm. At the top of the pedal stroke—or 12 o'clock—you should be moving the pedal directly forward. At 6 o'clock, move the pedal backward. The only time you should be pushing directly down on the pedal is at exactly 3 o'clock. At 2 or 4, you'd be moving

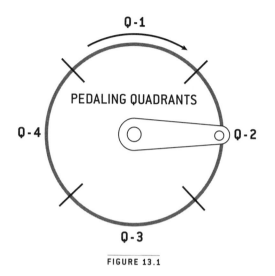

FIGURE 13.1

the pedal slightly forward and down or slightly back and down, respectively. It is nearly impossible to manage this all the time, but just understanding the idea and making improvements in your force application to the pedals will help.

Cyclists will often find themselves still pushing down on the pedal at the bottom, or 6 o'clock, in an attempt to stretch the crank arm. This also "lifts" you off the saddle, since you are pushing directly down with your leg at that moment and the force has to go somewhere, so it lifts you up. This can cause bouncing on the saddle and is common during higher-rpm efforts when it's more difficult to coordinate the movement of the legs to sync with the pedals. You are essentially falling behind the pedals and still pushing down when you should be moving your feet backward.

Push the pedal over or across the top of the pedal circle (quadrant 1). Start your pedal stroke by pushing the pedal up and over the top. This creates a longer power stroke by starting force application before the downstroke begins. Think of the pedaling circle as being four overlapping quadrants: top, front, bottom, and back (see Figure 13.1). The top quadrant is from about 10 or 11 o'clock to about 1 or 2 o'clock, the second quadrant starts at about 1 or 2 and ends around 4 or 5, then the bottom quadrant starts and ends around 7 or 8, and the back quadrant is from there until the top quadrant starts again.

Make some effort to move the pedal up over the top, rather than just letting your foot and leg go along for the ride. I'm not suggesting that you push as hard as you can; rather, push just enough to help move the cranks along and to get the power stroke (the front quadrant) started earlier.

Push down on the downstroke (quadrant 2). This tip may sound obvious, but one of the things that separates faster cyclists from average cyclists is how hard they push down on the pedals. You'll notice how hard you can push on the pedals when you're riding up a steep hill at a low cadence. You don't need to be pushing that hard all the time, and you certainly shouldn't be riding at superlow cadences, but keep in mind that this is the power stroke, or quadrant, where you can produce force most effectively. So use it to push the cranks harder when you need to accelerate the bike or keep it moving. Low-rpm drills outlined in Chapter 11 are useful for developing this ability.

Pull through the bottom of the pedal stroke (quadrant 3). This will assist in keeping a more constant force or continuous movement throughout the entire pedaling circle and will help the leg that's moving the pedal up over the top of the stroke. This motion has been described as many things, including scraping mud (or worse) off the bottom of your shoe.

Unweight the pedal as it is coming up (quadrant 4). A leg that is resting on the rising pedal creates more resistance for the leg pushing down to overcome. It's not necessary to pull up on the pedal; just make an attempt to unweight it. The goal is not to use up a lot of energy or pull your foot out of your shoe. Don't think of this as creating more power but rather as reducing the amount of power necessary to push the other pedal down. Try lifting your knee like you're stepping up onto a box.

Don't try to improve all of these areas at the same time or expect to see huge gains in power from doing this. At the same time, even slight improvements in efficiency are welcome. Work on one aspect of pedaling efficiency at a time. This will help you improve your pedal stroke more quickly and then gradually piece it all together as one cohesive movement.

As with any workout, the following drills should be preceded by an adequate warm-up. I suggest choosing a couple of drills before each ride and focusing on them throughout that training session.

Back and Forth

The back and forth drill emphasizes the pedaling movement in the areas that are usually in the most need of improvement (the top and bottom quadrants). During this drill, you'll be focusing on pushing the pedals over or across the top quadrant and pulling them back through the bottom. Think about moving the pedals back and forth rather than up and down. This will feel odd at first, but after a while you'll become more comfortable with applying force earlier in the top quadrant and assisting with this by moving the pedal back through the bottom.

As with the other drills, work on keeping the muscles relaxed. This drill can be done on any ride at any time and works especially well during steady, moderate efforts. Try to include it as often as possible.

Pedal Like Pistons

When climbing, focus on lifting your knees. This is intended to unweight the pedal, and you should notice slightly less resistance from the pedal you're pushing down on. Think about bringing your knees straight up and pushing straight down over the top of your foot. Move your knees straight up and down like pistons. If you're riding indoors, place a large mirror in front of you so you can see whether your knees are tracking up and down well. You can also use black tape to create vertical lines on the mirror to help with this.

If you find that this drill is very difficult to do or causes any discomfort, then you may need to have your bike fit analyzed by a licensed cycling coach or a qualified bike fitter at a bike shop, and you might want to have your stabilizer muscle strength checked as well. Many physical therapists are well qualified to do this. Ask your local cycling community for referrals in your area.

This drill focuses on the front and back quadrants, but you should incorporate all four quadrants in it. Do 30 seconds of up and down and then add the back and forth motion to complete all four quadrants. Note how it feels when you are just moving up and down, or back and forth, and try to include that sensation to your complete pedaling so that you are active in all four quadrants.

Single-Leg or Dominant-Leg Pedaling

Single-leg or dominant-leg drills are intended to teach your muscles how it feels when you are actually working to move the pedals through all of the pedaling quadrants, rather than just pushing down on them. Single-leg drills should be done on a stationary trainer, while dominant-leg drills can be done while riding outdoors with both feet clipped into the pedals.

Riding down the road with one leg unclipped and dangling by your side may create muscle usage problems. Indoors, you can place short stools, chairs, or milk crates next to the bike and trainer. Unclip one leg and rest it on the milk crate and pedal with just the other leg. The crate, or whatever you place your foot on, should be at a height that allows you to keep your hips level on the saddle as if you were still clipped in.

Keep the cadence, resistance, and duration low until you develop your technique. Alternate legs about every 10 to 20 seconds (or when you get fatigued), then gradually (over several weeks of practicing) increase the duration, cadence, and then resistance. This is not a strength workout, so keep the resistance on the low end.

Pedaling with one leg will force you to move the pedal through all four quadrants. You will notice right away how much work it is to pull through the bottom of the pedal stroke and lift the pedal back up and over the top. You'll really feel this in your hip flexors (the muscles responsible for lifting your upper leg toward your chest). Focus on moving the pedals from the bottom quadrant up and through the top quadrant, and keep the pedaling motion as even and smooth as possible. Don't use momentum to "throw" the pedal up over the top. Slow down and move it purposefully. This will seem difficult at first, but you should begin to see some improvement after a few weeks of single-leg pedaling for 5 to 10 minutes 2 to 3 times a week.

Again, focus on keeping the legs relaxed and smoothing out the transition from one direction of pedaling movement to another. As with the leg speed drill, you should listen for the consistent, steady whirling sound that the tire makes on the trainer roller.

You can practice a similar dominant-leg drill on the road as well. Focus on favoring one leg at a time. Pull through the bottom, lift the knee as it comes up, and push your foot up over the top. Be sure to give each leg equal time. Try doing 90 seconds, or to fatigue, with one leg, and then alternate to the other leg.

As you do these drills, you may notice that one leg seems to be able to put out more effort than the other. This could be an indication that you have a muscle imbalance. When riding with both legs, you may not notice this because the stronger leg just does more work. If you suspect that this is the case for you, then you'll want to be sure to do single-leg presses, hamstring curls, and leg extensions, as outlined in Chapter 12, until you find that your leg strength is balanced.

Leg Speed

Some muscles in your legs oppose one another, which can create resistance to the pedaling movement. This resistance can waste energy and inhibit performance. As with any other physical skill, the muscles can be taught to do this better. By developing leg speed, you'll be able to ride more smoothly at higher cadences and become more efficient at your selected cadence.

You can do this drill on a stationary trainer or outside on a slight downhill. Use light to moderate resistance. Gradually (over about 10 seconds) increase your rpms until you begin to bounce on the saddle. Back off to the point where you smooth out, and then hold that cadence for about 20 seconds. Gradually bring your rpms back down.

Keep your leg muscles relaxed and the spin smooth. Think about relaxing your toes and ankles. Don't force the movement. Try to release the tension in your legs and let the energy flow. You're looking for a smooth, fast, yet effortless motion.

If you do these drills on an indoor trainer, you should be listening to the whirling or whooshing sound that the tire makes on the roller. If the sound is "whoosh-whoosh-whoosh," then try to get the sound to be continuous and constant. A continuous, steady sound means that you're transferring power from one pedal to the other smoothly, pedaling more in one single motion than in two separate motions.

Smooth pedaling is also very important for off-road cycling. When you're climbing on loose and/or steep terrain, that whoosh-whoosh will become "slip-slip" as your rear tire loses traction. Spinning your tires was cool in high school, but it's a waste of energy in cycling.

Heart rate will rise during or, more likely, right after these, but effort levels should be in a comfortable zone. What you're doing is developing the neurological pathways responsible for instructing the muscles to fire at the appropriate times. As you practice this, you will be developing muscle memory. Eventually, it will happen automatically, but it takes practice.

You can do leg speed drills throughout long rides or as a transition from warming up to high-intensity training. Try to include three to five repetitions during every endurance ride throughout the base training. Make it a habit when you reach a moderate downhill to spin up the legs for 20 to 30 seconds.

Endurance Spinning

The idea behind endurance spinning is to ride for steady durations at a slightly higher cadence than normal. Although everyone will have a preferred cadence, the goal is to ride at higher cadences more smoothly and comfortably. At a higher cadence, each pedal revolution requires less force to produce the same power output than at a lower cadence. Power is force times speed. So, if you pedal faster in the same gear, your power output will increase; or if you pedal at the same cadence in a harder gear, your power output will also increase.

You need to be able to pedal effectively at a variety of rpms. This is especially true for mountain bike racing, in which you may find yourself stuck grinding up a short steep climb or blasting down a fast fire road. Road races can have steep hills that bring you down to 40 rpms and fast accelerations that require that you pedal at over 120 rpms for short durations. Sprinting also demands that you can spin the pedals effortlessly and at very high rpms. Being efficient at all these rpms can be an advantage. Most cyclists practice riding at low rpms because the terrain forces them to do so, but they avoid riding at higher rpms because it feels awkward. Practice it.

To practice endurance spinning, ride along at a moderate speed, maybe 14 to 16 mph with a tailwind, on a flat to rolling route. Shift into an easier gear and maintain the same speed by pedaling faster. The gearing you choose should bring you up to the very top of your comfortable cadence range. Ride steadily at this higher cadence for about 5 minutes. This is not intended to be a high-intensity interval, so keep the speed down enough that you don't blow a heart gasket. If your heart rate is increasing, then you're trying to move the bike or pedals too fast. Keep your heart rate and power level low, in zones 1–2. Pedaling fast is the goal, but you may be trying to go faster than you are ready for now. Pedaling should be smooth with no bouncing. There is no benefit from practicing bad form. Try to be smooth by applying all of the pedaling drill motions that you've been practicing. Include two or three of the 5-minute efforts throughout your endurance rides.

Record your average cadence, power, and heart rate for each 5-minute work interval so that you can see your progress.

Spin through Zone 3

Later in base training, when we are adding more upper endurance efforts, you can do endurance spinning that is more challenging. Find a steady pace at the top end of your heart rate zone 2. Check your speed and then shift down into the next easier gear, but this time challenge yourself with both higher rpms and bike speed so that your heart rate will start to climb through zone 3. When your heart rate reaches the top of zone 3, slow your pace down until you recover (back to the top of zone 2). Pace yourself so that it takes 2 or 3 minutes to reach the top of zone 3. Repeat this drill three to five times throughout an upper endurance level workout.

SPRINTING DRILLS

Success in sprinting depends on many factors. Power output is certainly one of them, but you also need good positioning, timing, skills, luck, and some courage.

Developing your sprinting capabilities is a yearlong process that starts during base training. You should start out by working to improve and develop your form and then move to increasing sprinting-specific strength. Good form and strength will allow you to develop more power. Power is a product of how hard you can push on the pedals and how fast and effortlessly you can move them. You will also want to maintain all of these elements of sprinting throughout the training year and race season.

I recommend doing sprinting drills outdoors on the road. Working on a stationary trainer can be counterproductive, since it doesn't allow the bike to move so that you can develop your technique. Also, the forces you are applying to the bike while it's locked into the trainer may damage the frame. If you are very experienced on rollers, you may be able to do sprint drills on them successfully.

Form Sprints

This is where your sprint takes shape and develops into a smooth, efficient action. These are not high-intensity intervals, and you should focus on form rather than power output. Form sprints should last just 10 seconds. The idea is to get accustomed to the movements and muscle activity of sprinting.

Do form sprints on a moderate downhill or with a tailwind, so you can keep your speed up and the pedaling resistance low. Begin your sprint from a rolling start at moderate speed and with your hands in the drops. Just as your pedal is dropping over the top quadrant, stand on that pedal and thrust yourself up and forward with your upper body. Try starting out with the right pedal first and then the left to see which is more comfortable for you.

After reaching the maximum rpm you can handle while standing, smoothly transition to sitting down. Don't drop onto the saddle—ease down onto it instead while still driving the bike forward. You can shift gears after you sit, but try to start in a gear that you can stay in for the entire sprint and keep increasing your rpms instead. Your goal is to be able to sprint smoothly with your cadence reaching higher than 130 rpms. During the form sprints, you want to get your rpms up very quickly. You should be "undergeared" for these so that you spin up quickly.

Work on smooth form rather than high power output. Stay in your drops and keep your upper body low, hips back over the cranks, wrists slightly rotated out, elbows bent and out, and head up. Remember to watch where you're going. Your hips should still be over the cranks when you're standing, so don't lean forward on or over the bars. It should not feel like you're supporting your upper body by leaning on the bars. You need to be using your upper body to help you drive the pedals forward and down. Your upper body should be low with your elbows bent close to a 90-degree angle. Stick your elbows out, not down (see Figure 13.2). This is a more powerful position that allows you to use your upper body more effectively. Try rocking your upper body and hips slightly from side to side and forward. Aim for your shift levers rather than the side of the road when you do this. Use the rocking motion of your upper body to help create more forceful pedal strokes that drive the bike forward using your upper body strength, not just your legs. Avoid rocking the bike from side to side excessively. The fastest way to reach the finish line is to move the bike forward. Try this at slower speeds until you feel comfortable with your form, then gradually increase the pace.

If you are going to race in road events, you should try to do three to five form sprints during your long rides two or three times a week. Once you're comfortable with your form and sprinting at higher speeds, start practicing alongside other riders to simulate race conditions.

Correct Sprinting Form

FIGURE 13.2

Strength Sprints

Strength sprints teach your body to recruit as many muscle fibers as possible. This is done by turning over a big gear slowly while applying the maximum force possible to the pedals.

Start by bringing the bike nearly to a complete stop while in a very large gear. Stand and pull on the handlebar as you drive the pedals down and the bike forward with as much force as you can produce. Be sure to use your upper body as described in the form sprints, but you shouldn't be able to move the pedals quickly. The gear should be large enough that you're not able to "get on top of it," or reach 90 rpms, even after 12 pedal strokes.

Do strength sprints on a slight uphill to maintain resistance without having to shift gears as you begin to accelerate. Don't use a steep hill. You may have heard these referred to as "standing starts." This is the same idea, but you should incorporate your sprinting form into this drill. Use the muscles as you would in a sprint, only with much greater force than you would be sprinting with.

Using heart rate or power on these is not as useful as just driving the pedals as hard as you can, starting out at a very low cadence. Record your maximum and average power to track your progress.

Power Sprints

Developing power means being able to overcome a heavy resistance quickly—in other words, turning over a big gear fast! Start out in a big gear, but not as big as you would use for the strength sprints. At a moderate to fast speed, launch yourself up out of the saddle, and drive the pedals forward and down as quickly and forcefully as you can. Start with the foot that feels most comfortable to begin sprinting. Stand as it crosses over the top of the pedal stroke and start the sprint the way you've practiced your form. Consider these maximum efforts for 10 seconds, or up to 24 pedal strokes. The effort should remain hard throughout the sprint, but you should "get on top" of the gear quickly. You should reach at least 130 rpms during power sprints.

Power workouts are best done using a power meter, since heart rate will lag behind. A power meter will tell you when you're finished. If power output drops off, then you should stop for the day. Power level for these is CP2, or the maximum average power that you can maintain for 12 seconds, but just go as hard and fast as you can.

For variety, you can also do power sprints up a hill with a fast rolling start. Approach the hill in a big gear at a fast speed. As you hit the bottom of the hill, explode out of the saddle and drive the pedals over the top and down while pulling on the handlebars. Efforts can be up to 20 to 30 seconds long with long rest intervals between them.

To develop power, your sprints should be done early in the workout when the legs are fresh, and you should have at least 5 minutes of recovery between power sprints. Later, as you get closer to your high-priority events, you can include power sprints at the end of your long and harder workouts to simulate the demands of sprinting at the end of a race.

Reaction Time

Reaction time is an important aspect of successful sprinting. Whether you're the one who is jumping first or you have to react to someone else, the faster you can respond, the greater your advantage will be. This ability involves training the neuromuscular system. Reflexes can be trained by practicing the activity that you're trying to improve.

One of the best ways to do this is to practice sprinting with another rider and take turns jumping first. Start out riding side by side and matching the pace of the other rider. Try to stay relaxed (because relaxed muscles respond more quickly and more smoothly while using less energy) and wait for the other rider to jump. Remember to keep breathing. When you see his body flex or move more quickly, take off with everything that you've got. Once you jump, don't hesitate—just go. Don't question if you've left too early. It doesn't matter at this point; just commit to the sprint. I've seen several sprints be lost because a rider hesitated. The more you practice this drill, the faster your reaction time will become. Teams can practice this one together, too, by having one rider on the side of the road blow a whistle as your cue to go.

Lead-Outs

I'm amazed by how few teams will practice their lead-outs before the race season starts. Dialing this in is important, and when it's done well, it's an art. You may not reach the level of top ProTour teams, but the better you can do it, the more likely it is that your designated sprinter will be successful. Base training may be a bit earlier than you need to be practicing lead outs, but getting an early start will pay off.

You'll need several riders to accomplish this drill. If you don't have four or more riders who will be there at the end of the race and able to put out power, then you'll have to come up with some other ideas for your sprinter, like using another team's lead-out train. You can have just one or two riders lead out your sprinter, but you'll have to start your drive to the finish later and won't be able to control the pace for as long.

The idea behind forming a long train of riders to pull your sprinter to the finish is to string out the pack and create a pace that is too fast to allow anyone else to get up and around your sprinter. The more riders you have, the farther from the finish line you can start your drive and the longer you can keep the pace up. If you're starting far enough out from the finish, you may also have to rotate your riders back into the train to keep it going. In this case, the riders with the greatest endurance can start at the front of the train and rotate back in. The goal is to take the sprinter to 200 meters from the line with her at the front of the pack. If you do this, she should have a bike-length advantage over the riders behind her; or, if you have enough riders, you can place a sweeper behind your sprinter so that no other teams can get on your sprinter's wheel.

The sprinter can direct the train by calling out instructions: slow down, faster, drop left or right. The riders dropping off the train can actually be used to slow other riders or teams that may be trying to swarm up around your sprinter. If riders are coming up on the left, the sprinter is in a position to see this and can direct the lead riders to drop off on that side. Be careful, as this can be dangerous, especially in lower category races. If you drop off and slow down too much, you may create a pileup behind you. If you don't have the entire road open to you, then space is also limited and can cause problems. Any rider who is going to be dropping off and not sprinting should drop off before the 200-meter mark. Once you hit that mark, you should hold your line and not move left or right.

By practicing this, you can also develop your pacing strategy. If you go into a race not knowing how fast and how long your team can keep the train going, you may go out too hard and blow up before the finish. This can leave your sprinter stranded and waste your team's efforts. Try doing a couple of lead-outs at the end of a long team ride.

If you have a strong team that will be leading you out for a fast finish, then you may want to do your power sprints in a way that better simulates these conditions. To do this, find a hill that is long enough to easily build up your speed but then drops down to a flat run-out. Use the downhill to get your speed high; when you hit the flat section, it will feel like you're coming out into the wind when the last of your lead-out train of riders drops off. Start your sprint at the bottom of the hill with the goal of accelerating and maintaining a high speed as long as you can.

RIDING DRILLS

Riding skills are one of the most neglected aspects of cycling. More cities, towns, and teams are adding skills clinics each year. Although these have been aimed mainly at helping cyclists who are new to racing, they can provide help for all cyclists.

Balance

Balance is the basis of nearly every riding skill, so I suggest working on this aspect first. Other skills—like braking, cornering, drafting, riding in the pack, and in a pace line—are all dependent on balance. For mountain biking, balance becomes critical when you're trying to ride over obstacles, climb slow technical sections, or maneuver in tight corners. The slower you ride, the more your balance skills become apparent. At faster speeds the bike's wheels act as gyroscopes that help keep you balanced. If you can maintain your balance at very slow speeds, you will be able to do it better at all speeds. This is why practicing a track stand is popular. You don't need to be able to wait at a traffic light with your feet clipped in and standing on the pedals; but if you can, then your balance is well developed.

Your body balances through feedback from your eyes, ears, and muscles. If you stand on one leg, you can feel your muscles firing on and off in an attempt to maintain balance. This is your body sending signals back and forth between the brain and muscles. Your brain is getting information from the muscles in your leg and trying to connect it with the information coming in from your eyes and inner ears. This is called *proprioception* (perception of movement and spatial orientation in space based on stimuli from the body). Through practice, your body develops the ability to fire the muscles appropriately so that you maintain your balance. If you look down while trying to balance, then the information from your eyes and inner ears becomes less useful in this process, so keep your head up and level.

Start by riding the bike as slowly as you can without stopping or falling over. You should learn to clip out of your pedals quickly before trying this. One way to make this easier is to do it on a forgiving surface, like firm grass, and on a slight downhill. Place your pedals so they are nearly level with the ground and start applying the brakes to gradually slow you down. You may find that you are most comfortable with the forward pedal slightly higher than the other. Slow the bike down as much as you can. If you feel yourself losing your balance, just let go of the brakes and roll forward. This should help you regain your balance. You can do this on a flat

Balanced Position

FIGURE 13.3

road, but you need to be prepared to pedal if you start to lose your balance. That means keeping the chain tight and one pedal slightly up above level so that you can apply pressure to it as you let go of the brakes. The bike will move forward to help you regain your balance. Keep working on this until you can slowly bring the bike to a complete stop before you have to roll again. Once you can do this, then you can see how long you can hold steady at a complete stop.

If you're on your road bike, start with your hands in your drops, keep your elbows bent, and try to breathe and stay relaxed. Tense muscles are prone to make sudden or jerky movements; you need to make supple, light adjustments or you will overcompensate. When you feel comfortable doing this in your drops, you can also try it on the hoods. Also, remember to keep your head up and level while doing this. It also helps if you're up off the saddle so that you have your weight on your feet. Try pinching the nose of the saddle with your inner thighs to help keep you "grounded" to the bike. Having the weight on your feet helps your body better maintain balance because you'll be getting signals from the muscles in your feet and legs regarding your body's position in space (see Figure 13.3). Since the brain is more accustomed to receiving these signals from your feet and legs rather than your butt, you should be able to pick it up faster this way. As you get better at this, you'll be able to balance at slower speeds while staying seated.

Once you feel relaxed and balanced at slow speeds, you'll find that taking technical turns, riding through tight places, having to stop suddenly, making evasive moves, and riding on slow technical mountain bike trails will all feel more comfortable. You'll also be able to move on to more advanced skills once you develop your balance.

Wheelie

Once you are comfortable with your balance at slow speeds, you can attempt a small wheelie. If you are a mountain biker, you need to be able to lift the front wheel up to help clear roots, rocks, and curbs. You can also use this skill on your road bike to get the front wheel up over a bump in the road or a curb if necessary.

Start by practicing this on a slight uphill. This keeps speed down and makes it easier to get the front wheel up. Find a gear that requires a bit of force to move so that you can "power" the front wheel up as you pull up and back on the bars. Just before you power it up, bend your elbows to bring your chest closer to the bars, and then pull up on the bars and shift your weight back at the same time you power it up. Try a few different gears to see what works best.

Keep your fingers poised on the rear brake lever when you do this drill. If you power up too forcefully and the front wheel comes up too high, grabbing the rear brake will bring the front end back down. If you're doing this on your road bike, it is easier to wheelie with your hands on the hoods because it allows you to keep your weight back. Be sure that you can still keep your fingers on the rear brake. Once you get the hang of it, you'll be able to do it while riding along without having to use power. You'll be able to just shift your weight back and lift the bars to get the front wheel up off the ground several inches to clear objects.

Bunny Hop

If you've mastered getting the front wheel up, you can move to getting both wheels up off the ground. Called a bunny hop, this skill is used to clear potholes and debris on the road and roots, rocks, and varmints on mountain bike trails. This is best done while riding at a moderate to fast speed, but you can learn it at a slower speed.

Start by learning to get the front wheel over something small and then bring the rear wheel up over it as well. Approach the obstacle at slow to moderate speed and coast with pedals close to level, as in your balance drills. Do a small wheelie that lifts the front wheel high enough to clear the obstacle by pulling on the bars and shifting your weight back. Drop the front wheel down on the other side of it, and then "torque" on the bars at the same time that you lift up on the pedals. To torque on the bars, twist on them as if you were trying to rotate them forward and down at the same time that you shift, or thrust your weight forward and up. You can also try bringing both knees up at the same time. If you're clipped into your pedals, this should lift the bike. If you keep your weight forward and you torque on the bars, it should lift the rear wheel.

To lift both wheels at the same time, you need to develop a sense of timing for the movements just described. Ride along, coasting in your standing balance position, and then crouch down on the bike by bending your elbows and knees and bringing your chest toward the bars like you're getting ready to wheelie. This time, spring your body up and simultaneously pull back on the bars and twist them forward as you lift both knees straight up. At first you'll probably find that the front wheel comes up first, followed by the back wheel. That's fine, since you need to get the front wheel up first to clear an object. After practicing and getting the timing down, you'll be able to bring both wheels up at the same time.

Seeing

It may seem odd that we would need to learn to "see" better while riding our bikes, but we do. Our bodies are not built for speed. We process information quite well up to a fast running pace. When we get on a bike and start moving along at 20 mph or more, our brain is not processing the information around us as well. To assist our brain, we need to look farther down the road. The faster we go, the farther we need to be "seeing." The more time our brain has to process the information (pothole, parked car, mountain lion), the better it can direct the body to react to the information. If you're looking down and admiring your new front wheel and a pothole appears, you won't see it until it's a foot in front of you. Give yourself more time to steer around the pothole by seeing it when it's still 40 feet or more in front of you.

Of course, if you have a bunch of riders in front of you, this is not always possible. Look between, over, and under the riders in front and alongside of you. The most common error is fixating on the wheel in front of you. You certainly don't want to run into it, so you stare at it to make sure you don't hit it. What can happen, for example, is when a herd of deer run across the road, all the riders in front of you have to swerve or stop, but you don't realize it until you hit the wheel that you're fixated on. Before you know it, you're eating the gels out of the back pocket of the rider who owns that wheel.

It's important to keep your peripheral vision alert as well. You should be aware of riders around you without having to actually look over at them. Practice this by looking as far down the road as you can see while riding alongside a friend. Notice how you can still tell, or see, that your friend is there. Developing a sense of what is going on around you without having to take your attention off what you are approaching allows you to stay focused on the road ahead rather than the road directly underneath you.

The bike tends to want to go where you're looking. Keep this in mind when you see something that you don't want to hit. If you stare at it, you're more likely to hit it than avoid it. This phenomenon is called *object fixation.* Practice looking where you want to go, not where you don't want to go.

You will find that seeing is critical when descending fast, cornering, riding technical single track, and riding in a large group. If you're in a pack of riders, you should be looking up the pack as far as you can. If you see helmets up at the front start bobbing, then you know they are stepping on the gas, and you'd better get going or you'll be left behind. If you see bikes leaving the ground, you want to have enough time to steer around them or stop. Steering around something is usually the better choice as long as you don't have to veer into a more dangerous place, like oncoming traffic. Stopping may cause the riders behind you to pile into you if you brake too hard or too quickly. If you've been seeing what is ahead of you and are aware of what is around you, then you have a better chance of taking the best way out.

Sometimes there is no way out. Learning to tumble is actually a good skill, too. You don't want to go into the ground hands or face first. Tucking and rolling is usually safer. Practice tumbling on thick foam mats while wearing protective gear.

Riding without Hands

It can take some time to feel comfortable riding with your hands off the bars. If you'll be racing, this will allow you to take off a jacket or vest, swap bottles more easily, and raise your hands in the air when you cross the finish line.

If you're struggling with this, try starting with your hands on top of the bars and take one hand off the bars while riding with just the other hand holding the bar lightly. Swap from one hand to the other for a while. Then, slowly release the hand that is holding the bar but keep it near the bar. Try to remain calm and keep your muscles relaxed. If you can stretch your arms out to your sides, it is actually easier to balance yourself. The one drawback is that the bars are farther away if you need to get back to them. You have to be able to steer and balance with your hips when you don't have your hands on the bars. This is another instance when proprioception comes into play.

One way to practice steering, or balancing, from your hips off the bike is to sit on a large gym ball and grip the sides of the ball with your feet off the ground. This will force you to maintain your balance by adjusting your hips and upper body. Just as when you are trying to balance on your bike, you should keep your head up and level to help your brain communicate with your body regarding its position in space.

Riding in a Straight Line

Ever hear someone yell "Hold your line"? This seems to be the most overused gripe in the lower racing categories. The message is not always clear, but evidently something that you're doing is making the rider even more nervous. He may be telling you that he doesn't like the direction that you are choosing to go in, or that you are riding unpredictably, or wandering from side to side. Usually, the peloton is dynamic and needs to move side to side. However, you do need to be able to ride in a straight line. It's hard to hold a straight line if you are not looking far enough down the road (seeing), are riding with stiff arms, or are steering the bike in a different direction than you are looking. This comes back to stiff muscles making dramatic, jerky movements rather than the supple movements that more relaxed muscles are capable of, and not giving your brain the time to process what is coming. Try keeping your upper body loose, elbows bent, shoulders dropped, and head up and looking down the road.

If you steer the bike off a straight line when you look to the side or back over your shoulder, this may be because as you turn your upper body, you are also turning the bars. Stand with your arms straight out in front of you as if you're holding your bars. Now, rotate your head to the side as if to look over your shoulder. You'll notice that as you turn to the left, your left shoulder is moving back and pulling your left arm and hand with it. This will redirect the bike. Try dropping your left hand off the bars and looking back until you get the hang of not steering the bike left when you look over your left shoulder.

Braking

Braking is necessary from time to time, and being able to do it well in an emergency is something that practice can improve. The front brake will do more to stop the bike than the rear brake will. However, when you grab the front brake suddenly, you are also causing your weight to move forward. This is one reason why you'll see riders go over the bars. When your weight shifts forward the rear brake becomes less effective because with the rear wheel unweighted, it is more likely to lock up and skid.

To brake hard and effectively, you need to shift your body weight back at the same time that you apply the brakes. This becomes even more important if you're riding downhill, since your body weight is already more on the front wheel because of the hill. To shift your weight back, straighten your arms as if to push yourself away from the bars, and slide your butt back on the saddle. Move to your balance position, only farther back on the bike. I still suggest gripping the nose of the saddle with your inner thighs so you can maintain more contact with the bike to help you stabilize it, but have the grip be further down your legs. Mountain bikers can move their butt clear off the back of the saddle to compensate for going down very steep hills. You'll need to lower your upper body to do this.

Practice this drill often so that you will be able to stop quickly if it suddenly isn't safe to steer around something. Make sure no one is behind you when you decide to practice braking. Apply pressure to the brakes quickly and firmly but not abruptly. Grabbing very hard and suddenly can cause the wheels to lock up and skid the tires. It can also send you over the bars in search of a place to land. Once you have applied the brakes, you can begin squeezing them more tightly.

When applying the brakes hard, be sure that the bike is upright and moving in a straight line. When the bike is upright, the largest portion of tire is contacting the ground. When you lean the bike over, the tire rolls over onto its side with less rubber to grip the ground. You also are calling on the tires to handle the cornering forces in addition to any braking forces that you demand of them. I often see riders slide out in corners because they are using the brakes too much when the bike is leaned over. Try to brake when you are riding in a straight line. If you are setting up for a corner, brake early enough so that when you need to turn into the corner, your speed is low enough that you can let go of the brakes just before you lean the bike over.

Cornering

Going around corners fast can make cycling fun. It can also be scary if you're not comfortable cornering fast. In motorcycle racing, the art of cornering can fill an entire book. Some of the drills we've already reviewed will help you develop your cornering skills so that you can have more fun and ride more safely while maintaining higher speeds through turns. Be especially sure that you develop your balance, braking, and seeing.

Try to keep your weight balanced between the front and rear tires and push down on the outside pedal. The inside pedal should be up for better ground clearance. You need to be able to see around, or through, the corner as far as possible. Being able to see where you want to go makes it easier to steer the bike there. If you're looking down in front of you, you will find it difficult to steer the bike smoothly through the turn. Look where you want to go. Point your nose (the one on your face) exactly where you want the bike to go.

Keep your hands in the drops and your upper body low by dropping your inside elbow and shoulder when you turn into the corner. This will make you lean your body into the corner and make it easier to point with your nose. Lowering your upper body also lowers your center of gravity, which helps the bike corner better. Keeping your elbows bent and loose will make steering smoother, too.

Push on the bar with your inside hand. This is called countersteering, because if you are moving very slowly and want to steer the bike to the left, you have to turn the tire to the left by pushing the right side of the bar forward. When you are cornering at faster speeds and push the right side of the bar forward, the bike will actually turn to the right rather than the left. This is the fastest way to get the bike to turn into a corner. You don't have to push very hard to make this happen, and you probably already do it without even being aware of it. Try to do this as one motion of dropping your inside shoulder, pointing your nose, leaning the bike over, and pushing the inside of the bar forward.

Leaning the bike will make it turn, but you can also lean your body. The more you lean the bike over, the tighter and faster it will turn. As discussed under braking skills, one drawback to this style is that the farther you lean the bike over, the less tire surface is contacting the ground. If you lean your body more and lean the bike less, you can still get your bike to turn, but you will have more of the tire in contact with the ground. This is why motorcycle racers hang so far off the inside of the bike in corners. This position will allow you to corner faster on loose trails and wet pavement.

When the bike is leaned over and you hit a wet or oily spot, loose gravel, or a bump, the tire may slip. If you "stand" the bike up, or take the lean out of it, you may regain traction before it slides out from under you. Most riders will not have adequately developed the reflexes to do this unless they have ridden mountain bikes fast for years and are accustomed to having the tire slip. The natural response is for muscles to tighten and freeze. The bike will slide out from under you if you react this way, so practice leaning your body more and the bike less until you get comfortable with the tires slipping. You can go into corners with the bike leaned a bit and then stand it up as if the tires did slip. This may help you develop your reflexes and sense of timing. Keep your body leaned into the turn, but push the bike upright.

The fastest way through a corner is to make it as straight a line as you can. To make the corner straighter, start out wide, drop in, and exit out wide. If you are making a right turn, you would start on the left side of the lane, turn into the inside of the corner, and exit out to the left side again. The point at which you are closest to the inside of the corner is called the *apex*. The route that you take through the turn is called your *line*. Although this is the fastest way through a corner, it is not the only way. You can take the corner as a constant radius that follows the same curve as the corner itself. This is often necessary if you're riding alongside another rider or have riders on either side of you. The group will usually be going slower through the turn if it is bunched up like this. When the pack gets flying and is strung out in single file, that's when it will more likely be taking the fast line through the turn. If you are riding in a group, be aware of other riders around you, and keep in mind that they may be seeing a different line through the turn. Try to be predictable and not make any sudden deviations from your line. If you're going to start out wide and drop into the apex, be sure to glance over your shoulder to check for riders whom you might "cut off" if you do this.

If you're approaching a turn that you're not familiar with and cannot see around the entire corner (called a *blind corner*), it may be safer to go deeper into the corner before turning in to the apex. This allows you to get farther into the turn before committing to a line. This is called a *late apex*. Wait until you can see where the turn exits before committing. Turning in too soon can force you to go wider on the exit of the turn than you want and may send you out into the oncoming lane.

Look for three main points within the corner: your turn-in point, apex, and exit point (see Figure 13.4). As you approach the turn, you need to find the point where you'll drop your shoulder and turn in. Don't stare at that point. Once you find it, start looking for your apex because when you reach your turn-in point, you'll need to know where to point your nose. As you turn in, you should be looking past your apex point and pointing your nose to the exit of the turn. Follow your nose. The goal is to make one turn into the corner and not have to make a lot of adjustments as you travel through the corner.

Start out practicing skills like cornering and descending (described next) at less than 75 percent of what would be your fastest pace. This allows you to stay more relaxed and gives you more room for error. If you're riding on the edge of control, you tend to be more tense and less able to think about what you're doing. By holding back some, you'll be able to practice good skills and then build your speed up

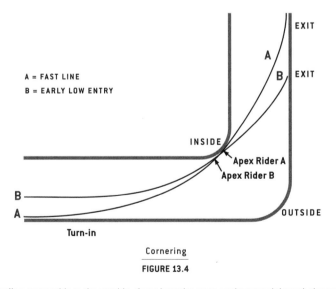

Cornering

FIGURE 13.4

A **fast line** starts wide to the outside, drops in to the apex, carries speed through the apex, and exits wide to the outside. An **early low entry** turns in too early and too close to the inside. If the rider carries his speed, he may have to turn too wide and ride off the road or trail.

from there. Build confidence through competence. Slow down to practice. You have to slow down to get faster.

Descending

To descend well, you must be able to brake, turn, and see well. As with cornering, descending can be the most fun you'll have on a bike, or the most intimidating. You can build your skills so it becomes more fun and so that you may gain time on the competition in a race.

If you are descending and a corner is approaching, be sure that you get your speed to a point that will allow you to make the turn comfortably. Braking takes more distance when you're going faster and downhill. Use the setup described earlier for cornering, and "pick up" or see the next turn as soon as possible, so you can set up on the correct side of your lane and straighten the next corner out. You should be looking for your next turn as you are exiting the turn you're in.

When descending off-road on a loose surface, be careful not to apply the front brake too suddenly or forcefully. Since there is more load on the front tire from the weight being shifted forward, it is more likely to lock up. If it locks up and you have the tire turned at all, it will slide out or "wash out" from under you. The steeper the descent, the farther back you need to slide on the saddle to balance your weight between the front and back wheels. This will also put you in the appropriate position for braking when necessary.

If you have developed your balance well, you can keep your speed down on steep, technical off-road descents. This allows you to keep the bike in control better. When you get very proficient, you can actually lock the tires up while still keeping the bike upright. Skidding the rear tire can also be used to steer the bike off-road. If the rear tire is skidding and you lean the bike to the right, it will turn tighter to the right. It may also slide out from under you and dump you on the ground, so practice at slower speeds. Some trails get eroded, and skidding your tire increases the erosion, so don't do it in areas that are in danger of eroding.

Very steep off-road sections require you to keep your weight farther back. Push your butt back behind the seat. With some practice you can get it so far back that you are resting your stomach on the saddle. This prevents you from going over the bars and balances your weight over the tires equally so you have better traction and can use the brakes.

On what is called "dropping in" where the trail drops out from under you, it may be necessary to wheelie the front tire up so that it doesn't drop down first and send you over the bars. Pull up on the bars enough so that you land on your rear wheel first, and drop the front wheel down next. This style distributes the load better between the front and rear wheels and can make the landing softer.

When descending fast off-road, you can bunny hop over some obstacles or simply lift the front wheel and let the rear suspension do its job getting the rear wheel over it. The bigger the obstacle, the more likely you'll need to get the rear wheel over it by bunny hopping. With full suspension, you can "load" the suspension by pushing down on the bars and pedals just before you want to bunny hop. As you lift up to bunny hop, the suspension pushes back up and assists you in getting the bike off the ground.

Your aim when riding off-road is to move down trails smoothly. By looking farther ahead, you'll be able to move through and around obstacles like water flowing around rocks rather than slamming into and over things like a monster truck.

Drafting

Once you are comfortable with seeing and riding in a straight line, you should be ready to draft and ride in a pace line or a pack of riders. Drafting is the most effective way to conserve energy on a bike. When you're close behind another rider, the power needed to maintain the same speed goes down dramatically. The closer you are to the wheel in front of you and the more riders there are in front of you, the greater the advantage you gain from the draft.

There is a limit to this advantage, however. If you're at the back of a very large group, you may be getting hit by the wind as it goes up and over the group and comes down at the back. If the group or field also speeds up and slows down a lot, then you'll be wasting energy because by the time the movement of the pack gets to the back, it's already strung out and you have to consume energy to catch back up. It takes more energy to increase your speed than it does to maintain it.

Start out within three feet of the rider in front of you. Keep your fingers near the brakes, but don't stop suddenly. Grabbing the brakes hard while drafting in a pack of riders is a bad habit to develop since there may be riders behind you. You can scrub off some speed by gently applying the brakes if you find you're getting too close to the wheel you're following, but be subtle and light on the brakes. The goal is to be able to maintain your position without having to use your brakes. You can also move slightly to the side of the rider in front of you to move out of the draft, and you will find that the wind may slow you down enough. Be careful doing this if other riders are alongside you, since they may be overlapping your rear wheel with their front wheel and you don't want to hit them. You also should avoid getting so close to the wheels in front of you that your front wheel overlaps any of their rear wheels. If that rider makes a move to one side or the other and her rear wheel hits your front wheel, there is a good chance that you'll lose control and crash.

Sometimes, overlapping wheels just happens. If you have a wind coming from the side (crosswind), then your best drafting position will be just on the opposite side of the rider in front. So, if the wind is coming from the left, you'll want to be just behind and slightly to the right of the rider in front to get the best draft. Try to find the position that provides the most protection from the wind. Make sure that the rider in front is aware of your position so he won't move over into your front wheel. Another time that you may find yourself overlapping wheels is when you're sitting within a large group of riders. As long as the riders next to you are "boxed in," meaning they have riders alongside them and won't be able to move left or right, you are less likely to have your wheels hit even if they are overlapped.

As you become more comfortable and relaxed while riding close behind other cyclists, you'll be able to stay up closer to their wheels and gain more benefit. Try to stay between one and three feet from the wheel ahead of you.

Bumping

When you start riding within a large group of riders, you will inevitably get bumped or bump into another rider. But if you keep your upper body loose and relaxed, you will absorb the bumps more easily. If your hands are tight and elbows locked, you're more likely to be deflected by the bump. Think back to Newton's Third Law of Physics: for every action, there is an equal and opposite reaction. Either your body absorbs the bump, or your body and bike move somewhere you may not want them to go. Practicing bumping into other riders will make you more comfortable when this does happen.

To practice bumping, you'll want to find a rider who has similar or better riding skills and is about the same height as you. You may also want to start out wearing sneakers so that you're not clipped in. Find a firm grassy field that you can ride on. It also helps if there is a very gradual uphill. Practicing while riding uphill helps to keep your speed down without having to use the brakes. Start out by just riding alongside each other at the same slow speed. One rider should have her hands in the drops, while the other rider has her hands on the hoods and then one hand placed on the shoulder of the rider next to her. Try pushing very lightly on each other to see how it feels when you get "pushed" by another rider. To "hold your line," you need to lean back into the other rider or you'll get moved over. If you lean in too much and then she stops pushing on you, you'll suddenly move over toward her. So, lean into her only as much as is necessary to keep your position, and be ready to stop leaning into her when she stops leaning into you.

Once you are comfortable pushing and leaning on each other with your hands, try doing the same thing with your shoulders. Start out shoulder to shoulder. You can also try using your hips. Do this in your drops and don't slam into the other rider; just lean and lightly push on her until you're comfortable. When you get very skilled at this, you can bump more firmly, but not before. I coached a category 2 female rider who would try to knock her category 1 boyfriend over by slamming into him. They were both very skilled and used this drill to practice what might happen in a race. At times, I thought they were using this drill to work out some aggression, but they usually seemed to be smiling and laughing when they were doing it, so maybe not.

Avoid riding with your handlebars in a position where they are slightly behind the other rider's bars or between her knees and bars. If you are in this position and the other rider moves into you, there is a chance that your bars will move in between her knees and bars and will get smacked by her knees as she pedals. When your bars get smacked this way, you tend to lose control.

When you become comfortable bumping shoulders and hips, you can try touching bars, but don't do this unless you are on a soft surface and are very comfortable with your riding skills. Start out by just having someone you trust reach over, gently place her hand on your bars, and apply light pressure. If you are okay with this, then you can progress from there.

Pace Line Riding

Pace line riding takes on many forms. There is the standard group ride form, in which you ride at the front, "pulling" until you get tired, and then drop to the back of the line or somewhere along the way. There is also a rotating pace line, an echelon, and a team time trial line. All of these are done slightly differently but with a similar objective, which is to take several riders farther and faster than if they were working on their own.

The keys to an effective pace line are maintaining a constant pace and finding the spot in the draft that is most effective. If the speed varies a lot, then you waste energy accelerating back up to speed again. Remember, you use more energy to increase your speed than you use to maintain it. If you find yourself riding with a group of riders with varied ability or freshness in their legs, you can adjust the pace line by having the stronger riders take longer pulls, or by adjusting the pace to accommodate the slower riders. Steady may or may not win the race, but it uses less energy.

Finding the "sweet spot" in the draft means knowing what direction the wind is coming from and how to adjust your position to stay out of the wind as much as possible. You may also have to adjust your position as the road turns, since the wind will effectively be coming from a different direction. If you want to drop back, be sure to look before you move. A rider may be coming up alongside or a car may be overtaking the group. Use your drafting and seeing skills and keep your movements smooth and predictable.

The exact dynamics of the pace line will vary depending on the group. Don't be afraid to ask what the intent is. I often see someone start rotating out of line who acts like he expects that everyone else knows what he wants them to do.

Climbing

Long climbs are about pacing and, to some extent, drafting. If the grade is moderate enough that the pace is 14 mph or more, then you may benefit from drafting. If there is a headwind, you may benefit from drafting at even slower speeds. As the grade gets steeper and the pace slower, drafting will no longer help and you're on your own.

In a race, the pace is often very hard at the start of long climbs while the faster climbers try to bust the pack up, but they usually settle into a slightly slower pace. If you are a strong climber, then try to keep up during this initial surge so you can stay with the leaders. If climbing is not your strength, then make sure that you start out near the front of the group so that you have some room to drift back.

When climbing, it's important to be efficient and relaxed on the bike. Use your upper body to help you pedal strong, but don't overuse those muscles. Keeping your upper body relaxed, pull lightly on the bars to help stabilize your upper body and counteract the forces of pushing on the pedals. On steep sections where your cadence drops below 60 rpms, you can benefit by pulling on the bars a bit more as you pedal, but don't pull so hard that you're wasting energy.

Sliding back on the saddle can give you a bit more leg extension and will activate the glutes and hamstrings more. Moving forward on the saddle will engage the quadriceps more. If it is a long climb, try moving around on the saddle from time to time to distribute the muscle usage. This can also be useful during long, flat time trials.

Stand periodically to stretch out and use your body weight to help drive the pedals on steeper sections. When you stand, keep your elbows slightly bent and hips centered over the cranks, and use your upper body to gently rock yourself from side to side along with your pedaling. Rock your body, not the bike, but keep your upper body relaxed.

Upper Body Relaxation

One area that is often overlooked in attempts to become a more efficient cyclist is the use of muscles other than those that are used to actually propel the bike. Any unnecessary or nonproductive muscle tension or motion consumes energy. If you can learn to keep your hands, arms, and shoulders loose and relaxed, then you will reduce their tension and the likelihood of developing aches and pains in your neck, shoulders, arms, or hands.

Practice relaxing your grip on the handlebars, keeping your elbows slightly bent and your shoulders dropped and relaxed, and you'll be on your way to becoming more efficient and more comfortable (see Figure 13.5). You'll probably have to keep reminding yourself to do this for a while before it becomes a habit. I suggest a sticky note on your handlebars that says, "Relax."

BREATHING DRILLS

For some reason, we're taught to expand our chest when we breathe. This is not how our bodies are designed to inhale. The diaphragm is the muscle designated for expanding the lungs and bringing air into them. It's located under the lungs. To breathe efficiently by using the diaphragm, think about drawing air into the bottom third of your lungs as you expand your belly like a balloon. Try doing this

Tense (left) and Relaxed (right) Form

FIGURE 13.5

while inhaling through your nose. You should begin to notice a relaxing sensation throughout your body.

Take a few moments before each workout to sit quietly and practice breathing through your nose and with your diaphragm. This will start you out in the right frame of mind and breathing correctly. Keep reminding yourself how to breathe with the diaphragm throughout your workout and return to it if you fall back on incorrect breathing. You can also practice diaphragmatic breathing while you're lying in bed. Breathe through your nose and expand your belly. It'll help you develop the habit and relax yourself to sleep. You may also find this useful when you're sitting at the start line and your anxiety level is too high, but try not to fall asleep at the start line.

Another breathing aid is to focus on exhaling during climbing and hard efforts. Once you've developed the habit of filling your lungs by breathing with the diaphragm, your body will take care of the inhaling portion on its own. By forcing the air out of your lungs, you'll develop a more complete, efficient breathing cycle. Short, shallow breaths don't completely fill or empty the lungs and can lead to diluting the incoming oxygen with carbon dioxide that you should be exhaling. If you find yourself breathing rapidly during very hard efforts, try to slow your breathing rate down by taking fuller, deeper breaths rather than shallower, shorter ones.

If you find that you get nervous, remind yourself that everyone gets nervous, from the first-time racer to the top pros. One idea that works for some athletes is to actually slow down physically. If you get rushed or hurried, it can increase your nervousness. Try physically moving more slowly. It can make a difference and bring your anxiety down a notch. It also helps to show up early enough before your event starts so that you do have more time.

●———●

Efficiency is best achieved through a series of drills that develop your riding, sprinting, pedaling, and breathing skills. This aspect of fitness development is often ignored, yet can make the biggest difference for many cyclists. Base training is the time to identify areas that may be holding you back and to work to improve them. Make it a point to include skill work in every workout. Start with basics, like balance and seeing, and progress from there. Practice skills at slower speeds so that you can remain relaxed and able to focus on them. Confidence will come through competence. Increasing your skill levels will also increase your confidence. The physical elements of base training are critical for success in cycling, and so are the all-important mental aspects of training, discussed in the next chapter.

14

TRAINING THE MIND FOR COMPETITION

Base training is the perfect time to develop your mental fitness. Mental skills can be a limiter for many athletes, yet they seldom recognize or address them. They'll go to the gym, do their rides, and watch what they eat, but they won't work on the one thing that may be holding them back from achieving their goals: their mind-set.

Mental training is an entire subject that fills many good books, so I'm going to touch only on the areas that I've found most commonly interfere with an athlete's progression. These mental skills are commitment, self-talk, and focus.

COMMITMENT

Passion is a necessary element for what you do as an athlete. You make sacrifices in your personal life and allocate a significant portion of your finances and time to the cause of obtaining your objectives and personal goals. You get up early to train, ride in hostile weather, or labor through tedious indoor workouts week after week. You'll skip a dessert but not a gym workout. This is where the commitment begins but is also where it ends for some athletes.

I often see an athlete's commitment to the day-to-day activities or workouts, but not to the details that can make the difference in the efficacy of the process. Regular, consistent workouts must be completed to meet your objectives and progress to your goals, but athletes may make the mistake of believing that doing the training means they are fully committed to achieving their goals.

Commitment to being the best possible athlete must go beyond following a schedule and completing workouts. Commitment is in the details of how you live your daily life, how you track your training, how you listen to and take care of your body, and how you act to change whatever is holding you back from reaching your goals.

Maintain Your Balance

Not everyone can plan a day around workouts as professional athletes do, but there are options, and you must choose carefully. If you make a commitment to fitness or performance goals, make sure your goals are realistic given all the other obligations in your life. From this point on, you need to be careful not to take on any extra obligations in your life unless you carefully measure how they will affect your athletic goals. I'm not suggesting that you risk losing your job or family to win a race. In fact, I'm suggesting just the opposite. Be realistic and fully understand what it will take to reach your goals before making a commitment to them and going on to make the necessary adjustments and sacrifices in your life. Yes, it is necessary to sacrifice something to gain something here.

To illustrate this problem, if an athlete expects to train to be competitive in category 1 and 2 races, but she also works 50 hours a week, is raising three children single-handedly, and is going to school part-time, she is not being realistic and is not likely to succeed. In fact, every aspect of her life may suffer. She will be too tired to work, study, or spend quality time with family, and her training may be less productive as well. Something has to go, and it's not likely that it will be the kids! On the other hand, I have seen a spouse leave an athlete who was apparently spending more time training than with his family.

Make commitments that take into account your entire life and keep a balance. I'll be one of the first to say that cycling is life, but I've learned through personal experience and from working with athletes that cycling can enhance your life or complicate it. If cycling becomes a burden, then it can also become like a job or an obligation that is hard to fit into everything else we need to do each day. Spend as much time as you can cycling, but make sure that you actually have that time available.

Know When to Say When

The athlete with a commitment to her long-term goals also knows that skipping a workout when her body is not up to the task will not set her back but will actually keep her moving forward. Committed athletes know the benefit of maintaining balance in their lives. When the committed athlete asks herself, "What can I do today to make myself a better athlete?" the answer may be "Rest."

The athlete who attempts to train through an injury rather than adjust his goals always believes he is committed, but he is not. He is acting obsessively rather than remaining committed to his objectives. Remaining injured is not the way to progress, and by not resting he only creates long-term setbacks. This is when obsession is mistaken as passion or commitment.

Don't Just Ride Along

If you have poor pedaling mechanics, don't just put that thought in the back of your mind and continue as usual. Make it your priority to work on your pedaling mechanics each and every day you ride. If you're just out "riding" your bike, what advantage do you have over everyone else out riding their bike? View every workout as an opportunity to improve. Spend time during each ride practicing something. Focus on improving your breathing technique, body relaxation, concentration, riding skills, and pedaling mechanics. The ideas in this book provide you with the information on how to improve, but it is your job to follow through and work on it as often as possible.

Improvements in technique, fitness, and structure begin in the mind. You must first get it clear in your mind what you want to do before you can get your body to engage. Take a few moments before starting a workout to get your mind on the right track. This will get your body on track, too. Don't just jump on your bike and start riding without first fully understanding the objective of that ride. Ride your bike with a purpose. It's okay to just go out and ride now and then, but give yourself an advantage over the other riders out there.

Riding your mountain bike will improve your skills, but give yourself an opportunity to improve more quickly, and the potential for even more progress, by thinking about what you're doing and setting aside time to actually practice specific skills.

Track Your Training

Write your goals down and place them where you will see them daily. Think about your goals each time you get on your bike. What may be missing in an athlete's commitment is the accurate tracking of the quality of the workouts and recovery. Noting how your legs felt on a given day can lead to more successful workout planning and adjusting than knowing what the pro down the street or your teammate did today.

If you don't track how your workouts are going and how your body is feeling and responding, then you are missing out on an opportunity to get more from your training. When I review training logs, I look for patterns that give insight into how an athlete's body is responding to his training. If the athlete's comments are simply, "I did this workout," how do we know whether his body was recovered enough going into the workout and whether he performed the workout effortlessly or struggled?

When an athlete gets sick or becomes too tired to train, the first thing I want to know is when this condition started and why. This is one of the important functions of the daily log, and filling it out with useful information is your responsibility. It may not seem valuable each day, but keeping accurate detailed training logs will help you down the road.

You may reach a point when your body is telling you that it's had enough and needs additional rest. It's important to know why. Was it the training load? Was it inadequate nutrition? Was it an increase in work or family obligations? Was it caused by weather that made training more challenging, and did you do the workouts as scheduled? To make the necessary adjustments in your schedule, you need this information. Daily information about your personal life balance and training is a critical part of the process of developing and adjusting your training plan.

You will see improvements by following an appropriate training plan, but getting the highest possible return for your investment requires your full attention to detail. Take personal responsibility for your success.

Here is a list of some of the habits you should develop as a committed athlete:

- Eat before, during, and after breakthrough workouts and races.
- Get 8-plus hours of sleep every night (more when necessary).
- Record morning resting heart rate daily.
- Recording daily vital signs (e.g., stress, sleep, soreness).
- Accurately log daily workout details, including comments on how the body felt and responded during the workout.
- Have all equipment ready well in advance of a race, important workout, or event.

- Stick to your workout rather than keeping up with a training partner.
- Practice skills every day, even when not scheduled.
- Develop a mental training regimen and practice it regularly.
- Know when to say when.
- Fill out detailed race reports.
- Track daily calories to ensure that nutrition is adequate.
- Monitor personal life balance regularly.
- Set short- and long-term goals.

SELF-TALK

I'm surprised by how many athletes have a negative mind-set in training and competition. If you're beating yourself up verbally—"I screwed up" or "I can't climb" or "I never do well at this race"—you'll most likely find ways to fulfill your assertions. Try being easier on yourself: "I learned some things in that race" or "I'm working on improving as a climber" or "This time I'm better prepared for this race."

Don't underestimate the power of your words. During a 24-hour mountain bike race, they shot a flare into the night sky at the 12-hour mark. One athlete saw the flare and energized herself by saying, "Yes! I'm halfway done—only 12 more hours to go!" while another drained his energy by saying to himself, "Damn, I'm only halfway done. I still have another 12 hours to go." Say both of those phrases and you may feel the difference. What are you telling yourself?

Sticks and Stones

I've seen very talented athletes being held back by low self-esteem and negative self-talk. Most of the time, you won't even realize when you're beating yourself up verbally. It can become such a regular part of your life that you don't even notice it. Your negativity can ultimately exist as an inner dialogue that you don't verbalize. Listen to what you're telling yourself, and work to make adjustments. When you catch yourself being negative, stop and make an adjustment in how you phrase something, verbally or internally.

An athlete may never be able to fully reprogram his brain, but by recognizing, acknowledging, and "owning" the areas that are holding him back, he will be on his way to improving his mental skills. If you don't "own" your thoughts, they'll own you. I see a lot of athletes who are controlled by their emotions. If this is an area that may be holding you back, make it a priority to work on improving it during this base training phase.

Enjoy the Process

If you find that you measure your self-worth by how well you did rather than what you did, you're less likely to enjoy the sport and your attitude can actually inhibit your performance. Use each training session, race, or event to learn something about yourself as an individual and an athlete rather than as a measurement of your self-worth. If you can focus on the process rather than the outcome, you'll be on your way to better results. It's okay to seek victory; but by placing less emphasis on results and moving your focus to enjoying and learning from the process, you will feel less stress and more relaxed. Relaxed muscles perform better, making it more likely for you to achieve better results.

Here are two examples of different responses I've had from athletes I coach to the question "So, how did your race go?" See if you can identify the athlete who enjoys what he is doing. Keep in mind that both of these athletes have very successful careers outside of cycling and that cycling is a "hobby," not a profession.

Athlete A

Thomas, it was great! I went off the front with a group early on and got to work in the break for five laps. I worked really hard when I got to the front to try to help keep the breakaway. I love riding hard! I blew up because the pace was too hard for me, and I had to drop back to the pack and recover. I recovered after a few laps and started working my way back up to the front, but there was a crash in front of me, and I lost contact with the main group. I hooked up with a couple of riders, and we chased hard for the rest of the race. We didn't get back on, but it was great to have been in the break for a while and then working with a group and finishing. I realize that I need to watch my power when I'm in a break and not take such hard and long pulls. Did you see how much power I put out? It was great! I was really excited to be in the break, so I worked harder than I should have. Next time, I'll pace myself better and make the other guys work more!

Athlete B

It sucked. My legs felt like crap. I couldn't keep up on the hills and had to chase back on a couple of times. My heart rate was really high, and I couldn't breathe. It was a terrible race, and I kept thinking about giving up racing altogether. Oh, and I won.

What is your objective? Is it to enjoy what you do and be happy, or do you think you have to win to be happy? You may be surprised. Winning is a great feeling, but it lasts for only a while. Winning is also out of our control, since things like crashes, equipment failures, and other riders can interfere with our plans. Find enjoyment in what you do, not how well you do. View every race or training session as an opportunity to learn. Try to remain optimistic and resilient, and adopt a positive perspective of what you've done. If you struggle to enjoy the process, win or lose, then you may want to find out why.

Confidence

Winning takes calculated gambles. Race to win. Don't be afraid to lose, or you may never learn to win. To win, many things have to be in place. Your fitness, tactics, nutrition, the competition, and your head all have to be working in your favor to put together a great race.

Believe in yourself. It's easy to be confident when you win. Challenge yourself to believe you can be successful regardless of whether you're winning.

When you get to the start of your event, be confident in the training that you have done. Realize, too, that there is nothing more you can do at this point anyway.

FOCUS

What happens when it gets tough in a race and you feel yourself suffering? There is a point when going harder than you have before is more dependent on your mental will than on your fitness.

The Body Will Follow the Mind

A talented amateur triathlete was on the run at mile 20 of the Ironman® World Championships. He was suffering and surviving from mile to mile on Coca-Cola.

His body was shutting down. His goal for the race was to be the top amateur finisher. He was currently the second amateur. He was questioning whether he could maintain his pace or even finish when he saw the current first-place amateur up the road. Suddenly, and with determination, he picked up his pace. He closed and passed his closest rival with a pace that ensured there would be no possible response. He finished sixteenth overall as the top amateur.

There was more left in this athlete's tank than he believed, but he had lost his focus and detoured from his task. His pace slowed because he was giving in to the fatigue and was willing to accept that slowing down was not only possible but necessary. Once he saw his competitor, his task came back into focus, and he tapped a source that many of us seldom, if ever, find.

Is It a Physical or Mental Gap?

A female road racer was a strong sprinter but she was struggling on hilly courses. She described feeling a loss of energy and motivation when she would start getting gapped on climbs. She knew that if she could stay with the bunch, she could beat them in the sprint, but she felt defeated when she would start to drop off on hills. I told her that the gap was not a physical gap but a mental one. I told her that the strength to hang in on the climbs was there, that she could stay with them if she was as mentally strong as she was physically.

On the next hilly road course, her goal was to think of the gap as mental, not physical. She started to get gapped on the first climb and decided that she could close it and stay with the bunch. She did close the gap (even though her heart rate was maxed out) and went on to win that race. Her body followed her mind, but her mind had to know it was in charge first.

Finding ways to perform at your full potential when your body is telling you that it's done is essential for success in tough endurance sports like cycling. That gap between you and your competitors may be a mental gap rather than a physical one.

Some research indicates that the body may have a mechanism designed to prevent it from fully depleting itself by convincing our mind that we need to slow down and conserve. Have you ever pushed yourself beyond what you thought was possible during a workout or race despite your body's wanting you to slow down? Although there certainly is a point when we must slow down or stop to avoid injuring ourselves, for some of us that point may be beyond when we actually do. Find ways to flow with fatigue rather than fight it and you may tap further into your potential.

Use Mental Strength to Fight Physical Challenges

If you find yourself focusing on or distracted by fatigue or suffering during training and racing, try redefining it as merely "discomfort" or a challenge. Then move your focus to your breathing or pedaling form to help you get back on task. If you find yourself spending time dwelling on the fatigue, you might tell yourself that you just can't hang on to a wheel or maintain a pace any longer. This will surely be self-defeating.

Another idea is to choose a mantra of three words or less that will help keep you focused on your task rather than on your discomfort. Your task may be maintaining a pace, staying relaxed, or getting to the finish. Choose mantras that empower you and are task-specific. One example would be for a mountain biker to use "strong, steady, relaxed" for long climbs and "smooth and relaxed" for descents.

Your inner dialogue should enhance the focus on your task, increase confidence, and help reduce anxiety. The words of your mantras should have meaning to you that fulfill these elements. "Strong, steady, relaxed," for example, could mean "I've done the training (strong), I can maintain this pace (steady), and I'm feeling great (relaxed)." "Smooth" used in descending could remind you to look ahead and flow like water over obstacles rather than slamming into them like a monster truck.

Identify Your Mental Strengths and Weaknesses

Your emotions can affect your physical energy, and, conversely, energy levels can directly affect your emotions. Learn to identify things that drain or charge your physical and mental energy.

Identify ways that you can calm yourself when your energy is too high and is making you anxious or nervous. Try focusing on your breathing or relaxing tight muscles, for example. Identify ways to get yourself going when your energy level is too low and you're feeling lethargic, unmotivated, or unconfident. One idea is to try visualizing past success or reviewing your goals. Learn to use these methods when you need them.

You can also create mantras to use when you're experiencing a variety of emotions like weakness, fear, nervousness, ennui, frustration, or whatever you tend to experience before and during competition that may be holding you back. Select words can have a positive effect on your emotions. Repeating calming words can help reduce anxiety, and using energizing words can get you going when you're dragging.

Practice to Get Better

Mental skills become habits if you practice them frequently. Set out on every workout with a goal of staying focused as long as possible by using mantras, breathing, and form drills. When you catch yourself drifting off, bring yourself back into focus. Challenge yourself to stay focused as long and as often as possible. It's not easy, but you'll get better.

•———•

Adequate and appropriate physical training is, of course, necessary; but without being able to stay focused on your task and push yourself to your true limits, you may never realize your full potential. Appropriate inner dialogue or self-talk can improve your performance, but it needs to be task-specific, constructive, and rehearsed. Commit to your goals and pay attention to the details of your training and recovery. By developing mental and physical base fitness you will be adequately prepared for advanced fitness training, the topic of the next chapter.

15

ADVANCED FITNESS ELEMENTS

Once your base fitness foundation is developed, you are ready to move on to the advanced training phase. The objective of the advanced training phase is to bring your training as close to the specific demands of your important events as possible. This is when your training moves to developing the advanced fitness elements introduced in Chapter 6. As a reminder, the advanced fitness elements are strength endurance, anaerobic endurance, and power.

You should allow 9 to 12 weeks before the specific event you're preparing for to focus on developing the advanced fitness elements. Be careful during advanced training. You want to increase the training load, but as the intensity goes up, you need to reduce the overall volume. By decreasing the volume, you can provide more time for recovery to help ensure that your advanced workouts are of high quality. The exception to this is the ultraendurance athlete. If you're training for ultraendurance events, then your advanced training will continue to build in duration to prepare you for the specific demands of your events.

Advanced training is not the time to try to lose weight, since your training will be demanding a higher percentage of carbohydrates, and you are at higher risk of carbohydrate depletion at this time. Carbohydrates should make up about 60 percent of your total intake during advanced training.

Introduce advanced workouts into your weekly schedule by having one during the week and one on the weekend. If you find that you are able to tolerate a lot of training load, then you can do up to three advanced workouts a week—Tuesday,

Thursday, and Saturday, for example. Strength training stays in the maintenance phase during advanced training.

The following sections outline the advanced training phase workouts.

STRENGTH ENDURANCE

You will be well on your way to developing strength endurance if you complete your base training because late base training begins to focus on developing this fitness aspect. Continue to build strength endurance with longer durations of SE-3, level 4 rides, and add a second day of interval training in the advanced training phases. If this is your first year of training, your limiters will probably include climbing and time trialing. If ultraendurance events are your focus, then developing strength endurance should be your main priority.

Cyclists often believe that increasing the intensity level of SE-3 intervals (pushing higher than level 4) will bring more benefit. I recommend increasing the duration instead of the intensity. Gradually build your efforts to 60 minutes in level 4 and 90 minutes in level 3. Break these into intervals of 15 to 30 minutes, with 5 to 10 minutes' recovery. Save your efforts above level 4 for anaerobic endurance development.

Ultraendurance Rides

As mentioned before, you won't need to ride for 24 hours straight if you're preparing for a 24-hour race. I have my ultraendurance mountain bike racers build up to a point where they can ride 14 to 18 hours over a 2- to 3-day period. This might break down as 6 hours Saturday morning, 5 hours Saturday night, and then 5 hours Sunday afternoon, for example. By segmenting your training this way, you get a challenging stimulus with some built-in rest between the workouts. The more advanced you are in your training years, the shorter the rest durations between these rides can be. You can also reduce the training load by doing the Sunday ride on the road bike. Use the rest time between the rides to eat and nap.

Table 15.1 offers some suggestions for how to use a weekend to prepare for ultraendurance events. Keep in mind that you must add more recovery leading up to, and following, these ultraendurance training sessions. Practice your race nutrition and pacing during these workouts.

TABLE 15.1: ULTRAENDURANCE WEEKEND PREPARATION

EVENT	THURSDAY	FRIDAY	SATURDAY	SUNDAY	MONDAY	TUESDAY
24-hour mountain bike race	Easy ride or day off	Day off	AM: Ride 3–6 hours in levels 1–2; eat and sleep. PM: Ride 3–5 hours in levels 1–2; eat and sleep.	AM: Ride 3–5 hours in levels 1–2; eat and sleep. You can also sleep in and ride later in the day if needed.	Day off	Day off
Multiday stage race	Day off	LTR	Fast endurance group ride	LTR	SE-1 and 2	LTR
Multiday tour	Day off	LTR	SE-1 and 2	LTR	SE-1 and 2	LTR

ANAEROBIC ENDURANCE

The base fitness elements needed for anaerobic endurance, endurance and efficiency, are developed in the base training phases. Once you have them in place, you can begin doing advanced training by riding hard for shorter durations in your level 5b or CP 5- to 6-minute power level. If this is your first year, start out with 30-second intervals with equal rest, and don't do them more than one day per week. Intermediate riders can do longer intervals of 2 or 3 minutes. Advanced riders can do 3-minute intervals also with equal rest intervals, and may be able to do them two times a week for 3 to 5 weeks. After doing these intervals for three weeks, you can begin doing them on hills, both seated and standing.

Keep in mind that effort should remain within your appropriate training level. It's common for athletes to go as hard as they can for the duration of the work interval. That is not the objective. If your CP6 power is 350 watts, then stay at 350 watts for the interval. You will need a couple of recovery days after these efforts before your next breakthrough workout. Table 15.2 gives some examples of anaerobic intervals that you can adjust as needed.

		TABLE 15.2: EXAMPLES OF ANAEROBIC INTERVALS AE-1, TRAINING LEVEL 5B INTERVALS			
WEEK	TIMES PER WEEK	BEGINNER (TOTAL MIN. WORK PORTION)	INTERMEDIATE (TOTAL MIN. WORK PORTION)	ADVANCED (TOTAL MIN. WORK PORTION)	DRILLS
1	1	10 × 30 × 30 sec. (5)	8 × 1 × 1 min. (8)	6 × 3 × 3 min. (18)	Upper body relaxation and breathing
2	1	10 × 30 × 30 sec. (5)	8 × 1 × 1 min. (8)	6 × 3 × 3 min. (18)	Upper body relaxation and breathing
3	1	15 × 30 × 30 sec. (7.5)	5 × 2 × 2 min. (10)	8 × 3 × 3 min. (24)	Upper body relaxation and breathing
4 Add hills	1	15 × 30 × 30 sec. (7.5)	5 × 2 × 2 min. (10)	8 × 3 × 3 min. (24)	Upper body relaxation and breathing
5	1	20 × 30 × 30 sec. (10)	7 × 2 × 2 min. (14)	2 × per week: 8 × 3 × 3 min. (24)	Upper body relaxation and breathing
6	1	20 × 30 × 30 sec. (10)	8 × 2 × 2 min. (16)	2 × per week: 8 × 3 × 3 min. (24)	Upper body relaxation and breathing

Note: Adjust as needed.

POWER

You begin to bring power development together in late base training with power sprints. You'll continue to improve it by adding hill sprints in your advanced training phases. You'll also want to move your sprints to the end of long rides during advanced training to prepare for sprinting with tired legs at the end of a race. Be sure to keep sprints at the start of workouts on other days because power is developed better on fresh legs. Power workouts are done at your level 5c or at a power that you can average for 5 to 12 seconds.

If your focus is on track, criteriums, or road races, then you should include plenty of power development training in your advanced phases. I've found that most athletes can tolerate two or three days of power workouts during advanced training weeks. You can add them to your long aerobic or strength endurance training days. Watch your power maximum and average during these workouts. When your power starts to drop off, stop the workout. If you continue, you will no longer be training power.

Building Advanced Fitness in Group Rides and Races

Table 15.3 outlines some advanced training weeks. During this time, you can also use fast group rides to improve your anaerobic endurance and strength endurance. This is your opportunity to "open it up" and challenge yourself during group rides. Be sure that you are still listening to your body, however. If you are carrying a lot of fatigue or struggling, drop out of the group ride. Know when to back off.

TABLE 15.3: EXAMPLE OF ADVANCED TRAINING SAMPLE WEEK

MON.	TUES.	WED.	THURS.	SAT.	SUN.
Workout 1: Day off; example of advanced training week	Workout 1: Bike AE, warm up, do power sprints, recover, and do anaerobic endurance intervals	Workout 1: Bike SE	Workout 1: Day off	Workout 1: Bike FGR or Bike UER or Race	Workout 1: Bike LTR, include form sprints and drills; Workout 2: Strength core

Low-priority races and events that have demands similar to your most important events can also serve as workouts during the advanced training. A criterium can take the place of an anaerobic endurance and power workout. A road race can be a strength endurance workout. A century or double century could be an ultraendurance workout.

———

During advanced training, you develop your strength endurance, anaerobic endurance, and power. Strength endurance is especially critical for ultraendurance cyclists, who can use a weekend to cover up to 18 hours of training rides. Base training has developed your endurance and efficiency, ingredients of anaerobic endurance. Power sprints and criterium races can help increase your short-duration power output. Fast group rides and road races offer opportunities to train in all the advance fitness elements, especially strength endurance. Use the sample workout plans in this chapter to devise the best training for your needs.

APPENDIXES

A

RESOURCES

TRAINING LEVELS						
LEVEL	NAME	% OF CP30	POWER RANGE	HEART RATE RELATIVE TO UTT	HEART RATE RANGE	RPE
1	Active Recovery	< 55%		30 or more beats below		1–2
2	Endurance LTT	55–75%		20–30 beats below		2–4
3	Tempo	75–85%		10–20 beats below		4–6
4	Upper Threshold UTT	85–95%		5–10 beats below and up to your LTT		5–7
5a	CP30	95–105%		UTT, plus up to 10–15 beats		6–8
5b	VO$_2$max	CP5–8 min. power		N/A		7–9
5c	Neuromuscular Power	CP5–12 sec. power		N/A		9–10

STRENGTH TRAINING LOG

Athlete: ______________________________ Year: ______________

EXERCISE	DATE									
										Weight
										Reps
										Sets
										Weight
										Reps
										Sets
										Weight
										Reps
										Sets
										Weight
										Reps
										Sets
										Weight
										Reps
										Sets
										Weight
										Reps
										Sets
										Weight
										Reps
										Sets
										Weight
										Reps
										Sets
										Weight
										Reps
										Sets
										Weight
										Reps
										Sets
										Weight
										Reps
										Sets
										Weight
										Reps
										Sets
										Weight
										Reps
										Sets

B

PERFORMANCE TESTING GUIDELINES

In order for testing to be a reliable measure of the athlete's state of fitness progression and recovery, a specific protocol leading up to the test and during the test must be followed. This is to ensure that any outside variables can be eliminated.

Here are the parameters to pay attention to, the idea being to treat the test like race day:

Two recovery days before test. The two days before the test should be active recovery or days off. No strength training!

Fully fueled and hydrated. Be sure to eat plenty of carbohydrate-rich meals (about 60 percent of total calories from carbohydrates) during the days leading up to the test. Fluid intake also needs to be adequate leading up to the test. Be sure to take in at least half your body weight in ounces of water, plus an additional 30 to 40 ounces for every hour of training.

Pretest meal. The meal and/or snack that you eat the morning of the test should be the same each time you test. It should also be consumed at the same time prior to the test.

Time of test. The time of day that you do the test should be the same.

Warm-up. The warm-up before the test should be the same each time.

Environment. Note the temperature. It is better to test indoors so that wind, temperature, and other variables are eliminated, but power output is often slightly higher outdoors when compared with indoor efforts.

Tensions. The tire pressure, the tension of the tire against the roller on the stationary trainer, and the resistance setting on the trainer should be recorded and the same each time.

Record. Record all of the above information so that you can be sure to repeat it for the next test.

PERFORMANCE TESTING GUIDELINE

ATHLETE:

DATE										
DURATION										
AVG. POWER										
MAX. POWER										
AVG. HR										
MAX. HR										
RPE 1–10										
TEMPERATURE										
TIME										
TIRE PRESSURE										
TRAINER SET										

Pretest meal: _____

_____

Warm-up routine: _____

_____

Notes: _____

_____

_____

C

SAMPLE BASE TRAINING PLANS

Use the beginner, intermediate, and advanced training plans that follow as sample outlines for your base training. These plans may not include all of your training needs and they should be adjusted to accommodate your weekly training hours, personal limiters, level of experience, and season goals. Use Chapters 11, 12, and 13 to adjust the plans as needed. As always, consult with your doctor (and maybe your spouse) before starting an exercise program.

Workout Codes and Abbreviations

WU	Warm-up
MS	Main set
CD	Cool-down
btw	between

AA	Anatomical Adaptation Strength Phase
ES	Endurance Spinning
FGR	Fast Group Ride
FR	Force Reps
LHR	Long Hill Ride
LR	Long Ride
LTR	Lower Threshold Ride
MGR	Moderate Group Ride
MS	Maximum Strength Phase

MT   Maximum Transition Strength Phase
PS   Power Sprints
RR   Recovery Ride
SE   Strength Endurance
SM   Strength Maintenance Phase
XT   Crosstraining

Notes for all training plans:

1. Strength workouts

Weight training: Complete 6 weeks or more of AA strength phase and 2–3 weeks of MT phase before moving on to MS phase at start of your early base training. See Chapter 12.

Core strength: After warm-up do step-ups, step-downs, and 4-way hip exercises. Also do 15 minutes of abs and lower back exercises.

2. Suggested drills for LTR

WU: Back and forth and breathing drills. If indoors, include single-leg pedaling and leg speed drills; if outdoors, include dominant leg pedaling and form sprints.

MS: Pedal like pistons and personal limiter.

CD: Breathing drills

3. Suggested drills for FR

WU: Personal limiters and leg speed drills or form sprints.

MS: Push pedal over top and down front side during force reps, relax upper body.

CD: Personal limiter

4. Suggested drills for SE

WU: Pedal like pistons and personal limiter; leg speed drills or form sprints.

MS: Lift knee and push over top, relax upper body.

CD: Personal limiter

5. Suggested drills for LHR

WU: Personal limiters and leg speed drills or form sprints.

MS: Lift knee, upper body relaxation on climbs.

CD: Breathing drills

6. Suggested drills for MGR and FGR:

WU: Endurance spinning and leg speed.

MS: Pack riding, drafting, seeing, upper body relaxation.

CD: Breathing drills

Advanced Plan Notes:

See Chapter 11 for workout descriptions.
See Chapter 12 for strength workouts.
See Chapter 13 for drills.

SAMPLE TRAINING PLAN FOR BEGINNING CYCLIST

		MONDAY	TUESDAY	WEDNESDAY	THURSDAY
PRE-BASE: ALL WEEKS		Day off	XT 20–30 min., level 2 AA strength workout	Bike 1:00 LTR *(2)* WU: 20 min., level 1 MS: 1 × 30, level 2 CD: 10 min., level 1	XT 20–30 min., level 2 AA strength workout
PRE-BASE: FINAL WEEK		Day off	AA strength workout	Bike 1:00 LTR WU: 20 min., level 1 MS: 1 × 30, level 2 CD: 10 min., level 1	Day off
EARLY BASE: WEEK 1		Day off	XT 20–30 min., level 2 AA strength workout	Bike 1:00 LTR WU: 20 min., level 1 MS: 1 × 30, level 2 CD: 10 min., level 1	XT 20–30 min., level 2 AA strength workout
EARLY BASE: WEEK 2		Day off	XT 30–40 min., level 2 AA strength workout	Bike 1:30 LTR WU: 20 min., level 1 2 × 5 × 5 ES MS: 2 × 20 × 5, level 2 (recover in level 1) CD: 10 min., level 1	XT 20–30 min., level 2 AA strength workout
EARLY BASE: WEEK 3		Day off	XT 40–50 min., level 2 AA strength workout	Bike 1:30 LTR WU: 20 min., level 1 2 × 5 × 5 ES MS: 2 × 20 × 5, level 2 (recover in level 1) CD: 10 min., level 1	XT 40–50 min., level 2 AA strength workout
EARLY BASE: WEEK 4 RECOVERY		Day off	AA strength workout	Bike 1:00 LTR WU: 20 min., level 1 MS: 1 × 30, level 2 CD: 10 min., level 1	Day off
MID-BASE: WEEK 1		Day off	XT 60 min., level 2 AA strength workout	Bike 1:30 LTR WU: 20 min., level 1 2 × 5 × 5 ES MS: 1 × 30, level 2 4 × 1 × 1 FR CD: 10 min., level 1	XT 60 min., level 2 AA strength workout
MID-BASE: WEEK 2		Day off	Bike 1:00 LTR WU: 20 min., level 1 MS: 1 × 30, level 2 CD: 10 min., level 1 AA strength workout	Bike 1:30 LTR WU: 20 min., level 1 2 × 5 × 5 ES MS: 1 × 30, level 2 4 × 1 × 1 FR CD: 10 min., level 1	XT 60 min., level 2

FRIDAY	SATURDAY	SUNDAY	
Day off	Bike 1:30 LTR WU: 20 min., level 1 MS: 2 × 30, level 2 CD: 10 min., level 1	XT 20–30 min., level 2 AA strength workout	PRE-BASE: ALL WEEKS
Day off	Test 30-min. TT (See Chapter 4)	Bike 1:30 LTR WU: 20 min., level 1 MS: 2 × 30, level 2 CD: 10 min., level 1 AA strength workout	PRE-BASE: FINAL WEEK
Day off	Bike 1:30 LTR WU: 20 min., level 1 MS: 2 × 30, level 2 CD: 10 min., level 1	XT 20–30 min., level 2 AA strength workout	EARLY BASE: WEEK 1
Day off	Bike 1:30 LTR WU: 20 min., level 1 2 × 5 × 5 ES MS: 2 × 20 × 5, level 2 (recover in level 1) CD: 10 min., level 1	XT 20–30 min., level 2 AA strength workout	EARLY BASE: WEEK 2
Day off	Bike 2:00 LTR WU: 20 min., level 1 3 × 5 × 5 ES MS: 2 × 30 × 5, level 2 (recover in level 1) CD: 10 min., level 1	XT 30–40 min., level 2 AA strength workout	EARLY BASE: WEEK 3
Day off	Test 12-min. TT (See Chapter 4)	Bike 1:30 LTR WU: 20 min., level 1 2 × 5 × 5 ES MS: 2 × 20 × 5, level 2 (recover in level 1) CD: 10 min., level 1 AA strength workout	EARLY BASE: WEEK 4 RECOVERY
Day off	Bike 2:00 LHR (5) WU: 20–30 min., levels 1–2 MS: moderate climb, stay in levels 2–3 at 80+ rpms 3 × 1 × 1 FR CD: 10 min., level 1	Bike 1:30 LTR WU: 20 min., level 1 2 × 5 × 5 ES MS: 2 × 20 × 5, level 2 (recover in level 1) CD: 10 min., level 1	MID-BASE: WEEK 1
Day off	Bike 2:30 LHR WU: 20–30 min., levels 1–2 MS: moderate climb, stay in levels 2–3 at 80+ rpms CD: 10 min., level 1	Bike 2:00 LTR WU: 20 min., level 1 3 × 5 × 5 ES MS: 2 × 30 × 5, level 2 (recover in level 1) CD: 10 min., level 1	MID-BASE: WEEK 2

(continues)

SAMPLE TRAINING PLAN FOR BEGINNING CYCLIST (CONTINUED)

	MONDAY	TUESDAY	WEDNESDAY	THURSDAY
MID-BASE: WEEK 3	Day off	Bike 1:00 LTR WU: 20 min., level 1 MS: 1 × 30, level 2 CD: 10 min., level 1 AA strength workout	Bike 1:30 LTR WU: 20 min., level 1 2 × 5 × 5 ES MS: 1 × 30, level 2 4 × 1 × 1 FR CD: 10 min., level 1	XT 60 min., level 2 Core strength workout *(1)*
MID-BASE: WEEK 4 RECOVERY	Day off	AA strength workout	Bike 1:00 LTR WU: 20 min., level 1 MS: 1 × 30, level 2 CD: 10 min., level 1	Day off
LATE BASE: WEEK 1	Day off	Bike 1:30 LTR WU: 20 min., level 1 2 × 5 × 5 ES MS: 1 × 30, level 2 4 × 2 × 2 FR 3–5 strength sprints or standing starts CD: 10 min., level 1 AA strength workout	Bike 1:30 LTR WU: 20 min., level 1 2 × 5 × 5 ES MS: 2 × 20 × 5, level 2 CD: 10 min., level 1	Bike 1:30 SE WU: 35 min., levels 1–2 MS: 3 x 10 x 5, level 3 CD: 10 min., level 1 Core strength workout
LATE BASE: WEEK 2	Day off	Bike 1:45 LTR WU: 20 min., level 1 2 × 5 × 5 ES MS: 1 × 30, level 2 4 × 2 × 2 FR 3–5 strength sprints or standing starts CD: 10 min., level 1 AA strength workout or Core strength workout	Bike 1:00 LTR WU: 20 min., level 1 MS: 1 × 30, level 2 CD: 10 min., level 1	Bike 1:45 SE WU: 35 min., levels 1–2 MS: 3 x 10 x 5, level 3 CD: 10 min. level 1 Core strength workout
LATE BASE: WEEK 3	Day off	Bike 2:00 LTR WU: 20 min., level 1 2 × 5 × 5 ES MS: 1 × 40, level 2 4 × 3 × 3 FR 3–5 strength sprints or standing starts CD: 10 min., level 1 AA strength workout or Core strength workout	Bike 1:00 LTR WU: 20 min., level 1 MS: 1 × 30, level 2 CD: 10 min., level 1	Bike 2:00 SE WU: 35 min., levels 1–2 MS: 3 x 20 x 5 level 3 CD: 10 min. level 1 Core strength workout

FRIDAY	SATURDAY	SUNDAY	
Day off	**Bike 2:30 LHR** WU: 20–30 min., level 1–2 MS: moderate hills, stay in levels 2–3 at 80+ rpms CD: 10 min., level 1	**Bike 2:30 LTR** WU: 20 min., level 1 MS: 2 × 45 × 5, level 2 3–5 strength sprints CD: 10 min., level 1	MID-BASE: WEEK 3
Day off	**Test 30-min. TT** (adjust zones accordingly)	**Bike 1:30 LTR** WU: 20 min., level 1 2 × 5 × 5 ES MS: 1 × 30, level 2 4 × 1 × 1 FR CD: 10 min., level 1 **AA strength workout**	MID-BASE: WEEK 4 RECOVERY
Day off	**Bike 2:30 LHR or MGR** (include strength sprints or standing starts)	**Bike 2:00 LTR** WU: 20 min., level 1 3 × 5 × 5 ES MS: 2 × 30 × 5, level 2 CD: 10 min., level 1	LATE BASE: WEEK 1
Day off	**Bike 3:00 LHR or MGR**	**Bike 2:30 LTR** WU: 20 min., level 1 3 × 5 × 5 ES MS: 2 × 45 x 5, level 2 CD: 10 min., level 1	LATE BASE: WEEK 2
Day off	**Bike 3:00 LHR or MGR** (include strength sprints or standing starts)	**Bike 3:00 LTR** WU: 20 min., level 1 3 × 5 × 5 ES MS: 2 × 60 x 5, level 2 CD: 10 min., level 1	LATE BASE: WEEK 3

SAMPLE TRAINING PLAN FOR INTERMEDIATE CYCLIST

		MONDAY	TUESDAY	WEDNESDAY	THURSDAY
PRE-BASE: ALL WEEKS		Day off	XT 0:30–0:40, levels 1–2 AA strength workout *(1)*	Bike 1:30 LTR *(2)* WU: 20 min., level 1 2 × 5 × 5 ES MS: 2 × 20 × 5, level 2 (recover in level 1) CD: 10 min., level 1	XT 0:30–0:40, levels 1–2 AA strength workout
PRE-BASE: FINAL WEEK		Day off	AA strength workout	Bike 1:30 LTR WU: 20 min., level 1 2 × 5 × 5 ES MS: 2 × 20 × 5, level 2 (recover in level 1) CD: 10 min., level 1	Day off
EARLY BASE: WEEK 1		Day off	XT 1:00, levels 1–2 MS or MT strength workout	Bike 1:30 LTR WU: 20 min., level 1 2 × 5 × 5 ES MS: 2 × 20 × 5, level 2 (recover in level 1) CD: 10 min., level 1	XT 1:00, levels 1–2 MS or MT strength workout
EARLY BASE: WEEK 2		Day off	XT 1:00, levels 1–2 MS or MT strength workout	Bike 1:30 LTR WU: 20 min., level 1 2 × 5 × 5 ES MS: 2 × 20 × 5, level 2 (recover in level 1) CD: 10 min., level 1	XT 1:00, levels 1–2 MS or MT strength workout

EARLY BASE: WEEK 3		Day off	XT 1:00, levels 1–2
			MS or MT strength workout
				Bike 2:00 LTR
				WU: 20 min., level 1
				  3 × 5 × 5 ES
				MS: 2 × 30 × 5, level 2
				(recover in level 1)
				CD: 10 min., level 1
					Bike 1:30 LTR
					WU: 20 min., level 1
					  2 × 5 × 5 ES
					MS: 2 × 20 × 5, level 2
					(recover in level 1)
					CD: 10 min., level 1

EARLY BASE: WEEK 4 RECOVERY		Day off	XT 1:00, levels 1–2 MS or MT strength workout	Bike 1:30 LTR WU: 20 min., level 1 2 × 5 × 5 ES MS: 2 × 20 × 5, level 2 (recover in level 1) CD: 10 min., level 1	Day off

FRIDAY	SATURDAY	SUNDAY	
Day off	Bike 2:00 LTR WU: 20 min., level 1 3 × 5 × 5 ES MS: 2 × 30 × 5, level 2 (recover in level 1) CD: 10 min., level 1	Bike 1:30 LTR WU: 20 min., level 1 2 × 5 × 5 ES MS: 2 × 20 × 5, level 2 (recover in level 1) CD: 10 min., level 1 AA strength workout	PRE-BASE: ALL WEEKS
Day off	Test 30-min. TT (see Chapter 4)	Bike 1:30 LTR WU: 20 min., level 1 2 × 5 × 5 ES MS: 2 × 20 × 5, level 2 (recover in level 1) CD: 10 min., level 1 Core strength workout *(1)*	PRE-BASE: FINAL WEEK
Day off	Bike 2:00 LTR WU: 20 min., level 1 3 × 5 × 5 ES MS: 2 × 30 × 5, level 2 (recover in level 1) CD: 10 min., level 1	Bike 2:00 LTR WU: 20 min., level 1 3 × 5 × 5 ES MS: 2 × 30 × 5, level 2 (recover in level 1) CD: 10 min., level 1 MS or MT stength workout	EARLY BASE: WEEK 1
Day off	Bike 2:30 LTR WU: 20 min., level 1 3 × 5 × 5 ES MS: 2 × 45 × 5, level 2 (recover in level 1) CD: 10 min., level 1	Bike 2:30 LTR WU: 20 min., level 1 3 × 5 × 5 ES MS: 2 × 45 × 5, level 2 (recover in level 1) CD: 10 min., level 1 MS or MT strength workout	EARLY BASE: WEEK 2
Day off	Bike 3:00 LR, levels 1–3 or MGR*(6)* long, steady aerobic climbs no more than 10% of ride above level 2	Bike 2:30 LTR WU: 20 min., level 1 3 × 5 × 5 ES MS: 2 × 45 × 5, level 2 (recover in level 1) CD: 10 min., level 1 MS or MT strength workout	EARLY BASE: WEEK 3
Day off	Bike 1:45 Test 12-min. TT (see Chapter 4)	Bike 1:30 LTR WU: 20 min., level 1 2 × 5 × 5 ES MS: 2 × 20 × 5, level 2 (recover in level 1) CD: 10 min., level 1 Core strength workout	EARLY BASE: WEEK 4 RECOVERY

(continues)

SAMPLE TRAINING PLAN FOR INTERMEDIATE CYCLIST [CONTINUED]

	MONDAY	TUESDAY	WEDNESDAY	THURSDAY
MID-BASE: WEEK 1	Day off	Bike 2:00 FR*(3)* WU: 35 min., levels 1–2 MS: 75 min. hilly course, levels 2–3 3 x 2 x 2 FR, up to level 4 CD: 10 min., level 1 **SM** or **AA** strength workout	Bike 1:30 LTR WU: 20 min., level 1 2 x 5 x 5 ES MS: 2 x 20 x 5, level 2 (recover in level 1) CD: 10 min., level 1	Bike 1:45 SE*(4)* WU: 40 min., levels 1–3 MS: 3 x 15 x 5, level 3 CD: 10 min., level 1 (include 3–5 strength sprints or standing starts) **SM** or **AA** strength workout
MID-BASE: WEEK 2	Day off	Bike 2:00 FR WU: 35 min., levels 1–2 MS: 75 min. hilly course, levels 2–3 3 x 3 x 3 FR, up to level 4 CD: 10 min., level 1 **SM** or **AA** strength workout	Bike 1:30 LTR WU: 20 min., level 1 2 x 5 x 5 ES MS: 2 x 20 x 5, level 2 (recover in level 1) CD: 10 min., level 1	Bike 2:00 SE WU: 40 min., levels 1–3 MS: 3 x 20 x 5, level 3 CD: 10 min., level 1 (include 3–5 strength sprints or standing starts) **SM** or **AA** strength workout
MID-BASE: WEEK 3	Day off	Bike 2:00 FR WU: 35 min., levels 1–2 MS: 75 min. hilly course, levels 2–3 4 x 3 x 3 FR, up to level 4 CD: 10 min., level 1 **SM** or **AA** strength workout	Bike 1:30 LTR WU: 20 min., level 1 2 x 5 x 5 ES MS: 2 x 20 x 5, level 2 (recover in level 1) CD: 10 min., level 1	Bike 2:00 SE WU: 45 min., levels 1–3 MS: 2 x 30 x 5, level 3 CD: 10 min., level 1 (include 3–5 strength sprints or standing starts) **SM** or **AA** strength workout
MID-BASE: WEEK 4 RECOVERY	Day off	XT 1:00, levels 1–2 **SM** or **AA** strength workout	Bike 1:30 LTR WU: 20 min., level 1 2 x 5 x 5 ES MS: 2 x 20 x 5, level 2 (recover in level 1) CD: 10 min., level 1	Day off
LATE BASE: WEEK 1	Day off	Bike 2:00 PS (see Chapter 13) WU: 35 min., levels 1–3 MS: 75 min. 3 sets of 3–5 sprints 5 min. level 1 btw sprints 10 min. level 1 btw sets CD: 10 min., level 1 **SM** or **AA** strength workout	Bike 1:30 LTR WU: 20 min., level 1 2 x 5 x 5 ES MS: 2 x 20 x 5, level 2 (recover in level 1) CD: 10 min., level 1	Bike 2:00 SE-3 WU: 60 min., levels 1–3 MS: 2 x 20 x 5, level 4 CD: 15 min., level 1 **SM** or **AA** strength workout
LATE BASE: WEEK 2	Day off	Bike 2:00 PS WU: 35 min., levels 1–3 MS: 75 min. 3 sets of 3–5 sprints 5 min. level 1 btw sprints 10 min. level 1 btw sets CD: 10 min., level 1 **SM** or **AA** strength workout	Bike 1:30 LTR WU: 20 min., level 1 2 x 5 x 5 ES MS: 2 x 20 x 5, level 2 (recover in level 1) CD: 10 min., level 1	Bike 2:00 SE-3 WU: 60 min., levels 1–3 MS: 2 x 20 x 5, level 4 CD: 15 min., level 1 **SM** or **AA** strength workout

FRIDAY	SATURDAY	SUNDAY	
Day off	Bike 2:30 LTR, levels 1–3 or **MGR** long, steady aerobic climbs no more than 10% of ride above level 2	Bike 2:00 LTR WU: 20 min., level 1 3 x 5 x 5 ES MS: 2 x 30 x 5, level 2 (recover in level 1) CD: 10 min., level 1 **Core strength workout**	MID-BASE: WEEK 1
Day off	Bike 3:00 LR, levels 1–3 or **MGR** long, steady aerobic climbs no more than 10% of ride above level 2	Bike 2:30 LTR WU: 20 min., level 1 3 x 5 x 5 ES MS: 2 x 45 x 5, level 2 (recover in level 1) CD: 10 min., level 1 **Core strength workout**	MID-BASE: WEEK 2
Day off	Bike 3:00 LR, levels 1–3 or **MGR** long, steady aerobic climbs no more than 10% of ride above level 2	Bike 3:00 LTR WU: 20 min., level 1 3 x 5 x 5 ES MS: 2 x 60 x 5, level 2 (recover in level 1) CD: 10 min., level 1 **Core strength workout**	MID-BASE: WEEK 3
Day off	Bike 2:00 Test 30-min. TT (see Chapter 4)	Bike 1:30 LTR WU: 20 min., level 1 2 x 5 x 5 ES MS: 2 x 20 x 5, level 2 (recover in level 1) CD: 10 min., level 1 **Core strength workout**	MID-BASE: WEEK 4 RECOVERY
Day off	Bike 3:00 LHR*(5)*, levels 1–3 or **MGR** long hilly ride	Bike 3:00 LR, levels 1–3 or **MGR** no more than 15% of ride above level 2 **Core strength workout**	LATE BASE: WEEK 1
Day off	Bike 3:30 LHR, levels 1–3 or **MGR** long hilly ride (see Chapter 11)	Bike 3:00 LR, levels 1–3 or **MGR** no more than 15% of ride above level 2 **Core strength workout**	LATE BASE: WEEK 2

(continues)

SAMPLE TRAINING PLAN FOR INTERMEDIATE CYCLIST (CONTINUED)

	MONDAY	TUESDAY	WEDNESDAY	THURSDAY
LATE BASE: WEEK 3	Day off	**Bike 2:00 PS** WU: 35 min., levels 1–3 MS: 75 min., 3 sets of 3–5 sprints 5 min. level 1 btw sprints 10 min. level 1 btw sets CD: 10 min., level 1 **SM** or **AA** strength workout	**Bike 2:00 LTR** WU: 20 min., level 1 3 x 5 x 5 ES MS: 2 x 30 x 5, level 2 (recover in level 1) CD: 10 min., level 1 or **Bike 1:00 RR, level 1**	**Bike 2:15 SE-3** WU: 60 min., levels 1–3 MS: 2 x 30 x 5, level 4 CD: 10 min., level 1 **SM** or **AA** strength workout
LATE BASE: WEEK 4 RECOVERY	Day off	**XT 1:00, levels 1–2** **SM** or **AA** strength workout	**Bike 1:30 LTR** WU: 20 min., level 1 2 x 5 x 5 ES MS: 2 x 20 x 5, level 2 (recover in level 1) CD: 10 min., level 1	Day off

FRIDAY	SATURDAY	SUNDAY	
Day off	Bike 4:00 LHR, levels 1–3 or MGR long hilly ride (see Chapter 11)	Bike 3:00 LR, levels 1–3 or MGR no more than 15% of ride above level 2 **Core strength workout**	LATE BASE: WEEK 3
Day off	Bike 1:45 Test 6-min. TT (see Chapter 4)	Bike 1:30 LTR WU: 20 min., level 1 2 x 5 x 5 ES MS: 2 x 20 x 5, level 2 (recover in level 1) CD: 10 min., level 1 **Core strength workout**	LATE BASE: WEEK 4 RECOVERY

SAMPLE TRAINING PLAN FOR ADVANCED CYCLIST

	MONDAY	TUESDAY	WEDNESDAY	THURSDAY
PRE-BASE: ALL WEEKS	Day off	XT 1:00, levels 1–2 Strength workout*(1)*	Bike 2:00 LTR*(2)* WU: 20 min., level 1 3 x 5 x 5 ES MS: 2 x 30 x 5, level 2 (recover in level 1) CD: 10 min., level 1	XT 1:00, levels 1–2 Strength workout
PRE-BASE: FINAL WEEK	Day off	XT 1:00, levels 1–2 MT strength workout	Bike 2:00 LTR WU: 20 min., level 1 3 x 5 x 5 ES MS: 2 x 30 x 5, level 2 (recover in level 1) CD: 10 min., level 1	Day off
EARLY BASE: WEEK 1	Day off	XT 1:00, levels 1–2 MS strength workout	Bike 2:00 LTR WU: 20 min., level 1 3 x 5 x 5 ES MS: 2 x 30 x 5, level 2 (recover in level 1) CD: 10 min., level 1	Bike 1:30 LTR WU: 20 min., level 1 2 x 5 x 5 ES MS: 2 x 20 x 5, level 2 (recover in level 1) CD: 10 min., level 1 MS strength workout
EARLY BASE: WEEK 2	Day off	XT 1:15, levels 1–2 MS strength workout	Bike 2:30 LTR WU: 20 min., level 1 3 x 5 x 5 ES MS: 2 x 45 x 5, level 2 (recover in level 1) CD: 10 min., level 1	Bike 1:30 LTR 2 x 5 x 5 ES MS: 2 x 20 x 5, level 2 (recover in level 1) CD: 10 min., level 1 MS strength workout
EARLY BASE: WEEK 3	Day off	XT 1:30, levels 1–2 or Bike 1:30 LTR MS strength workout	Bike 2:30 LTR WU: 20 min., level 1 3 x 5 x 5 ES MS: 2 x 45 x 5, level 2 (recover in level 1) CD: 10 min., level 1	Bike 2:00 LTR WU: 20 min., level 1 3 x 5 x 5 ES MS: 2 x 30 x 5, level 2 (recover in level 1) CD: 10 min., level 1 MS strength workout
EARLY BASE: WEEK 4 RECOVERY	Day off	XT 1:00, levels 1–2 MS strength workout	Bike 2:00 LTR WU: 20 min., level 1 3 x 5 x 5 ES MS: 2 x 30 x 5, level 2 (recover in level 1) CD: 10 min., level 1	Day off

FRIDAY	SATURDAY	SUNDAY	
Day off	Bike 2:30 LTR WU: 20 min., level 1 3 x 5 x 5 ES MS: 2 x 45 x 5, level 2 (recover in level 1) CD: 10 min., level 1	Bike 2:00 LTR WU: 20 min., level 1 3 x 5 x 5 ES MS: 2 x 30 x 5, level 2 (recover in level 1) CD: 10 min., level 1 **Strength workout**	PRE-BASE: ALL WEEKS
Day off	Bike 2:00 **Test 30-min. TT** Establish training zones (see Chapters 4–5)	Bike 2:00 LTR WU: 20 min., level 1 3 x 5 x 5 ES MS: 2 x 30 x 5, level 2 (recover in level 1) CD: 10 min., level 1 **Core strength workout**	PRE-BASE: FINAL WEEK
Day off	Bike 2:30 LTR WU: 20 min., level 1 3 x 5 x 5 ES MS: 2 x 45 x 5, level 2 (recover in level 1) CD: 10 min., level 1	Bike 2:00 LTR WU: 20 min., level 1 3 x 5 x 5 ES MS: 2 x 30 x 5, level 2 (recover in level 1) CD: 10 min., level 1 **MS strength workout**	EARLY BASE: WEEK 1
Day off	Bike 3:00 LR, levels 1–3 long, steady level 2 efforts no more than 10% of ride above level 2	Bike 2:00 LTR WU: 20 min., level 1 3 x 5 x 5 ES MS: 2 x 30 x 5, level 2 (recover in level 1) CD: 10 min., level 1 **MS strength workout**	EARLY BASE: WEEK 2
Day off	Bike 3:30 LR, levels 1–3 no more than 10% of ride above level 2	Bike 2:30 LTR WU: 20 min., level 1 3 x 5 x 5 ES MS: 2 x 45 x 5, level 2 (recover in level 1) CD: 10 min., level 1 **MS strength workout**	EARLY BASE: WEEK 3
Day off	Bike 1:45 **Test 12-min. TT** (see Chapter 4)	Bike 2:00 LTR WU: 20 min., level 1 3 x 5 x 5 ES MS: 2 x 30 x 5, level 2 (recover in level 1) CD: 10 min., level 1 **Core strength workout**	EARLY BASE: WEEK 4 RECOVERY

(continues)

SAMPLE TRAINING PLAN FOR ADVANCED CYCLIST (CONTINUED)

	MONDAY	TUESDAY	WEDNESDAY	THURSDAY
MID-BASE: WEEK 1	Day off	Bike 2:30 FR*(3)* WU: 45 min., levels 1–2 MS: 95 min. hilly course levels 2–3 3 x 3 x 3 FR, up to level 4 CD: 10 min., level 1 SM strength workout	Bike 3:00 LTR WU: 20 min., level 1 3 x 5 x 5 ES MS: 2 x 60 x 5, level 2 (recover in level 1) CD: 10 min., level 1	Bike 2:00 SE*(4)* WU: 40 min., levels 1–3 MS: 3 x 20 x 5, level 3 CD: 10 min., level 1 (include 3–5 strength sprints or standing starts) SM strength workout
MID-BASE: WEEK 2	Day off	Bike 2:30 FR WU: 45 min., levels 1–2 MS: 95 min. hilly course levels 2–3 4 x 3 x 3 FR, up to level 4 CD: 10 min., level 1 SM strength workout	Bike 3:00 LTR WU: 20 min., level 1 3 x 5 x 5 ES MS: 2 x 60 x 5, level 2 (recover in level 1) CD: 10 min., level 1	Bike 2:00 SE WU: 45 min., levels 1–3 MS: 2 x 30 x 5, level 3 CD: 10 min., level 1 (include 3–5 strength sprints or standing starts) SM strength workout
MID-BASE: WEEK 3	Day off	Bike 2:30 FR WU: 45 min., levels 1–2 MS: 95 min. hilly course levels 2–3 4 x 4 x 4 FR, up to level 4 CD: 10 min., level 1 SM strength workout	Bike 3:00 LTR WU: 20 min., level 1 3 x 5 x 5 ES MS: 2 x 60 x 5, level 2 (recover in level 1) CD: 10 min., level 1	Bike 2:30 SE WU: 45 min., levels 1–3 MS: 2 x 45 x 5, level 3 CD: 10 min., level 1 (include 3–5 strength sprints or standing starts) SM strength workout
MID-BASE: WEEK 4 RECOVERY	Day off	XT 1:00, levels 1–2 SM strength workout	Bike 2:00 LTR WU: 20 min., level 1 3 x 5 x 5 ES MS: 2 x 30 x 5, level 2 (recover in level 1) CD: 10 min., level 1	Day off
LATE BASE: WEEK 1	Day off	Bike 2:00 SE–3 or FGR WU: 60 min., levels 1–3 MS: 2 x 20 x 5, level 4 CD: 15 min., level 1 (include 3–5 strength sprints or standing starts) SM strength workout	Bike 3:00 LTR WU: 20 min., level 1 3 x 5 x 5 ES MS: 2 x 60 x 5, level 2 (recover in level 1) CD: 10 min., level 1	Bike 2:30 PS WU: 60 min., levels 1–3 MS: 80 min., 3 sets of 3–5 sprints 5 min. level 1 btw sprints 10 min. level 1 btw sets CD: 10 min., level 1 SM strength workout
LATE BASE: WEEK 2	Day off	Bike 2:30 SE–3 or FGR WU: 65 min., levels 1–3 MS: 3 x 20 x 5, level 4 CD: 15 min., level 1 (include 3–5 strength sprints or standing starts) SM strength workout	Bike 2:30 LTR WU: 20 min., level 1 3 x 5 x 5 ES MS: 2 x 45 x 5, level 2 (recover in level 1) CD: 10 min., level 1	Bike 2:30 PS WU: 60 min., levels 1–3 MS: 80 min., 3 sets of 3–5 sprints 5 min. level 1 btw sprints 10 min. level 1 btw sets CD: 10 min., level 1 SM strength workout

FRIDAY	SATURDAY	SUNDAY	
Day off or Bike 1:00 RR	Bike 3:30 LHR*(5)*, levels 1–3 or MGR*(6)* long hilly ride (see Chapter 11)	Bike 3:00 LR, levels 1–3, or MGR no more than 10% of ride above level 2 **Core strength workout**	**MID-BASE: WEEK 1**
Day off or Bike 1:00 RR	Bike 4:00 LHR, levels 1–3 or MGR long hilly ride (see Chapter 11)	Bike 3:30 LR, levels 1–3, or MGR no more than 15% of ride above level 2 **Core strength workout**	**MID-BASE: WEEK 2**
Day off or Bike 1:00 RR	Bike 4:30 LHR, levels 1–3 or MGR long hilly ride (see Chapter 11)	Bike 4:00 LR, levels 1–3, or MGR no more than 20% of ride above level 2 **Core strength workout**	**MID-BASE: WEEK 3**
Day off	Bike 2:00 Test 30-min. TT Adjust training zones (see Chapters 4–5)	Bike 2:00 LTR WU: 20 min., level 1 3 x 5 x 5 ES MS: 2 x 30 x 5, level 2 (recover in level 1) CD: 10 min., level 1 **Core strength workout**	**MID-BASE: WEEK 4 RECOVERY**
Day off or Bike 1:00 RR	Bike 4:30 FGR, levels 1–4 or repeat Tuesday's SE–3 or FGR (see Chapter 11)	Bike 4:00 LR, levels 1–3, or MGR no more than 15% of ride above level 2 **Core strength workout**	**LATE BASE: WEEK 1**
Day off or Bike 1:00 RR	Bike 4:30 FGR, levels 1–4 or repeat Tuesday's SE–3 or FGR (see Chapter 11)	Bike 4:00 LR, levels 1–3, or MGR no more than 15% of ride above level 2 **Core strength workout**	**LATE BASE: WEEK 2**

(continues)

SAMPLE TRAINING PLAN FOR ADVANCED CYCLIST (CONTINUED)

	MONDAY	TUESDAY	WEDNESDAY	THURSDAY
LATE BASE: WEEK 3	Day off	Bike 2:30 SE–3 or FGR WU: 65 min., levels 1–3 MS: 2 x 30 x 10, level 4 CD: 15 min., level 1 (include 3–5 strength sprints or standing starts) SM strength workout	Bike 2:30 LTR WU: 20 min., level 1 3 x 5 x 5 ES MS: 2 x 45 x 5, level 2 (recover in level 1) CD: 10 min., level 1	Bike 2:30 PS WU: 60 min., levels 1–3 MS: 80 min., 3 sets of 3–5 sprints 5 min. level 1 btw sprints 10 min. level 1 btw sets CD: 10 min., level 1 SM strength workout
LATE BASE: WEEK 4 RECOVERY	Day off	XT 1:00, levels 1–2 SM strength workout	Bike 2:00 LTR WU: 20 min., level 1 3 x 5 x 5 ES MS: 2 x 30 x 5, level 2 (recover in level 1) CD: 10 min., level 1	Day off

FRIDAY	SATURDAY	SUNDAY	
Day off or Bike 1:00 RR	Bike 4:30 FGR, levels 1–4 or repeat Tuesday's SE–3 or FGR (see Chapter 11)	Bike 3:00 LR, levels 1–3, or MGR no more than 15% of ride above level 2 Core strength workout	LATE BASE: WEEK 3
Day off	Bike 1:45 Test 6-min. TT (see Chapters 4–5)	Bike 2:00 LTR WU: 20 min., level 1 3 x 5 x 5 ES MS: 2 x 30 x 5, level 2 (recover in level 1) CD: 10 min., level 1 Core strength workout	LATE BASE: WEEK 4 RECOVERY

LIST OF ABBREVIATIONS AND ACRONYMS

AA	anatomical adaptation	PR	personal record
AE	anaerobic endurance	RMR	resting metabolism rate
AeT	aerobic threshold	RPE	rate of perceived exertion
AT	anaerobic threshold	rpm	revolutions per minute
ATP	adenosine triphosphate	SE	strength endurance
CP	critical power	SM	strength maintenance
FG	fast glycolytic (fibers)	TDEE	total daily energy expenditure
FOG	fast oxidative glycolytic (fibers)	URTI	upper respiratory tract infection
FTP	functional threshold power	UTT	upper training threshold
LT	lactate threshold	VO_2max	maximum aerobic capacity
LT1	lower training threshold	VT	ventilatory threshold
LT2	upper training threshold		
LTT	lower training threshold		
MLSS	maximum lactate steady state		
MS	maximum strength		
MT	maximum strength transition		
OTS	overtraining syndrome		

RECOMMENDED READING

The Cyclist's Training Bible, 3rd Edition
Joe Friel

The Paleo Diet
Joe Friel

Training and Racing with a Power Meter
Hunter Allen and Andrew Coggan, PH.D.

Working Out, Working Within
Jerry Lynch

GLOSSARY

Absolute power output average watts generated over a given duration of time

Absolute strength how much force an athlete can produce

Adaptation process of gaining new strength and fitness by applying a challenging training load and then allowing the body to recover and absorb that load

Adenosine triphosphate (ATP) biological compound that serves as the main source of energy for cells and muscles

Aerobic with oxygen present, or producing energy by using oxygen

Aerobic energy system energy system that requires oxygen to be present in production of energy

A-lactate energy produced through the anaerobic system without releasing lactic acid by-products

Anaerobic without the presence of oxygen, or producing energy without using oxygen

Anaerobic A-lactate system anaerobic energy system that produces immediate energy for durations up to 12 seconds without creating any lactic acid by-products

Anaerobic endurance (AE) combination of efficiency and endurance; ability to move quickly with less effort

Anaerobic lactate system energy system that converts carbohydrates to fuel and releases lactic acid as a metabolic by-product

Anaerobic threshold (AT) physiological reference to the point at which the body begins to rely primary on the anaerobic energy system; typically measured in a lab and often used to establish training zones

Blood sugar level amount of glucose in the blood

Breakthrough workout challenging workout that serves to ultimately raise fitness levels

Cardiac drift an increase in heart rate during a long, challenging, and steady-state effort that is typically caused by heat and dehydration

Compact crank crank system with smaller chainrings to allow for higher cadences

Creatine phosphate metabolic substrate available within the muscles in limited supply for immediate muscle contractions of short durations

Critical power (CP) highest average power an athlete can sustain for a given duration

Crosstraining training that differs from the athlete's primary sport

Drafting riding behind a rider for windblock and increased efficiency

Efficiency using the least amount of energy required for a given effort

Endurance ability to resist fatigue

Glucose small amount of carbohydrates circulating in the blood

Glycogen carbohydrates stored in the liver or muscles

Individuality specific needs of an individual athlete

Intervals alternating between harder work efforts and recovery periods in training

Intensity effort level measured by heart rate, power, or rate of perceived exertion (RPE)

Lactate metabolic by-product released during anaerobic metabolism

Lactate threshold (LT) physiological reference point measured through blood samples and marked as a 1mmol increase in lactate levels above baseline

Limiter fitness ability that holds back an athlete; personal weakness

Lower training threshold (LTT) fitness and training reference point measured as a 1mmol increase in blood lactate levels above resting levels, or estimated as 55 to 75 percent of upper training threshold

Maximum aerobic capacity VO_2max, or the maximum amount of oxygen the body can process

Maximum lactate steady state (MLSS) maximum effort level that can be sustained without an increase in blood lactate levels

Overreaching necessary period of fatigue resulting from applied training stress; requires 1 to 10 days for recovery

Overtraining extreme physical and mental fatigue caused by inadequate rest and nutrition between workouts, often requiring several weeks or months of recovery

Periodization progressive structure of training that incorporates different levels of training volume and intensity at different points in the season

Personal adaptation threshold point at which the body can no longer absorb more training

Power combination of strength and efficiency or ability to move the pedals quickly and with force

Progressive overload increasing the training load above the previous load over time

Rate of perceived exertion (RPE) level of exertion based on the subjective perception of effort

Relative power output average watts divided by body weight, also known as power-to-weight ratio

Relative strength power-to-weight ratio as compared to absolute power output

Resting metabolism rate (RMR) number of calories burned daily before adding the calories required for daily acitivites

Reversibility the idea that training effect, or fitness, is temporary and that discontinuing training will reverse the fitness improvements, or result in a loss of fitness

Selected cadence revolutions per minute (RPM) that you will naturally select for riding

Specificity training in a manner that is specific to the demands of one sport

Strength ability to produce force; fitness ability in which the athlete is already proficient

Strength endurance (SE) combination of strength and endurance; ability to produce high levels of force for extended periods

Supercompensation body's adaptation to training stress, or load, whereby the body develops the ability to perform at a level higher

Tendinitis condition that occurs when the tendon is worked harder or longer than it is prepared for, becoming inflamed or damaged

Timing structuring or planning training for peak fitness at the appropriate time of the year

Total daily energy expenditure (TDEE) total calories burned during the day including resting metabolism rate and all activities

Training load measure of total training volume and intensity

Time trial all-out effort for a specific duration or distance

Type I muscle fiber aerobic, or oxidative, muscle capable of producing moderate efforts for extended periods

Type II muscle fiber muscle that includes both aerobic (oxidative) and anaerobic (glycolitic) fibers, capable of producing high force loads quickly

Upper training threshold (UTT) training and fitness reference point that is measured as the maximum lactate steady state, or estimated as 85 to 95 percent of CP30

Volume frequency and duration of training

VO_2max maximum aerobic capacity, or the maximum amount of oxygen that the body can process

INDEX

(continued)

(continued)

(continued)

ABOUT THE AUTHOR

Thomas Chapple, Ultrafit Coaching Associate, is a licensed elite-level coach for USA Cycling and USA Triathlon. Since Chapple began coaching full time in 1997, he has enabled athletes to successfully compete at national and worldwide races. His athletes have won their age groups and placed as top amateurs at the Ironman® World Championships in Hawaii, placed on the podium at the U.S. Pro/Elite National Criterium Championships, won their age groups in the NORBA National series, and won 24-hour solo mountain bike races.

Chapple is a regular contributor to training and cycling periodicals and Web sites. His coaching style emphasizes balance and consistency, with a focus on training process to reach short- and long-term goals. He has competed at the national level in downhill mountain bike racing, and regionally in road and track cycling. For more information, log on to www.coachthomas.com.